SUR-
FACE
RELATIO
-NS

FACE

R

Duke University Press   *Durham and London*   2022

SUR-

Queer Forms of Asian American Inscrutability

ELATIO
-NS
-NS

VIVIAN L. HUANG

© 2022 Duke University Press
All rights reserved
Designed by Courtney Leigh Richardson
Project editor: Bird Williams
Typeset in Warnock Pro by Westchester Publishing Services

Library of Congress Cataloging-in-Publication Data
Names: Huang, Vivian L., 1986- author.
Title: Surface relations : queer forms of Asian American
inscrutability / Vivian L. Huang.
Description: Durham : Duke University Press, 2022. | Includes
bibliographical references and index.
Identifiers: LCCN 2022004178 (print)
LCCN 2022004179 (ebook)
ISBN 9781478016359 (cloth)
ISBN 9781478018995 (paperback)
ISBN 9781478023623 (ebook)
Subjects: LCSH: Asian American art—20th century. | Asian
American art—21st century. | Asian American art—Themes,
motives. | Asian American artists. | American literature—Asian
American authors—Themes, motives. | Group identity in art. |
BISAC: SOCIAL SCIENCE / Ethnic Studies / American / Asian
American & Pacific Islander Studies | SOCIAL SCIENCE / LGBTQ
Studies.
General Classification: LCC N6538.A83 H836 2022 (print)
LCC N 6538.A83 (ebook)
DDC 700.89/95073—DC23/eng/20220628
LC record available at https://lccn.loc.gov/2022004178
LC ebook record available at https://lccn.loc.gov/2022004179

Cover credit: Detail, *Deep Cut.* © Hellen Jo. Courtesy of the artist.

Publication of this book is supported by Duke University Press's
Scholars of Color First Book Fund.

for 媽媽 婆婆 姐姐

CONTENTS

ACKNOWLEDGMENTS

This book and its author would not be what they are without the generosity, patience, and care of many. The pages cannot contain my gratitude in its liveness, but I submit this book as my attempt.

My profound thanks to Karen Shimakawa for the confidence, model, and mentorship you have offered me throughout my career. Karen, José Esteban Muñoz, and Ann Pellegrini have transformed me with their faith and radiance. I am forever grateful to you for making me feel possible. I was dazzled by the conviviality extended to me in the Department of Performance Studies at New York University. I thank Tavia Nyong'o, André Lepecki, Barbara Browning, Noel Rodriguez, Patty Jang, and Laura Elena Fortes for helping me make an intellectual home there. Thank you to J de Leon for your enduring friendship, feedback, and cheerleading. This book is better because of you. Thank you, Ariane Zaytzeff and Rüstem Ertuğ Altınay, for your delightful friendship. Thanks to Dasha Chapman, Kaitlin Murphy, Kathleen Tracey, and Tuo Wang.

Thanks to Kandice Chuh, Gayatri Gopinath, Joshua Chambers-Letson, and Mel Chen for your incredible generosity. Summer Kim Lee, Seulghee Lee, and Feng-Mei Heberer are dream interlocutors. Aisha Langford encouraged me with each check-in. Thank you to Christina León, Ivan Rámos, Leon Hilton, Hentyle Yapp, Josh Guzmán, James McMaster, Emily Hue, Lezlie Frye, Aliza Shvartz, Hella Tsaconas, Ethan Philbrick, Olivia Michiko Gagnon, Colleen Kim Daniher, Kelly Chung, Otis Ramsay-Zoe, Julia Steinmetz, Katie Brewer-Ball, Ren Ellis Neyra, Sarah Stefana Smith, Tina Post, Kyle Frisina, Elliott Powell, Wen Liu, Kadji Amin, Lakshmi Padmanabhan, Natasha Bissonauth, Alex Pittman, Krista Miranda, Gelsey Bell, Megan Nicely, Jih-Fei Cheng, and Mila Zuo. Thanks to Susette Min, Christine Mok, Mimi Thi Nguyen, Anita Mannur, Karen Tongson, Jasbir Puar, Nguyen Tan Hoang, Dean Saranillio, Sean Metzger, Eng-Beng Lim, Martin Manalansan, David Eng, Shinhee Han, Lisa Duggan, Anne Anlin Cheng, Kyla Wazana Tompkins, Amber Jamilla Musser, E. Patrick Johnson, Ramón Rivera-Servera, Juana María Rodríguez, Sandra Ruiz, Alex Vasquez, Joan Kee, and Jennifer Hayashida for your writing and collegiality. I thank Colleen Lye, Gautham Premnath, W. B. Worthen, and Ed Oh for encouraging my graduate studies. Thanks to Grace Kim, Chris Beirne, Keren Robertson, Roma Hammel, and Michael Smith for your formative literature classrooms.

I thank my colleagues and students in the Department of Communication Studies at San Francisco State University. Thanks to Amy Kilgard, Gust Yep, Chris Koenig, Constance Gordon, and Andrew Harris for your welcome of me. I look forward to continuing my work in your company.

I grew so much in my time at Williams College, and I feel thankful for the supports provided to me to bring this book to publication. Writing alongside Ianna Hawkins Owen has changed my life. I am so thankful to Ianna, Anthony Kim, Marshall Green, Christophe Koné, Natalie Bump Vena, Christopher Taylor, Franny Choi, VaNatta Ford, Lauren Williamson, Munjulika Tarah, Shayok Misha Chowdhury, Haydee Lindo, Kailani Polzak, and Angela Wu, who made the small town on Mohican land a home for me. Thanks to Monica Helm for providing vital dog care.

I thank Amy Holzapfel for her energizing mentorship and collegiality. Huge thanks to Gregory Mitchell for advocating for me. I thank my wonderful colleagues in Women's, Gender, and Sexuality Studies, including Kiaran Honderich, Greta Snyder, Emery Shriver, and Robin Keller. I thank Christopher Bolton, Katie Kent, Christopher Nugent, and Carol Ockman for their sustained support. Mea Cook, Scott Wong, Bernie Rhie, Mérida Rúa, Ondine Chavoya, Lucie Schmidt, Rashida Braggs, Jan Padios, Anjuli Fatima Raza Kolb, Jinhwa Chang, and Betsy Burris have shown me generosity. Shanti Pillai, Eli Nelson, Tatiana McInnis, Shawna Patterson-Stephens, Jackie Hidalgo, Amal Eqeiq, Kimberly Love, Sara Dubow, Kashia Pieprzak, Olga Shevchenko, Sophie St. Just, Sebastián Perez, Allana Clarke, Rhon Manigault-Bryant, Dorothy Wang, Li Yu, Helga Druxes, Jana Sawicki, Gail Newman, Gage McWeeny, Hannah Lipstein, Mari Rodríguez Binnie, Willie Binnie, Saadia Yacoob, Lu Kou, Anicia Timberlake, Jesús Hernández, Alma Granado, Kaye Shaddock, Justin Shaddock, Will Rawls, Jeffrey Israel, Sarah Allen, and Christina Yang have all offered me kindness and support for my work. Krista Birch, Elizabeth Gallerani, Stephanie Dunson, Lucy Green, Jim Reische, Dukes Love, John Gerry, Bridget Griffin, Bobbi Senecal, Denise Buell, Safa Zaki, and Maud Mandel have made my research and teaching more possible.

Natali Valdez cheered me on in the final pushes of this manuscript. Caroline Light, Annabel Kim, Hannah Frydman, Raji Harikrishna, Arvind Kannan, Nawab, Ju Yon Kim, Genevieve Clutario, Kareem Khubchandani, Lilian Mengesha, Takeo Rivera, Doug Ishii, Moya Bailey, Roanne Kantor, Terry

Park, Amy Parker, Robert Reid-Pharr, Iyko Day, Jina B. Kim, Britt Russert, Ren-yo Hwang, Elliot Montague, Treva Ellison, and Cameron Awkward-Rich have made the space between the mountains and the shore feel full of joyful connection. Thanks to the Asian American and Pacific Islander Studies Working Group at Harvard and the Five College Asian/Pacific/American Studies Program for intellectual community.

This book would not be what it is without conversations with my students over a decade of teaching in classrooms at Hunter College, City University of New York; New York University; Williams College; and Harvard University. Thank you for our work in the classroom. Thank you to Skye An, Julia Blike, Phuong Vo, Mei Kazama, William Oh, and Jamie Kasulis.

This book is indebted to the work of artists and writers such as Soomi Kim, TT Takemoto, Laurel Nakadate, Mika Tajima, Baseera Khan, Tseng Kwong Chi, Muna Tseng, Kimsooja, Barbara Takenaga, Young Jean Lee, Denise Uyehara, Hieu Minh Nguyen, Tamiko Beyer, Duy Doan, Jess X. Snow, Kit Yan, Kai Cheng Thom, Monique Truong, Kim Fu, Emma Sulkowicz, Canyon Sam, Tehching Hsieh, Yoko Ono, Ocean Vuong, Diana Oh, and Margaret Rhee. Thank you to Hellen Jo for blessing this book cover with your art work Special thanks to darien k n manning for proofreading this book.

Thank you to Courtney Berger for your steadfast support and guidance. Thank you to Sandra Korn and the Duke University Press editorial staff. Thanks to Liz Smith for project editing, Sheila McMahon for copyediting, Christopher Robinson for copywriting, Courtney Leigh Richardson for design, and Derek Gottlieb for indexing. My thanks to the editors, reviewers, and publishing staff who have made my work available to readers in *Women & Performance*, *Journal for Asian American Studies*, *Journal of Popular Culture*, *Diacritics*, *Theatre Journal*, *Criticism*, GLQ, and the *Oxford Encyclopedia for Asian American Literature and Culture*.

Many people, centers, associations, and institutions have hosted my presentations and research in the development of this book, including the Gaius Charles Bolin Dissertation Fellowship at Williams College; Association for Asian American Studies; Mellon Emerging Faculty Leaders Award from the Institute for Citizens and Scholars; Hellman Foundation; Center for Creative Photography at the University of Arizona, Tucson; Franklin Furnace; Center for the Study of Sexual Culture at the University of California, Berkeley; Northwestern Performance Studies Institute; Yale Performance Studies Working Group; Studies of Women, Gender, and Sexuality and Theater, Dance and Media at Harvard; and Alliance to Advance Liberal Arts Colleges (AALAC) Queer and Trans of Color Critique Seminar. Thanks to

API Equality–Northern California (APIENC), the Asian Pacific Islander Queer Women and Transgender Community (APIQWTC), and Plumeria and Shuly for hosting me in your Berkeley home.

So many loved ones have housed me and given me the physical space and emotional support to do my work. I couldn't have done this without you. Philippa Brentnall has been on the other end of the phone or laptop for the entirety of this book's writing. Thank you for encouraging me through everything. Martha Hoffman offers me refuge and direction. nar juiceharp castle emboldens me. Shona Ganguly, Sujay Pandit, Chelsea Burns, Carolina Borges, and Tanis Franco have shared laughter, rage, and care with me. Thanks to Susanne Fuchs and the Fuchs family. For unwavering support I thank Sue and Peter Brentnall. Thank you, Steph Lin, East McLaughlin, Tiffany Yao, Emily Yao, Emily Chien, Jean Hsu, Annie Shields, Emily Parker, Jessica Jacobs, Dexter Riff, Vanessa Banta, David Scanlon, Dominique Nisperos, Jason Hu, Jonathan Amores, Nick Wong, Emi Ikkanda, Jeena Yi, and Theatre Rice! Thanks to kris mizutani for your support and love. Thank you to Yoko Harumi, for the healing work, as well as to Cara Behrman and Brittney Cappiello.

My family inspires me and grounds me, and I am so thankful to be yours. Lily Huang, Chien Wen Yen, Chia-Hsi Yen, and Emily Huang have gifted me the trust, care, and distance that make this book possible. 謝謝! I am so proud of Dexter, Max, and Logan Beck. Thanks to Chien Hua Yen, to Su-Jane Hsieh, and to Kevin, Katherine, and Michael. Thanks to Rosa, Jessica, and Cheh Suei Yang. Thank you, Barnacle. You're a good dog and I love you.

And finally, thank you, reader, for giving this book a home.

INSCRUTABLE SURFACING

"Hello? Is anybody out there?"

Enrobed in a black acoustic sound blanket, artist Baseera Khan sits on the floor of a performance space surrounded by audience members in folding chairs. The audience cannot see the artist's body except for what might be glimpsed through a circular cutout in the fabric, embroidered with a sunburst design in gold thread. Khan's voice comes through surrounding speakers as they address the audience through a microphone. "Could someone with a red shirt approach me, please?" When an audience member responds, Khan asks them to remove their shoes, and the artist slowly extends a bare arm out of the cutout to retrieve one shoe at a time. Into the microphone, they comment on the shoes, trying one on before dedicating a song and dance to the audience participant. Throughout the performance, Khan switches between singing, dancing, conversing, directing, and sitting silently, all while under the blanket.[1] At times, Khan invites physical contact, for instance, extending their arm out of the hole and saying, "You can kiss my hand. I don't make you nervous, do I?" At other times, the artist sits alone in the middle of the space and asserts, "I don't want to talk to anyone. I'm not in a good mood. I feel isolated sometimes," before leading into their next pop song.

In iterations of their performance *Acoustic Sound Blankets*, Baseera Khan experiments with the bounds of sociality as contoured by the titular textiles.[2] Khan's performance under the sound blanket remixes tropes of Muslim, South Asian, and brown femme inscrutability that figure through visual cover and anxiety over women and femmes' capacity to voice. Through bossy, playful, and sullen interactions with the audience, Khan reminds us that their vision, too, is blocked, and their hearing is muffled from within the sound blanket. Yet what could be narrated as hindrances to sociality and creativity are instead the grounds upon which Khan constructs the performance.

Surface Relations: Queer Forms of Asian American Inscrutability considers minoritarian aesthetic and affective modes of inscrutability that negotiate formal legibility with sociopolitical viability. This book studies Asian American expressive cultures of surface, such as Khan's use of sound blankets, that invite the reader to the queer relational practices of inscrutability that are all too often invisibilized or written off as apathetic or apolitical. Khan's performance of inscrutability does not foreclose interaction but creates modes, space, and time through which to be together. Asian American, transnational, and diasporic writers and artists have reanimated and reconfigured inscrutability to strategically perform Asiatic difference as something that disturbs social conventions and shares alternative ways of being in time, space, and body. These performances of inscrutability are vital acts of world-making in a cultural landscape that has normalized the nonappearance of Asian American culture.

Historically, inscrutability has been employed as a powerful Orientalist discourse through which a masculinized Euro-American subjectivity emerges, producing the centrality of the Western knower who names the racial, gender, religious, and/or national other as "impenetrable or unfathomable to investigation; quite unintelligible, entirely mysterious."[3] The particulars of the Orientalized person, place, and/or thing are often flattened, homogenized, and objectified in the process, appearing as a surface that can or cannot be penetrated. When further considered, however, the casting of the Asian as "inscrutable other" also suggests a racialization wherein the other knows

FIGURE I.1. Baseera Khan, *Acoustic Sound Blankets*. Whitney Museum of American Art, July 21, 2017. Photograph by Filip Wolak.

something that cannot be accessed from without. To come into being as an inscrutable other is to have claim to modes of doing, knowing, and being that are inaccessible from an outside perspective. To claim inscrutability from an Asian diasporic positionality, then, is to protect a creative space and time in which minoritized lifeworlds may exist for their own audience.

The surface performance of inscrutability gives form to the fleeting, fluid qualities of Asian American sociality that do not appear under neoliberal optics. If legibility and meaning making are contingent on the repetition of conventions, then Asian American populations are often at a loss. Public convention erases Asian American history such that Asian American life is not believed to possess a legitimate culture. At the same time, Asian American communities face the generational grief, rage, and trauma of war, immigration, and exile, which disrupt the internal continuation of conventions as practiced through shared language, nationality, class, and, indeed, race. Forms of feminist, queer, trans, and Asian diasporic world-making are even more obscured for their deviation from inherited conventions of care and kinship. To theorize inscrutable relations through surface aesthetics, then, is to give time and space to these forms of being and becoming that elude—whether strategically or compulsorily—official narration.

Surface Relations explores aesthetic modes of inscrutability through queer racial forms of invisibility, silence, impenetrability, flatness/flexibility, distance, and withholding. Often these aesthetic modes overlap and amplify one another. These minoritarian modes are sensible through queer-of-color aesthetics that necessarily navigate and elude typical perception. Performing inscrutably is a minor racial performative that signals social epistemologies other than white nationalist frameworks that narrate Asian American life as white aspiration or nonexistence.[4] *Surface Relations* centers the work of contemporary art practitioners of Asian descent based in North American settled colonies, and theorizes inscrutable aesthetics through critical feminist, queer, and trans frameworks to expand possibilities for reading, feeling, and desiring beyond nationalist cis-heteronormative epistemic grids.

The common dismissal of Asian American, queer, and trans cultural life requires a confrontation with the xenophobia against esoteric knowledge. This book's meditations on inscrutability are intended not to alienate but rather to invite the reader to reconsider the racialization of engagement. Through performance analysis, I shift focus away from individual enlightenment and toward relational, contingent world-making with the contention that these inscrutable aesthetic modes vitalize social forms that stagnant models of subjectivity and community desperately need.

Inscrutability asks after the gender and sexual valences of Asian relationality, and the racial aesthetics of queer form. Asian and queer formations are entangled, not collapsible, and these entanglements warrant further thought in both ethnic studies and queer studies. "Asian American" and "queer" emerged as political hails through coalitional activisms of the sixties, seventies, and eighties. Yet under neoliberal capitalism, both terms have hardened into identities interpreted as model minorities, a white supremacist discourse that drains the terms of their revolutionary politics. To be Asian American or queer is often to be narrated toward white-adjacent, wealthy, coupled assimilation, as exemplified by model minority discourse or marriage equality progress narratives. To feel Asian American and queer can render one illegible to dominant epistemes of straight/gay, masculine/feminine, white/Black, citizen/foreigner, settler/Indigenous binaries. These racialized feelings of illegibility weigh heavily on psychic health and are symptomatic of racial violence. To survive, again and again, the reiterative racial erasure of Asian American becoming is to develop a supple creative response to forms and knowledges that slip out of identitarian legibility. Affective and aesthetic attunement to inscrutability equips us with tools to question the assimilationist narrative for queers and Asians in the United States, and to attend to non-identitarian practices of minoritarian world building.

Readers may hesitate to energize the xenophobic discourse of the inscrutable other, as Asian American cultural life remains underrepresented in major institutions of power. An incorporative impulse might dismiss a historic association between Asianness and inscrutability, and advocate for improved representation as a justified prerequisite for public care and claims to humanity. But what, and who, is further excluded in this wish for legibility? How might these flickering forms of the illegible occasion other modes of relating, attuning us to nuanced social practices not premised on racial, gender, and sexual fixity? Allowing for the legitimacy of political claims to public life, this book theorizes inscrutability as an intervention into liberal narratives of racial and sexual progress through assimilation.

Recognition and inclusion have not been freely granted to Asian Americans or queers, and histories of institutional exclusion have necessitated queer racial forms and affects for the survival of Asian American culture. This book reframes inscrutability as a dynamic anti-racist, feminist, and queer aesthetic through which Asian American life might become otherwise sensible and tenable in contemporary culture—not necessarily for majoritarian recognition but for minoritarian life and creativity. Chapter by chapter, *Surface Relations* analyzes Asian American culture through a queered lens of inscrutability by lingering in common criticisms of Asian American life as invisible, silent, impenetrable, flat, distant, and withholding. Rather than refute these judgments, this book lingers in the negative space that these stereotypes mold to see what has grown there and in this way makes a space for Asian American queer life.

Historical Productions of the (Queer) Inscrutable Asiatic

When I write of inscrutable surface, I point to the ways in which aesthetic judgments of spectacular exteriority and inaccessible interiority have produced conventions of Asian form premised on queer illegibility. The unknowability of what is behind the unspeaking surface, of what cannot be found out from an outside perspective, has occasioned deep anxiety and suspicion of Asian others throughout the modern age.[5] Yellow peril rhetorics visualized China and the Orient not only at the farthest edge of the map but also as queered objects that embody distance and pure exteriority, whether through trade goods, linguistic script, or bodies. The relational construction of the Orient and the Occident cannot be separated from heteropatriarchal constructions of gender in the time of colonial expansion. Rey Chow connects the construction of inscrutable China as pure surface with "traditional readings of women as passive, silent objects."[6] That Asia becomes disciplined as the West's other, characterized as so different in its values, customs, languages, and beliefs, is epistemically entangled with Christian European ideas of gender and power. Inscrutability gives shape to discourses of hyper(hetero)sexualized Asian and Asian diasporic women, of emasculated and asexualized Asian American men, and, as Mel Chen writes, the trans discursive and embodied practices of Asian American gender through regimes of modern racialization.[7]

Recall how the bodies of Chinese people created a problem for legal and political epistemes in the nineteenth century, which in turn structured material problems for Chinese and other Asian lives. Early characterizations of inscrutability cohered through remote encounters with Chineseness and moved from a discursive reliance on "inscrutable China" to a broader racialization of Asian inscrutability, compounding through US legal histories wherein Chinese immigrants revealed the limits of the law's existing racial categories. Early Asian immigrants to the United States were queerly unintelligible, as evidenced by the infamous Prerequisite Cases, where the inconsistent taxonomy of Asian bodies rendered immigrants legally inscrutable. This was reinscribed through their legal classification as "aliens ineligible for citizenship" and, in Mae Ngai's vernacular, "alien citizens."[8] Chinese inscrutability set US legal precedent for the inscrutability of Asian immigrants writ large.[9] The discourse of Chinese and Asian inscrutability made its way into US law as racial classification, systemically ensuring the foreign status of Asians by depriving them of the ability to claim citizenship. Karen Shimakawa shows how (white) US Americanness constructs itself in a subjective position through the reiterative abjection of Asianness, and that the provisional belonging of Asian Americans as Americans requires the jettisoning of one's Asianness, most pointedly through the rehearsal of gender and sexual norms.[10]

These nineteenth-century legal policies were of a piece with yellow peril discourses that constructed the inscrutable Chinese as unreadable screens from an alternate time and space. Consider, for instance, the following description from the *San Francisco Chronicle* in 1906: "Behind the slant eyes of the inscrutable yellow face one wonders what thoughts were flicking through the brain that has been forty-four centuries in the making, or with what subtle, shadowy Chinese contempt for all things Occidental the awakening infant was viewing the powwow of nations over his crib."[11] The Chinese, described with "slant eyes" and "yellow face," is constructed as a flat screen "behind" which lies the inscrutable thoughts of an ancient brain. The Chinese can be understood as a queer figure of time here.[12] Suspiciously withholding, the inscrutable Chinese is infantilized in relation to an occidental viewer, implying an aberrant or ace sexuality. Note the paradoxical historicity of the inscrutable other as both "the awakening infant" and "forty-four centuries in the making," suggesting a queer temporality embodied by the Chinese as both ancient and new to the modern era. This scene of inscrutability indexes a social encounter through a series of aesthetic judgments that construct the Chinese person as an epistemological limit, in relation to whose silence the occidental may speak. The voicelessness of the Chinese in this excerpt only ensures their inscrutability in relation to the enlightened occidental.[13] Nevertheless, the relationship drawn between the person who judges the inscrutable as such (the "one [who] wonders") and the inscrutable other (what lies "behind the slant eyes of the inscrutable yellow face") acknowledges the existence of multiple, potentially incommensurable knowledge systems.

Contemporary US American public life, with its continued denial of Asian American culture, inherits and reiterates this queer construction of Asian foreignness. The Asian racialization of face masks in the spring of 2020, with the initial outbreak of COVID-19, offers a contemporary case study for the surface aesthetics of national threat. How otherwise to understand US American resistance to mask wearing during a pandemic, in the name of patriotism and freedom, simultaneous to a rise in documented accounts of anti-Asian violence? The face mask operates as a layer that, while filtering air particles, obscures the face and stalls speech. Reanimating language of inscrutability that conflates visual obfuscation with suspicion, silence, and docility, Cathy Park Hong writes: "The masks depersonalized their faces, making the stereotypically 'inscrutable' Asian face even more inscrutable, effacing even their age and gender, while also telegraphing that the Asian wearer was mute and therefore incapable of talking back if aggressed."[14] These persistent conflations of inscrutability with racialized anti-American threat have material consequences, as documented in the devastating, racialized coronavirus death toll as well as anti-Asian racism.[15] Inscrutable surface as queer racial form can offer a way to understand the cultural (racialized, feminized, sexualized) coding of not only the face mask but also other head coverings (e.g., hijab, niqab, burqa), as the deployment of a long-standing construction of Asian/Eastern/Oriental styles as threatening surface. Further, we may connect racialized face masks to BDSM aesthetics, such that face covering is imagined as a queer racial threat. Such fear/fetish is premised on an Orientalist conflation of visual obfuscation with inaccessible interiority and suspicious passivity: the obscured face refusing speech and legibility, submitting to muteness.

These persistent racial aesthetics of Asian inscrutable surfaces are reproduced in and through modern epistemologies, including those that may claim no relation to Asia. When Asian form is disavowed as inscrutable surface, it often functions as a shorthand to reassert white or occidental mastery. Rey Chow's critique of Jacques Derrida's misreading brilliantly proves this point: that even the most celebrated critical thought in contemporary letters (deconstruction) relies on a fundamental Orientalism that "hallucinates China."[16] Derrida misidentifies the Chinese language as ideographic, instead of phonetic, evacuating the script of sound. Deconstruction serves as another example of the continued legacy of Western modern thought based on the prescribed, silent inscrutability of China. Chow writes: "At the moment of cultural encounter the other is thus crushed against on the outer edge, as a mere exterior. This exterior, which in this case is literally expressed as an impenetrable (sur)face, nonetheless returns to me (the non-Chinese subject) as my enlightening, my enhanced understanding, my epistemological progress. While the Chinese are inscrutable, I remain lucid; their objectlike obscurity constitutes my subjectivity, my humanity."[17] Derrida's productive construction of China as "the outer edge" repositions the cognizing "non-Chinese subject" as the knowing, enlightened ur-human. Chow's vital insight is that modern thought is so underpinned by the rehearsed casting of China as "mere exterior," vulnerable to another's judgment as to be "crushed against" itself, that critical theory is unspeakable without the axiom of Chinese inscrutability.[18] As Chow writes, "'Inscrutable Chinese' is no longer simply the enigmatic exterior of the oriental but also *an entire language and culture reduced to (sur)face, image, and ideogram.*"[19]

The abject inscrutability of the Chinese surface is precisely what renders Asian form queer. If, as Kadji Amin, Amber Jamilla Musser, and Roy Pérez write, "queerness is best understood as a series of relations to form," then Asian racialization takes a queer form through reiterative surface relations to Western critical thought. Orientalism occasions queer forms of Asian diasporic relationality, through the unreadable surface, the masked face, the impenetrable script. Asian American cultural practices, in turn, experiment with queer form by structuring other relationalities and delimiting the epistemic bounds of modern thought. More, aesthetic modes of inscrutability queer common sense by disorienting the circuitry of Western knowledge. Inscrutability resonates with Amin, Musser, and Pérez's description of queer form "as a name for the range of formal, aesthetic, and sensuous strategies that make difference a little *less* knowable, visible, and digestible."[20]

Queer forms make sensible inscrutable attempts to connect amid conventional sociality. Consider the force of not-knowing in the poem "Elegy for the First" by Hieu Minh Nguyen, wherein the speaker addresses a deceased uncle who "never married," "didn't have children," and appears in multiple photographs with a man identified as *the roommate*."[21] The family mourns the uncle's death collectively, yet the uncle's life appears as lack under heteronormative convention. Rather than refuse this negativity, however, the speaker "walk[s] toward" it. Note the play between presence and absence in the second half of the poem:

> Uncle, a story before you sleep:
> here, a child   dressed in dust.
> This time you wait for him
> before you leave.   Here, another:
> once, I ran, face first, into a mirror
>   because I didn't recognize
> my reflection, because I didn't see a reflection at all.
>   I feel each shard   open me
> as I walk toward you & that man, standing beside
>   your open casket. He is there
>   in every photograph
> of you smiling.   I want to kiss him.
>   I want to take him into me, soften his grief
> with my heat   & inherit
> any pulse you might've left behind.   *I'm sorry*
>   *for your loss*   I say   or he says
>   or neither of us say, I'm not sure.
> I have so many questions. I trace
>   your mouth counterclockwise
> but   you do not answer.

The speaker is a temporal misfit "dressed in dust" who sees no place for himself in the world as it is, underscored by the imperceptibility of his uncle's life even in death. His queer alienation from his family in this time of mourning is also what attunes him to the wordless presence of his uncle's devoted companion, brightening a capacity to inquire and to desire amid grief. Nguyen elegantly structures the poem with gaps in form and content. The speaker is not able to know his uncle's answers, nor is the reader granted access to the questions he would ask him. What awaits the reader, then, is not so much information about the uncle's life or the details of the speaker's curiosity.

Rather, the poem surges with the speaker's heated desire to reach for him and to attend to the quiet intimacies of his life that survive him. To wish to feel connected in the face of historical obscurity, and to give that desire a shape, is productive of his queer-of-color possibility. The vital relationality of the poem glimmers through this minor queer recognition that eludes as it appears.

Inscrutability refers to a way of sensing and relating that operates beside the normativizing pathways of family and citizenship, and in theorizing inscrutability, I wish also to theorize the shame, loneliness, and despair that may come from such racial formation. I find it helpful to consider the queer form of inscrutability like that of the closet, as modern epistemes that rely on an interplay between exteriority and interiority.[22] The figures of the inscrutable Asiatic and the closeted queer both obstruct a modern will to know through public spectacle, through "staying in" as opposed to "being out."[23] Jean Shin formulates the "foreign closet" for Asian Americans, as a need to "come out" as immigrant or Asian, where the Asian American is triangulated in a Black/white racial dichotomy as exceptional minority.[24] In these writings by Shin and Eve Kosofsky Sedgwick, curiously, queer and trans Asian Americans (as racially, sexually, and gender-closeted subjects) do not appear.[25] Their largely separate analysis of race and sexuality, however, must not foreclose the capacity to sense out their overlapping constituents. Often imagined as a shame chamber that the closeted wishes to break free from, the closet is constructed as a space that occasions the liberated subjectivity of others. But what if the closeted do not want to come out? In Nguyen's poem, the tacit space of the closet occasions queer kinship with his deceased uncle and his "roommate." To bring life to that space, as the poem does, is to reach for what may not be spoken or seen by the rest of the family—and is all the more precious for that reason. As Summer Kim Lee writes, opting to "stay in," as a tactical response to the "compulsory sociability" imposed upon Asian Americans, can remain a viable option that need not conflate asociality with antisociality.[26] What if inscrutable modes make certain worlds more livable and even proliferate social possibilities?

The Stakes of Obscured Internal Life

> There are many ways to hold water
> without being called a vase.
> To drink all the history
> until it is your only song.
> —Franny Choi, "Orientalism (Part I)"

The queer aestheticization of Asian surface has significant impacts on the legibility of Asian American internal life. The construction of Asian exteriority obscures racial interiority, shaping first-person Asian experience and material life chances. In this book, I grapple not only with the pain and damage of inscrutable aesthetics but also with their world-making capacities. Here my thinking follows the scholarship of David Eng, Shinhee Han, and Anne Anlin Cheng, as well as the writings of scholars across fields, including Sara Ahmed, Jeffrey Santa Ana, erin Khuê Ninh, and Sianne Ngai, to consider the negative affects and ugly feelings of Asian racialization that build rather than foreclose cultural and social life. Attending to the emotional impacts of Asian racial formation attunes us to the Asian feminist, queer, and trans forms of care that exist alongside and through inscrutability. This book emphasizes surface *relations* because the negative affects of racial surfacing do not preclude Asian American sociality but open the social horizon to feminist, trans, and queer affinities. Where Orientalist discourses of the perpetual foreigner and post-racial liberal projects isolate in their mandated individualism, queer aesthetic practices of inscrutability are ardently relational and reaching for something else.

When Asian American life appears in mainstream media, racial tropes of surface inscrutability are often reinforced. Consider, for instance, a recent incident when a dean at the Massachusetts Institute of Technology described a Korean American candidate as "yet another textureless math grind" who "looked like a thousand other Korean kids."[27] The indistinguishable, "textureless" surface imposed on this Asian American applicant, described without "American" claim, constructs not only a racialized surface exterior but also an unremarkable interior. Such evacuation of Asian American feeling reveals public neglect of Asian American life, care, and well-being. What is centered in these mainstream news items is not the particular lived experience of Asian Americans but a reiterated positioning of Asianness as social periphery, mute in the margins.

If Asia and Asian American history continue to be constructed as the outer limit, then Asian American psychic life bears the burden of holding histories that do not otherwise surface in national narratives. These lost histories and disavowed memories comprise a racialized loss formative of Asian American psychic life, one that reiterates spatial aesthetics of exteriority and interiority. As David Eng and Shinhee Han write, "These losses and voices are melancholically displaced from the external world into the internal world of the psyche."[28] Asian American bodies, rendered as inscrutable surface, function to create the bodily surface as the compartmentalized container to a private interior life. Asian American psychic health suffers from the public dismissal of Asian and Asian American histories. The losses brought on by external political and economic structures are internalized by Asian and Asian American people to constitute a racialized interiority founded in the absorption of such loss, trauma, and displaced history.

Depicted as ghostly, inconsequential, or forgotten, Asian American history, politics, and culture are often discounted as lacking real content. If there is no public recognition of Asian American history, politics, or culture, there can be no common ground on which violence and injustice, let alone grief, healing, and care, among Asian Americans are discussed. This lacuna occasions silent suffering in a neoliberal society. In an oft-cited line of the essay "Mourning and Melancholia," Sigmund Freud writes that "the patient is aware of the loss which has given rise to his melancholia, but only in the sense that he knows whom he has lost but not what he has lost in him."[29] As Eng and Han have written, the effect of the introjected lost "what" indexes the inscrutable factor as central not only to Asian racialization but to ego formation writ large. They write, "The pervasiveness of the model minority stereotype in our contemporary vocabulary works, then, as a melancholic mechanism facilitating the erasure and loss of repressed Asian American histories and identities. These histories and identities can return only as a type of ghostly presence."[30] Anne Anlin Cheng describes how the racialized American thus loses the self as a marker of legitimacy and instead feels the "installation of a scripted context of perception."[31]

Who benefits from this suffering? The evacuation and neglect of Asian and Asian diasporic lives have become normalized for the maintenance of global racial capitalism. Long-standing representations of Asians as silent exteriority are optimized in late capitalism to consolidate Asian tropes as ideal workers in racial hierarchies: self-regulating, cheap, in abundant supply, apolitical, eager to perform well. Whether model minority or migrant worker, the Asian American is often stereotyped as a robotic laborer whose social function revolves around economic efficiency, hard work, and professional success at all costs. The reality of complex Asian American feeling, of racial mourning and melancholia, is difficultly registered by a public gaze that depends on the exploitation and invisibilization of Asian labor (local, national, and transnational) in late capitalism. The racialization of transnational Asian flexible labor under neoliberalism, as studied by Aihwa Ong, is another form of hollow, disposable labor, evacuated of interior life relevant to public concern.[32]

This is all to locate the stakes of *Surface Relations* in the psychic, emotional, social, and cultural endurance of people enfigured by Asian racialization. If Asianness is configured as ahistorical exteriority under Orientalist discourse, then, what is it to be produced as a racialized Asian subject? The production of the Oriental as an unknowable other creates a subjective quandary for those racialized through Orientalist surface aesthetics. What counterdiscourses might we need to foster the psychic and somatic well-being of Asian Americans (whether or not they identify as such)?[33] How might a repurposed framework of Asian inscrutability allow for more supple self-understandings of race, gender, and sexuality?[34] Asian Americans lack collective language and frameworks for making sense of their own experiences as racialized beings, even as Asian Americans create and sustain vibrant social worlds.

The invisibilization of "Asian American" as a racial category is not something that only impacts Asian people. Inscrutability can be useful not only for analyzing the performative forms and force of Asian American racialization but also for interdisciplinary studies of race, gender, sexuality, and minoritarian aesthetics that may rely on the work of Asian American studies as an unspoken epistemic limit. The case studies in the following chapters focus primarily on artists of Chinese and Japanese ancestry; however, this is not to suggest that East Asians are the proper representatives of Asian America.[35] I write as the child of my single immigrant mother, who was born and raised in Taiwan, and as the grandchild of my maternal grandparents, whose arrival in San Francisco in the 1970s marked their second migration. It is from this positionality that I observe how East Asian racialization serves as a kind of racial limit not only for the reiterative consolidation of whiteness but also for coalition building among people of color (poc) in white-dominant spaces. Of course, not only Asian people are racialized as inscrutable, mysterious, and exotic. These social and political roles as the inscrutable other are textured and alchemized with other social conscriptions. Inscrutability can offer us a lither way to pursue interdisciplinary studies of race and its dynamic formations while fighting white supremacist practices and parsing the particularities and tensions within racial experience.

Contemporary scholars need to grapple with the "internal contradiction" posited by the Asian American for a capacious sense of the construction of difference.[36] Often, the Asian American is conjured, if at all, as the triangulated third to a Black and white racial binary, either visualized as in solidarity with Black and brown populations in provisional poc status or in complicity with a white monolith, thus reinforcing white supremacist hierarchies.[37] The Asian American racial position, as a shifting and contingent one, is relational, and its surface aesthetic is reiterated in theories of racial triangulation.[38] Asian Americans and immigrants can feel lost within discourses of "people of color," thus reinforcing a sense of unbelonging, foreignness, and cultural obfuscation. Might we consider the modularity of Asian Americanness as premised on the queer formal construction of Asia as surface limit?

A more robust discourse of inscrutability, from a subjective position not only about negation but also about productive space making, allows for better access and recognition of care networks that already exist, as constitutive of Asian American and minoritarian cultures.[39] While it is true that Asian American psychic formation relies on an endemic relationship to loss, these legacies of trauma through war, poverty, displacement, racism, and misogyny have also produced their own intergenerational cultures, through scholarly, artistic, and literary engagements with trauma, loss, and healing. Inscrutability's story does not end with the loss of legibility. In fact, loss is formative. Surface relations, as lived practices, may necessarily elude dominant optics but may be glimpsed in visual, literary, and performance art forms.

Performing Inscrutability as Reparative Knowing

To come into social life through surfaces is to figure queerly in a world premised on the exploration of depth. *Surface Relations* tends to the internal life and affective dimensions of Asian American racialization without overdetermining its content. Rather than attempt to penetrate a depth model of truth, this book notes the hetero-colonial tensions that arise from such a methodology, and instead focuses on Asian American appearance through this interaction of surface. How has the racial category "Asian American" itself taken on an inscrutable form: all exterior surface with ambiguous interior content? If we understand Asianness as that which is understood as pure screen for American projection, and "Asian American" as a still-questioned political signifier, then we must consider the productive work of inscrutable signs, known for emptiness, silence, or absence.

Asian inscrutability queers knowledge because it refuses the high valuation of modern thought as a kind of colonial capture. This book follows in the Indigenous, Black, anti-racist, feminist, and queer intellectual legacies that have destabilized modern foundations of knowledge by historicizing the violence exacted by Western thought. When queerness is informed by race and systemic violence, as desires and cultures that persist in the face of policing and violence, then the stealth expressions of queer lifeworlds can be better glimpsed through the language of inscrutability. Within such traditions, the limits of knowledge need not be threatening. As Audra Simpson writes, "Rather than stops, or impediments to knowing, those limits may be expansive in their ethnographic nonrendering *and in what they do not tell us*."[40] Inscrutability extends what Sedgwick posits as "practices of reparative knowing."[41] Reparative knowing practices of inscrutability can navigate forms of racial melancholia that Asian Americans face through persistent construction as hollow exteriority. An analytic of inscrutability can be understood as a kind of reparative surface reading, one that is attuned to the productive force of what can be sensed, including sensory negations in racial and queer forms.[42]

I write toward a reparative knowing practice that is for the Asian American becoming-subject whose social neglect can seem to foreclose modes of relating to the self and others. To cruise not only for an external object of desire but for a desirous future self is queer work.[43] As Eng and Han's theory of intersubjective becoming suggests, the search for oneself is not isolated from a search for a broader sense of belonging. The dearth of Asian American form in popular culture and national histories has necessitated a pedagogy of non-identitarian affinities and queer relations for those seeking Asian reflection. Animating Asian American sense is a queer form of minoritarian performance, because to sense out Asian forms within an American frame is necessarily to be in ambiguous, open, and reparative relation. The first chapter of this book will consider the vanishing point of Asian American visuality, particularly for Asian American women, as a productive horizon line in Asian American aesthetics. Relational aesthetics and embodied performance produce and share other ways of knowing and becoming.

Minoritarian performance of inscrutability is a mode of creating and inhabiting other worlds with one's body in relation to other bodies, if for the most fleeting of moments. *Surface Relations* begins with this premise that inscrutable Asian racial form produces a surface of internal and external life and documents how the body unfixes this dyad through relational performance. Those embodied moments potentiate relief from the stultifying loneliness and self-doubt from shame and racial melancholia. The performing body critiques and subverts the binarized deployments of Asian American experience as either pure exteriority or interiority. These moments of minoritarian performance occasion other forms of connection and possibility that exist from a vantage point that may not precisely be located but inhabited and moved through. The performing body can be said to experience, index, and ask after something through its movement as living form.

As queer and racial form, performances of inscrutability problematize the perceptibility of life. Made possible by the field of performance studies, this book's focus on aesthetic modes of inscrutability follows in a genealogy of José Esteban Muñoz's formulation of "the burden of liveness" for queers of color and minoritarian performers. Willful inscrutability in these pages follows Karen Shimakawa's theories of abject mimicry, that is, as an abject mime of the inscrutable other trope. As Shimakawa shows, Asianness has figured as the site of disgust and shame, that which should be abjected from the national body; moreover, the reiterative task of doing such racial abjection is labored on Asian Americans whose national belonging is contingent on successful performances of sexuality and nationality that mollify the perceived threat of Asianness. I name these two scholars and mentors here not only to credit their pivotal theories but also to index how Muñoz and Shimakawa together have mentored generations of performance scholars, such that to write "queer performance studies" or "minoritarian performance studies" as I almost do here feels redundant. This book is rooted, then, in the utopic part of the field that Muñoz and Shimakawa have tended, where the body's possibility and relational force are best understood through entangled rhetorics of performance, race, gender, sexuality, and nation. If "there are a (limited) number of preexisting ways of *reading* the abject Asian American body," then this book formulates the performance of inscrutability as a specific strategy of disidentification and mimetic abjection from the stereotype of Asian as inscrutable other.[44] Through performance methodology, the dynamic matter of the body, in its inscrutability and its imaginative interpretations and capacities, is the primary grounds of my readings. While performance seems to name that which disappears in its moment of appearance, its ephemerality does not delimit its perlocutionary effects. It is through performance's capacious temporality and liminality that inscrutability may be glimpsed. The body, whether conjured through written text or captured on film or labored through in performance art, troubles the abstraction that inscrutability could connote in its materiality, in its perception effects, and in its temporal and spatial specificities and decided critique of universalism. As Amin, Musser, and Pérez write, "To speak of the world-making capacity of aesthetic forms is not a willful act of naivety (though such acts of unknowing have their own value), but a way to keep critical practice vital and resist the downward pull of political surrender."[45]

Minoritarian Performance Aesthetics of Obfuscation

Inscrutable surfacing negotiates the burden of liveness that performers of color are taxed with on and off theatrical stages. The stakes of liveness, the burden to perform as a legible subject for a dominant gaze, and the impossibility of a neutral context shape most any imaginable conversation we can have about history, temporality, and futurity for minoritarian life. José Esteban Muñoz intervenes in the "obstructive fetish" of liveness in the field of performance studies and writes: "Some performances are structured through historically embedded cultural mandates that the body of color, the queer body, the poor body, the woman's body perform his or her existence for elite eyes. This performance is positioned within the dominant culture as a substitute for historical and political representation. Thus, performing beyond the channels of liveness and entering larger historical narratives seems especially important."[46] Listen for the resonance of Muñoz's words for Asian Americans, for whom "historical and political representation" remains tenuous, though some perform their "existence for elite eyes" as minorities offered provisional status in white-dominant institutions. Considering the charge of "negative personality" and evacuated interiority, Asian inscrutability can be said to index the burden of liveness as a burden of *liveliness*, of reassuring affective comportment that aligns one as a model minority who will not threaten dominant structures of liberal multicultural warmth and white fragility.[47] To focus on Asian American performance, as a vital part of a field of minoritarian performance, is to expand the study of compulsory liveliness for those who embody difference. Inscrutability is such a performance "beyond the channels of liveness" without forfeiting Asian American life. Through Muñoz's influential phrasing of "minoritarian performance" and "queers of color," this book resides in the relationship between these discursive formations and Asian American aesthetics.

Inscrutability troubles modern optics of and mandates for monolithic life and liveliness. Here I think with Mel Chen's writing on animacies and Sianne Ngai's writing on animatedness, with implications for queer and Asian temporalities. Asian and queer liveliness have symbolized twinned threats to the futurity of American modernity: Asianness as contagion and economic ruin through yellow perilism (as evidenced perennially through rhetorics of China as disease) and queerness as existential ruin through HIV/AIDS and non-heteronormative reproduction. Jasbir Puar's scholarship on Muslim / Arab / Middle Eastern terrorist assemblages, through Orientalist discursive formations of queerness, brilliantly shows the volatile movements of these forms.

If Asian life has been that which might infect and end the white supremacist state's economic virility, then what do Asian racial forms of inscrutability teach us about the performance of other lifeworlds and temporalities?

Inscrutability is aligned with racial, gender, and sexual performatives that cohere around what I call *minoritarian aesthetics of obfuscation*.[48] Aesthetic modes of inscrutability describe senses of racial, feminist, and queer performance that route political and cultural life away from identitarian fixity and representation as the desirable political horizon. We may note the centrality of Asian American diasporic feminist and queer thinkers in constellating such a study, namely in Karen Shimakawa's mimetic abjection, Gayatri Gopinath's discussion of impossibility and queer-sighted vision, Homay King's reworking of Jean Laplanche's enigmatic signifier, and Karen Tongson's remote intimacies.[49] Through their writings, the abject, the impossible, the enigmatic, and the remote signal other affinity formations, other sensory modes, and other doings that render being and becoming otherwise imaginable.

I align my thinking with feminist and queer scholars whose work on history, memory, culture, and the body are navigated through aesthetics of obfuscation, deferral, withholding, and nonappearance. Engaging the writings of Édouard Glissant, Christina A. León articulates how opacity "instead invokes the visual through a resistance to the kind of gaze that desires mastery, simplicity, and knowability, and which all too often aligns with sexist and colonial desires."[50] I also learn from Tina Post's writings on deadpan, surface, and monochrome in Black expressive cultures; Sarah Stefana Smith's work on surface and camouflage in Black feminist visual arts; and Colleen Kim Daniher's writings on racial ambiguity and racial modulation as a crucial rethinking of mixed-race discursive contributions to contemporary racial aesthetics.[51] I understand the writing of these scholars and *Surface Relations* to name and posit forth the urgency in swerving away from liberal impulses to cohere, to identify, in a word, to assimilate to existing terms of empathic life—all without forfeiting studies of "complex personhood" and historic dynamics of gendered racialization.[52] These scholars work with anti-identitarian aesthetics of obfuscation that maintain a relationship with difference at the same time as they refuse to perform essentialized difference, working in the debt and genealogy of women-of-color thinkers who refused a separatist politics that would forsake their intersectional activist commitments.[53] I constellate these scholars with a rich genealogy of performance scholars, including Daphne Brooks, Joshua Chambers-Letson, Summer Kim Lee, Roy Pérez, Iván Ramos, Sandra Ruiz, and Shane Vogel, from whom I learn about modes of being, becoming, and belonging that cannot be neatly segregated into analyses of gender, race, sexuality, or nation in a single axis but also cannot be encompassed through rhetorics of intersectionality or equality, as these spatial metaphors suggest the possibility of separating social axes into distinct or comparable specimens for study.

Within these minoritarian aesthetics is a need to consider the racialization of lively affect and its construction of social possibility. Inspired by Audra Simpson's work, Lilian Mengesha and Lakshmi Padmanabhan write, "Refusal asks us to reconsider the emotional, psychological, and embodied stakes of engagement—engaging in liberal state politics, engaging in representation, engaging in debate—because at the other end of that engagement for people of color, queer and trans bodies, is the punishment of excessiveness: we are too political, too sensitive, rude, loud, too argumentative. More succinctly, perhaps, we are often too much alive."[54] Yet, as we have seen through the racial construction of Asians as pure exteriority/interiority, these affective characterizations of excess can but often do not resonate for Asian American populations. In an American racial landscape, Asian Americans present a different kind of problem than being "too much alive" but rather not lively enough. The charge of not being lively, however, carries its own emotional, psychological, and political stakes, such that the very liveliness of Asian American culture and humanity is questioned. Asian Americans might be thought exceptional to racial excessiveness, such that to suggest a racial politics of inscrutability may stoke anxieties of Asian American apoliticality. So long as Asian Americans are formally conjured as hollow surfaces, Asian performativity is in a tense relation not only with white comportment but also with POC political affect.

Asian inscrutability disturbs the emotionality of political expression. While my task in the remaining pages of this book is to detail and think through the stakes of such an Asian American aesthetic theory, and how this racial form has occasioned an Asian American affective theory, I respect the caution that generations of scholars, from Mitsuye Yamada to Shireen Roshanravan, have voiced in noting the limitations of silence, invisibility, and infrapolitics.[55] This book does not build a "strong theory" for the inscrutability of Asian American and diasporic life.[56] More nearly, following Sedgwick, inscrutability can be understood as a weak theory in the service of minoritarian flourishing and queer speculative historiography.[57] Inscrutability warrants thought, as it allows for a more agile reckoning with Asian American subject formation that does not police Asian American life as always already needing to either defend its viability or apologize for existing. Asian American inscrutability is not only ever a reiteration of the status quo, of quiet passing, of model minority respectability. As with most strategies or tools, there is no inherent political agenda to inscrutability.[58] I offer my intellectual energy to formulate inscrutability as an aesthetic strategy that artists have used to destabilize binaristic racial, gender, and sexual knowledge production. Especially for the political, cultural, and social life of Asian Americans, engaging with inscrutability offers vital paths forward.

Aesthetic Modes of Inscrutability

Inscrutability as a feminist and queer-of-color aesthetic strategy contributes to conversations in anti-identitarian critique, post-racial neoliberalism, and queer formalism by offering a framework for sensing Asianness not as a racial form consistent with multicultural logics of assimilation but as a form latent with stealth obfuscation, political critique, and innovative social forms. As that which cannot be searched into or understood, and which may evade dominant terms of liveness, I think through inscrutability in performances of invisibility, silence, unreliability, flatness, and distance. I have identified these modes through reading and viewing cultural productions that use these racialized and gendered tropes as aesthetic form. Each of these modes functions, to some degree, as both aesthetic dynamic and affective mood. Each names a minoritarian aesthetic and affect in contemporary Asian American expressive culture. The chapters make their way through different material surfaces: film, canvas, skin, page, photograph, and cassette tape.

The first three chapters of this book think through the Orientalist romance of Asian female negation, through aesthetic modes of invisibility, silence, and impenetrability, to consider how it is that Asian woman, trans, and nonbinary artists navigate the conventional, Orientalist modes of engaging with their bodies. From this introduction, the book tackles the trope of invisibility and disappearance in Asian American performance cultures, whether that be in the language of a lack of media representation or in the operatic suicides of Asian female tragic lovers. Chapter 1, "Invisibility and the Vanishing Point of Asian/American Visuality," studies the trope of invisibility as one such mode whose productive force performs the nonappearance of Asian Americans as though a fact of contemporary life. Studying the aesthetic production of Asian invisibility allows us to contend with an American phenomenon where Asianness can only appear by disappearing. In this sense, the purported lack of representation of Asian Americans cannot be separated from misogynist and patriarchal nationalist forces that render feminine forms legible only through hyper-hetero-sexualization and colonial conquest. Put another way, the chapter on invisibility thinks through the trope of Asian female suicide, as romanticized in the butterfly character, where invisibility does not name the absence of Asian women but rather its spectacularized and sexualized self-erasure to uphold white Euro-American state power. I turn to the artwork of Asian American and diasporic artists, including Denise Uyehara, who use the vanishing point as the grounds for desire and sexual pleasure.

I argue that to resign inscrutability only to a position of victimization is to concede too much, as though suffering is the proper criterion for minoritarian life. Indeed, what a study of inscrutability allows is an observation of the blur between aesthetic form and circulated affect of Asian racialization. In an ocularcentric world of liberalism, affect may be the only way in which aesthetics of inscrutability may be sensed. In chapter 2, "Silence and Parasitic Hospitality in the Works of Yoko Ono, Laurel Nakadate, and Emma Sulkowicz," I consider artists who mime these tropes as conventions that provide a framework for interpretation and critique. Ono, Nakadate, and Sulkowicz are not so much reifying a stereotype of Asian/American silence and hospitality in my reading so much as each artist is in their own way identifying pervasive discourses of silence and hospitality that set the stage for their work. By acknowledging and working with these socio-environmental givens, the artists can navigate market and everyday demands and strictures of legibility as well as potentiate other readings of embodied performance and practice of ethical encounter.

My third and fourth chapters consider artists' invocation of Asian unreliability specifically through the materiality and penetrability of surface. In chapter 3, "Im/penetrability, Trans Figuration, and Unreliable Surfacing," I consider the role of skin cutting in three contemporary novels, where the surface of the queer and/or trans Asian protagonist's body is mutable. This changeability is also reflected in the protagonist's unreliable narration; this trans and feminine, and transfeminine, unreliability has not only distressed white nation-building efforts but is also what has historically occasioned masculinist anxiety in Asian American studies. This discussion of surface unreliability is continued in chapter 4, "Flatness, Industriousness, and Laborious Flexibility," through the installation work of Mika Tajima and the performance collective New Humans. I study how the inscrutability of Asiatic racial form is played with in Tajima's repurposing of 1960s modular office furniture, allowing for an economic analysis of Asian unreliability in the rhetoric of flexibility—that is, flexible labor. By retooling the flat monochrome canvases of cubicle furniture, as a kind of racialized modern form, Tajima critiques the optimization of economic efficiency in neoliberal capitalism.

In the last two chapters, the book turns toward a discussion of flatness and distance, both functioning as racialized affects and forms of inscrutability. For a recent example relevant to academic audiences, I write about the characterization of Asians and Asian Americans as having negative or low personality ratings in the admissions scandal at Harvard University, reminiscent of broader criticism of Asian/Americans as aliens or apathetic citizens. In chapter 5, "Distance, Negativity, and Slutty Sociality in Tseng Kwong Chi's Performance Photographs," I write about distance as racialized affect as well as artistic choice and material condition in performance artist Tseng Kwong Chi's use of geographic and temporal distance throughout his ten-year self-portraiture/landscape series during the HIV/AIDS emergency of the 1980s. The chapter analyzes Tseng's photographs to articulate a practice of slutty solidarity and queer coordination that is enacted through his performances of distance.

The book closes with "Something Is Missing," a consideration of the meticulous documentation practices of Tehching Hsieh and Linda Montano's famed year-long performance work, *Rope Piece*, in asking how inscrutability, via withholding, changes archiving practices. Taken together, these chapters offer a way to grapple with contemporary Asian racialization as something other than the missing identity, as a hollow and fading referent, in a list of races. Rather, attending to the productive force of this missing identification becomes the project of this book.

Surface Relations addresses the dangers of expectant self-sufficiency, diminishment, and invisibilization of Asian/American communities (commonly circulated through the model minority myth, persistent in academic institutions and elsewhere) as well as the need to collectivize comparative racialized and gendered feelings of inscrutability, urgent in a political climate that threatens both to disavow and to recruit difference—specifically Asian, feminine, and queer difference—under US neoliberal post-racial capitalism. I write this book with my students in mind, particularly Asian American, queer, and trans students who are working toward world-making in a reality that speaks in identity politics that often do not include them. With this book, I hope to offer conceptual frameworks for interpreting and practicing sociality otherwise, with critiques of the elevation of knowing over relating, and for extending curiosity for affective modes whose social potentials are currently dismissed. The broader significance of this project lies in the alternative world-making imagined, materialized, and made shareable through minoritarian aesthetic encounter. While under modernism, the inscrutable has been marginalized historically, politically, and legally, inscrutable practices of performance and spectatorship index that which cannot be anticipated. As such, inscrutability as a concept carries with it not only the threat of demise but also the prospect of hope in the unknown.

INVISIBILITY AND THE VANISHING POINT OF ASIAN/ AMERICAN VISUALITY

It is in these years at the waning of the twentieth century that the term "Asian" in the United States has achieved a certain highly productive invisibility (or at least opacity). Just a few years ago, in the inventorying of racial groups in the United States, "Asian American" was normally part of the cluster "Afro-American," "Native American," "Hispanic American," popularly evoked and presented as the essential markers of race and ethnicity in the United States. Now, however, one increasingly finds that "Asian American" is omitted.—DAVID PALUMBO-LIU, *Asian/American*

Apparently through a long conditioning process, I had learned how *not* to be seen for what I am. A long history of ineffectual activities had been, I realize now, initiation rites toward my eventual invisibility.—MITSUYE YAMADA, "Invisibility Is an Unnatural Disaster"

How does Asian American life appear? Many argue that it only appears through negation. In the classic 1981 essay "Invisibility Is an Unnatural Disaster," Mitsuye Yamada writes, "I had learned how *not* to be seen for what I am." In 1999 David Palumbo-Liu described the "highly productive invisibility," "opacity," and "omi[ssion]" of "Asian" and "Asian American." In 2021 Katie Li described to *Time* magazine how the Atlanta shootings on March 16 amplified "hundreds of years of history of exclusion, of erasure, of invisibility."[1] Disappearance has long been the expression, fate, and function of Asianness on a US national stage.

What does this absence have to do with cultural and aesthetic conventions? Cultural critics in recent years have commented on a historic lack of Asian American representation in popular media, often while reporting on efforts to cast Asian and Asian American actors in Asian and Asian American roles. Despite the success of the blockbuster film *Crazy Rich Asians* (2018) and the television sitcom *Fresh Off the Boat* (2015–20), contemporary films such as *Doctor Strange* (2016) and *Ghost in the Shell* (2017) continue theatrical and cinematic histories of yellowface performance and the whitewashing of Asian characters. In these ways, Asian visuality often circulates in its absence, lack, or disappearance.

The vanishing act of Asians and Asian Americans in popular representation is effected through not only outright omission but also the violent disappearance of Asian characters, and specifically of Asian woman characters. Consider the butterfly archetype popularized by Puccini's *Madama Butterfly* and the Broadway musical *Miss Saigon*, wherein the main Asian female character functions as a sacrificial foil, whose tragic love secures the futurity of white imperialism through heteropatriarchal reproduction. In these Orientalist narratives, the figure of the Asian woman exists primarily to serve the male protagonist's arc as well as the militarized systems of power that the man represents and upholds. Her ability to serve is underscored by her eventual suicide; the Oriental woman's aesthetic function is to make herself disappear in the maintenance of white heteropatriarchal rule.[2] This Orientalist narrative convention leaves Asian diasporic audiences without a script for a future. Any future relies on the Asian woman's compulsory heterosexuality, reproductive labor, and self-sacrifice. The plot quickly moves on from the Asian woman's suicide by sentimentalizing her legacy as carried on by her child. Thus, the Asian woman's future is paradoxically secured through biological reproduction and self-obliteration, all in the name of love. Her narrative value lies in a biologically dead and biologically reproductive future.[3]

The psychological effects of visualizing Asian women through the Orientalist romance of Asian female sacrifice are important to identify, especially when self-erasure becomes the primary, or exclusive, mode of appearance. The convention of Asian death as plot device has become a norm of modern life. One need only note the incidence of violence against Asian diasporic women and the occurrence of Asian American women's suicidal ideation to reckon with the stakes of these portrayals.[4] Consider the public response to the murder of eight people, including six Asian diasporic women, at three Asian spas around Atlanta, Georgia, in March 2021. A discourse of anti-Asian racism had been simmering throughout the coronavirus pandemic, but it was not until this mass shooting that Asian American pain and grief gained visibility, however briefly, in mainstream media. Asian American experience was overshadowed by the white gunman's right to complex interiority and the local state authority's refusal to see the mass shooting as racially motivated. Asian American and diasporic activists, artists, and scholars responded by connecting the murders to centuries of anti-Asian violence through vectors of imperialism, militarism, classism, and misogyny, and foregrounded ongoing histories of violence against Asian massage workers, whether or not they engage in sex work.[5]

Notably, authors used the rhetoric of sight and invisibility to critique violence against Asian diasporic women. The women's lives could not be seen on a public stage except through violence because of the active invisibilization of Asian/American histories. As Durba Mitra, Sara Kang, and Genevieve Clutario write, "To see these women's lives in fullness requires that we reckon with overlapping histories of racism, militarism, and policing that have made Asian diasporic women invisible to Americans except when condemned through ideas of illicit sex."[6] Community organizers with Red Canary Song write, "We see the effort to invisibilize these women's gender, labor, class, and immigration status as a refusal to reckon with the legacy of United States imperialism, and as a desire to collapse the identities of migrant Asian women, sex workers, massage workers, and trafficking survivors."[7] In both examples, the authors strategically employ a discourse of invisibility to describe the systemic dismissal of Asian American histories and imperialist violence against migrant Asian communities. The rhetoric of in/visibility serves to address the diminishment of Asian and Asian American existence since something invisible still exists whether or not it is seen. These powerful responses following tragic violence demonstrate the extent to which public recognition of Asian American experience relies on a framework of invisibility.

I worry, however, that invisibility has become such a common grammar of Asian America that visibility has become the telos of Asian American public life and, more broadly, of US cultural politics.

The dominant discourse of Asian American invisibility, that is, disciplines a liberal racial subject who is in a bind: they must plead for political recognition, but this "scramble for legibility," in the words of Dylan Rodríguez, only strengthens the "protocols of *legitimated* antiblack, colonial, class, and gendered state violence—criminalization, policing, prosecution, incarceration, civil expulsion, state punishment."[8] Meanwhile, this discursive framework of invisibility obscures political legacies and quotidian practices of coalitional, intersectional, and transnational activism that may never make it to national news. Such discursive invisibility belies activist and intellectual histories pursuing systemic change that care for the most vulnerable and least legible, including those for whom institutional visibility is unsafe.[9] When news sources did cover the Atlanta shootings, there was little attending to the archival lacunas of diasporic and multilingual lives, for instance, with reporters' mispronunciation of the murdered women's names, or the inconsistent acknowledgment that some of the victims' families did not wish for their relative to be identified publicly.[10] Such contingencies reveal some of the ways in which Asian American and diasporic lives operate beside or below the bounds of protocol and challenge frames of visibility and recognition.[11]

Where do we go from here? I open with this thematic of invisibility and violent obliteration as an aesthetic and political trope in Asian American representation, and specifically violence against Asian women, because there is no contending with Asian American inscrutability without going through vernaculars of invisibility, representation, and Asian female death. These discourses of disappearance and violence are symbolic and material. How are Asian American people to grapple with these violent terms of relevance and appearance?

Surface Relations theorizes Asian American aesthetics of invisibility less for external recognition and more toward the curiosity and capacity to recognize ourselves and, more, to ask after modes of visuality that are critical of the convention of disappearance. If Asian women appear in visual representation only to disappear spectacularly, then Asian American aesthetic practices pursue these harmful conventions to destabilize and revise them. Contemporary Asian American artists draw our attention to this trope of violent disappearance as a way to collectively identify and critique the normalization of Asian female self-obliteration as art or beauty. In a memorable penultimate scene of Young Jean Lee's 2006 play *Songs of the Dragon Flying* to *Heaven*, the four Asian woman characters (Korean 1, Korean 2, Korean 3, and Korean-American) line up to perform a grotesque series of suicides "*in a confident manner*" while Mariah Carey's hit song "All I Want for Christmas Is You" jingles through the speakers.[12] In addition to the identities suggested by the characters' names, the scripted forms of suicide are explicitly gendered and racialized. For example, Lee instructs: "*Korean 2 commits hara-kiri*," while "*Korean 3 stabs herself in the vagina with a knife*" and soon "*cuts off her breast, bites a chunk out of it, throws her breast into the audience, spits the chunk at the audience, and resumes scuttling.*"[13] The outrageous spectacle confronts the audience with the theatrical convention of Asian women's self-harm as feel-good entertainment. Played directly to the audience, the actors maintain eye contact with the crowd and compel them to *look* and see which violent histories are scripted onto their bodies and render their gestures legible. While such performance occasions momentary visibility, these violent representations of Asian women are difficult if not impossible to recuperate because of the psychological implications this has for viewers. When I have taught this play, as literature and performance, students have voiced intense discomfort in watching Asian American actors embody and hyperbolize the trope of Asian female suicide.[14] Perhaps most of all, students are disturbed by the audience's laughter. As Karen Shimakawa writes, "Reembodying abject personae, even insubordinately, nonetheless allows them to be bodied forth again."[15] Repetition may revise the mechanism and meaning but only insofar as it performs some fidelity to the previous iteration. However, these aesthetic conventions for Asian American legibility may be necessary to identify and mimic in order to move through them. As Shimakawa writes, "There is arguably a pleasure and a power, howsoever limited and inextricably linked with pain, in reclaiming the sign of abjection, miming it imperfectly and even hyperbolically."[16]

In this chapter, I shift from what Palumbo-Liu calls the "productive in-visibility" of Asian American life and turn to a theme of vanishing in Asian American performance and visual cultures. I identify these theatrical and everyday performances of violence against Asian and Asian American women in efforts to repeat this discourse of disappearance with a difference. There are distinctions to be drawn between externally scripted self-annihilation and strategically ephemeral appearance. How do we identify and perform forms of Asian American invisibility that function less as sacrificial romance and more as a critique of the terms of neoliberal visibility? From what epistemic regimes are these characters vanishing? Rather than merely advocate for the casting of Asian actors in Asian roles, might we not expand our frameworks for discussing Asian American visuality altogether? How might we repair this Orientalist vision and reframe vanishing otherwise?

The Queer Temporality of Asian American Life

but where are you really from? / yesterday is the wrong answer, tomorrow too
—HIEU MINH NGUYEN, "White Boy Time Machine: Software," in *Not Here*

The visual function of the Asian woman martyr figure is significant for her own undoing, for offering the beauty and morality of her erasure, for servicing the futurity of a white racial order.[17] The felicitous performance of Asian femininity has been aesthetically formalized as her constitutive disappearance. The spectacular annihilation of Asian women on American public and theatrical stages warrants thought alongside queer scholarship on self-obliteration and futurity. The Asian woman is a queer figure in her self-annihilation in the service of others, whose legibility is premised on her sexual deviance, her biological reproduction, and her self-harm.[18]

The symbolic and material effect of the Asian woman's violent disappearance is to throw Asian and Asian diasporic futurity into question. The future of Asian American life, like its past, is thrown into crisis and uncertainty. Inscrutability names a temporal problem for Asian American life, as a culture without collective origin point or a future horizon of biological reproduction. Consider the racial hail that commonly interpellates Asians and people of color across ethnic specificity in the United States, in the series of questions: "Where are you from? Where are you really from? No, what is your nationality?" Given undertaught histories of war, exclusion, and incarceration, Asian Americans are imagined to have a foreign origin point at the same time as they are made to embody the vanishing point of national belonging. To be questioned for one's origins could be understood as a queer diasporic placement, since one is simultaneously cast out of sexual and national imaginaries of time and space. As Martin Manalansan writes on queer undocumented world-making, "'Where are you from?' is a question that is posed to the foreigner, the non-citizen, and the queer. It is a question that comes from a power-laden state-centered vantage that demands a fixed reference, origin, or provenance from anyone seeking recognition."[19] As Hieu Minh Nguyen suggests, there are only wrong answers to this question. Rather than adhering to a normative sense of belonging to one fixed location, the Asian, foreigner, noncitizen, and queer figure indexes the multiplicity of points where one lives one's life. We might consider this threat to fixity as a queer threat, and take it up as queer insistence. I locate this as the work of inscrutability, of thickening the visualization of time and space as necessary origin or telos and instead elucidating other modes of relation in time and space, as exercised in Asian American aesthetics.

Asian Americanness is not yet here in at least two ways: a belated or deferred sense of belonging to the US nation—not yet here because perpetually foreign—and still questioned as a political identifier with traction or use value.[20] Muñoz's queer horizon resonates with my sense of Asian queer and trans utopia that is not yet here and toward which we must sense and work. Muñoz's turn to the not-yet and emphasis on queer futurity was ultimately with political consequences for concrete hope, especially for queer-of-color communities who, as he writes, are not the sacred princes of white reproductive futurity.[21] Horizon is not only before us in its teasing futurity but also surrounds us in indexing irrecoverable loss. While queer horizon beckons with seduction, there are horizons we could racialize as Asian that one would not want to return to, or anyway, one could not possibly return to. Muñoz's project is about the backward glance, "the *then* that disrupts the tyranny of the *now*" recognized as "both past and future," holding past and future as of the same fold.[22] As Ocean Vuong soothes, "Don't worry. Just call it *horizon* / & you'll never reach it."[23] In the poem "Someday I'll Love Ocean Vuong," the speaker connotes the safety and reassurance that can be found in distance, not only to the future (that muse for anxiety) but also to the past, as imaged in "the house with childhood / whittled down to a single red trip wire."[24] Here, the naming of "horizon" anesthetizes the tripwires of the past that would render the imaginability of the present impossible. This queer temporal holding is a mandatory survival strategy for Asian Americans, whose cultures and histories have figured in the United States as the spectral remnants of what is actively disavowed in the name of national progress.

As David L. Eng and Shinhee Han teach us, Asian American histories are repressed in the political unconscious such that it is unsurprising that Asian American life is registered in negation. This national melancholia produces "the Asian American model minority *subject*" as a "melancholic national *object*" and "haunting specter to democratic ideals of inclusion that cannot quite 'get over' the histories of these legislated proscriptions of loss."[25] Eng and Han's influential theory of racial mourning *and* melancholia suggests to me a correlative racial visual register, relevant to loss that neither multicultural nor neoliberal optics can bring into the visual field as more than a haunting or spectral form. This dual mode of becoming from, toward, and presently in loss makes clear the intimate relationships between Asian American becoming and queer negativity theory, as mutually invested in alternative aesthetic sensibilities and temporalities.

With the exclusionary pain, shame, and fear of these questions of impossible US origin also comes a queer power, a jettisoning from the prison house of the nation. I understand this questioning of origins, and the radical othering that this series of questions performs, as a queer racial performative. The painful exclusion of "Where are you from?" can be met not only with fear and isolation but also with a sense of relief in minoritarian becoming and world-making. The scene of questioning carries a subtext we can read queerly: *You did not come from only this, and you were not made for only this. You were made for a better world.* To reorient this relation to national belonging, however, is not to opt out of accountability.[26] Amid mainstream conversations about Asian representation, premised on imperialist optics of US raciality, Asian American visual cultures need to contend with queer theory's anti-identitarian verve, the critique of origins in performance studies, and what Kandice Chuh formulates as the *"subjectless discourse"* of Asian Americanist critique.[27] Engaging with contemporary artists, Asian American visual and performance studies can offer vitalizing frameworks for practicing and sharing out complex forms of life and feeling, including horizons of joy, grief, pleasure, and uncertainty as well as horizons of pain and alienation.

Queerness and Disappearance

It is time to consider how Asian American viewing and aesthetic practices have developed in a way that has less to do with mirror identification toward a telos of reflection and more about a queer disidentification. What I describe as the queer aesthetics of inscrutably becoming for Asian Americans names a disidentification from tropes of Asian as perpetual foreigner in the US American context, and suggests that strategic inscrutability is a mode of critique against presentist mandates for social and political legibility. A common emphasis on realist representation bespeaks an impoverished racial imaginary delimited by liberal values. In this chapter, I index invisibility as an Orientalist erasure of Asian life as well as a strategically abstracted visuality of Asiatic presence. These obscured ways of appearing are not to be confused with one another but rather thought together. The vanishing point of queer diasporic female subjectivity is identified in the work of Gayatri Gopinath, who opens *Impossible Desires* with a close reading of the film *My Beautiful Laundrette*. Gopinath writes:

The film's female diasporic character Tania, in fact, functions in a classic homosocial triangle as the conduit and foil to the desire between Johnny and Omar, and she quite literally disappears at the film's end. We last see her standing on a train platform, suitcase in hand, having left behind the space of the immigrant home in order to seek a presumably freer elsewhere. . . . She thus marks the horizon of Kureishi's filmic universe and gestures to another narrative of female diasporic subjectivity that functions quite literally as the film's vanishing point.[28]

The impossibility of Tania's visuality also marks her escape from the male cinematic gaze that can only focus on her through disappearance. To identify the female diasporic subject as the vanishing point to Western optics, and the vanishing point as the female diasporic subject, is to critique Orientalist representations of Asian women as necessarily tragic, heterosexualized, and self-sacrificing. There is political and aesthetic importance in figuring Asiatic feminine forms through a kind of para-visuality—as distinct from total disappearance but as a critical mode beside and against liberal appearance. It becomes imperative for those racialized as Asian to seek out other forms of visual reflection that do not result only in tragic disappearance and glamourized suicide. Here, I guide us to consider visual inscrutability as modes of appearing without conforming to white supremacist liberal aesthetic convention.

The notorious invisibility of Asian/American representation in mainstream US media and the vital modes of appearance in Asian American expressive cultures bring us to the work of Gopinath and other scholars of minoritarian aesthetics. Tina Campt's *black visuality* articulates "practices of refusal" of Black contemporary artists "who create radical modalities of witnessing that refuse authoritative forms of visuality which function to refuse blackness itself."[29] Campt's focus on "relationality and adjacency" and Black visuality's "ability to engage negation as generative" is instructive of this book's study of inscrutability. Similarly, Christina León, following Édouard Glissant, formulates *opacity* as "an aesthetic and ethico-political response to the demands for transparency" within performances of queer latinidades that can serve aesthetic analysis across ethnic studies.[30] As León writes about the work of performance artist Xandra Ibarra, "Such opacity at once conjures and resists the visual registers that so often form the contours of our political landscape; many such visual registers often presume simplistically that the inclusion or representation of certain bodies amounts to a kind of triumph."[31] León's formulation of queer-of-color opacity resonates with this work on Asiatic inscrutability as that which also "conjures and resists the visual registers" that have historically invisibilized Asian forms through strategies including yellowface. As the twenty-first century seems a time where more studio money is investing in Asian American and diasporic cultural production, we need opaque utopian aesthetics that refuse inclusionary identity politics as the best alternative to exclusion. My ideal horizon is neither oriented toward self-harm and suicide nor extravagant heteropatriarchal wealth consolidation but reaching toward something else.

The chapter will move us toward contemporary visual artworks that have grappled with dot and vanishing-point imagery as a mode of appearance that moves away from reproducing values of visual authenticity and toward other sensory modes that skirt realist figuration. My interest in dots and points in Asian/American aesthetics speaks to Phillip Brian Harper's theory of abstractionist aesthetics as a pointed critique against realist and compulsory positive images in African American expressive culture.[32] To view inscrutably is to think along Harper's definition of abstractionism as "the resolute awareness that even the most realistic representation is precisely a representation, and that as such it necessarily exists at a distance from the social reality it is conventionally understood to reflect."[33] The importance of insisting on and making space for abstractionist aesthetics, then, lies in the reorientation from fetishes of the real that marginalize if not outright dismiss the histories of those images as socially constructed and contingent to an idea of universal truth. Asian American visuality in its contemporary forms requires what Sarah Stefana Smith theorizes as "surface play," or that which "resists the impulse to make oppositional representation and abstraction by fraying the very lines of demarcation between the two."[34] To pursue inscrutability as a queer and Asian aesthetic is to languish in the socially and politically salient desire to feel the artistic and activist genealogies of Asian American movements—migrations, displacements, social activism, staged performance, and analytical efforts against the fixity of solo origin or telos—and to contribute to the aspirational space of their homing, without a single origin or destination point, as a proliferation of meaning, origin, destination, and significance.

Queer Erotics of the Vanishing Point

Does the absence of visual reflection foreclose fleshly presence or spectatorial pleasure? The answer must be no, out of an ethical need to attend to the fact of Asian American feminist, queer, and trans lives. Partly what the lack of mirrored identification of mainstream Asian American cultural forms has necessitated and trained in visually absented viewers is a creative op-positional viewing strategy, one that employs a disidentificatory visual prac-tice. Minoritarian inscrutability, then, indexes Asian visuality from a viewing position where Asian Americanness may not otherwise appear. An Asian American visual practice is melancholic not so much in its pathological con-notation but more so in its recognition of historic loss through exclusion and erasure. This form of creative looking, of looking with the aim of repairing, con-necting, and becoming, is minoritarian work. This creative labor—thinking, here, with Celine Parreñas Shimizu's writing on resistant spectatorial practice—is an everyday effort, one that can find company and muse in feminist, queer, and trans Asian diasporic visual and performance art.[35]

Denise Uyehara's 1994 solo performance piece *Hello (Sex) Kitty* helps me theorize the queer pleasures of showing up in forms that are not exactly vis-ible. In the vignette "The Vanishing Point," playing the character Woman, Uyehara recalls an art history professor who defines the vanishing point as "a point on the horizon line where two parallel lines meet, way off in the dis-tance."[36] As Uyehara speaks these lines, her arms zoom forward to represent straight lines and she brings her hands closer to one another to demonstrate the logic of Renaissance perspective (see figures 1.1–1.3). She concedes, "This may seem contradictory, since we are told parallel lines never meet, but go for infinity, without ever touching. But I will tell you, in real life, if you stand on a railroad track, you'll notice the tracks eventually merge together, way off into the distance, and where they meet, that is their vanishing point."[37] Woman invokes this memory to credit her art history professor as an early lesbian figure in her life. The character admits she was talking about the art history professor—identified endearingly as "a big ol' dyke"—in order to talk to the audience about sex, and begins to recount a "boring" night at a bar where people were standing around avoiding eye contact.[38]

To be sure, the lack of eye contact doesn't bother Woman; the character is not so much concerned with the optics of sociality as she is focused on the specific topic of sex. Looking elsewhere and not meeting another's eyes for her is an apt way to think through the relationship between visuality and sex-uality. Musing on the lack of eye contact, the character Woman quips, "Like how you ever gonna get laid doing that?"[39] Uyehara offers a theory to explain why people may be preoccupied from otherwise engaging with one another: "They're all secretly trying to reach orgasm. . . . Especially women because they can do that secret contraction thing, you know?"[40] She then returns to the gesture of the vanishing point, where the moment of contact of her fingers ("*blam, blam, blam, blam, blam, blam, zhoom*") maps onto the moment of

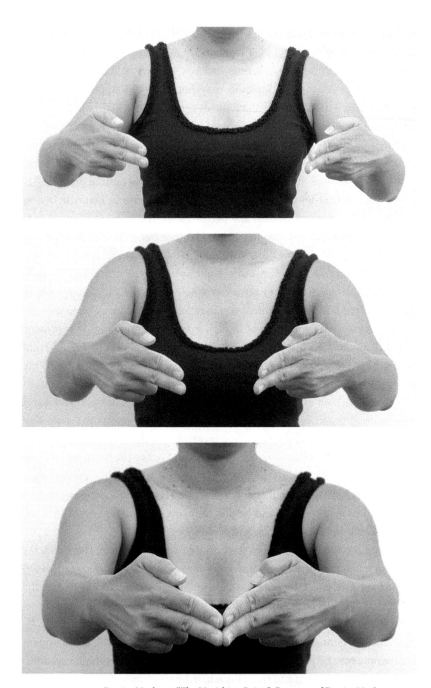

FIGURES 1.1–1.3. Denise Uyehara, "The Vanishing Point." Courtesy of Denise Uyehara.

orgasm. In this way, her arms come to stand in for not only the parallel lines of perspectivalism but also the crescendo of sexual stimulation toward orgasm. Her dialogue adds to this list, suggesting that her arms are also lovers who are coming closer to one another to attain "zero distance." She notes, "Yeah, sure your gender or color is important, but at that moment, it's about something else, it's about being zero distance apart. Once I made love with this woman and we watched each other the entire time. (BEAT) Okay, so some of you may be wondering how do two women reach orgasm while they look into each other's eyes at the same time. Well, go find out for yourself."[41] Here, eye contact is not essential to arousal between two women. Looking, and the particulars of "gender or color," is beside the points of sex, pleasure, or connection.

This moment in Uyehara's performance is instructive of inscrutable aesthetics since the art historical term of a vanishing point makes evident the simultaneous phenomena of two entities never actually contacting one another (therefore, in some sense, unrelatable and impenetrable to one another) *and* betraying such a projected logic in its visual experience and representation as undeniably reaching toward one another. Aesthetics of inscrutability help sense out a relational Asian American performativity, one that, despite its figuration as radical other or parallel line, maintains a reach toward and for one another from a specific perspective. In Uyehara's performance, what looks like social estrangement can be inscrutable sex, as in a kind of mutual masturbation via "secret contraction." The secretness of this bodily process is amplified by popular fascination around vaginal orgasm, one that is structured by the misogynist formation of the vagina as an inscrutable body part. Uyehara mocks this unknowability, however, not by teaching about vaginal anatomy, for instance, but by acknowledging sexual pleasure between women as something that is not for everyone to know unless it is from a first-person account.[42]

Through this vignette, the audience learns that the titular vanishing point is decidedly different from the self-vanishing of Asiatic femininity in Orientalist romances of compulsory heterosexual martyrdom. Instead, the vanishing point comes to figure pleasure and contact that operates outside an Orientalist heteronormative and ocularcentric universe. The vanishing point rather functions as an aspirational point of desire, a point one looks to on the horizon as an embodied pleasure that can be shared and does not rely on, but also does not exclude, the visual. The character Woman later asserts: "So when I talk about my passion, *that's* where I wanna go. The vanishing point. Cuz, like my teacher says, it's more than just a point."[43]

Uyehara's performance instructs me about inscrutable horizons, in that the two women can meet and achieve sexual pleasure in modes that defy visual representation, at the same time as they are gestured to through performance. In Uyehara's scene, the vanishing point names the moment of "zero distance," of orgasm between women. Although we could critique the privileged sexual metric of orgasm as the epitome of pleasure, Uyehara invokes the quotidian fact of sex between women and refuses the visual capture of such an act. Uyehara's horizon line is one of queer erotics (the "something else," the something "more than," from gender or color) that persist because they elude visuality. In this scene, Uyehara performs a disidentification with Renaissance perspectivalism in art history by hailing and critiquing the "some of you" who may not (yet) have insider knowledge about women having sex with women—schooling that "you" who would be the presumptively omniscient viewer through Enlightenment visual registers. Instead, Uyehara identifies the elusive vanishing point as the queer (and explicitly dyke, implicitly Asian American) moment of pleasure that, through normative optics, can only appear as vanishing.

Further, Uyehara cites the tropic fetishization and ignorance of lesbian sex to recommend self-exploration and cultivate curiosity in her audience. "Well, go find out for yourself," she encourages, withholding answers to how it is that two women can maintain eye contact and get off. Here, Uyehara harnesses the not-knowing in the audience and makes use of the sexual curiosity that may exist already in the room by promoting a method of humble ignorance. The sexualization of women, specifically Asian women, is not weaponized against women toward their aestheticized conquest. Their sexuality is not a plot point or accessory to a male character's storyline, nor is it something to know or study as static fact or subcultural ritual. Instead, Uyehara draws out the feminist potential in cultivating sexual curiosity as queer women, by refusing definitions, acknowledging limitations in knowledge, and promoting exploration through performance.

It is worth noting that Uyehara is not specific about which body parts these imagined women have. The nonparticularity of body parts allows for a formally fluid performance of gender, even as it is women's sexual pleasure that is prioritized in this scene. Asian American inscrutability is connected to femme invisibility and bi invisibility. The invisibility of Asian women's needs and pleasures in performance history highlights binaristic and androcentric privileging that can occur within queer cultures. How does the invisibility of Asian/American visual representation interface with broader structures of legibility that privilege cis-male and white identities as universal subjects?[44] Systemic Asian American invisibility, or the various systems that ensnare Asian American cultural power, is productively thought alongside bi and femme invisibility as that which cannot be sensed out in the institutional grip of patriarchal imperialism yet nevertheless shapes the social landscape.

Dot Formalism of Asian Feminist Queerness

My interest in this chapter and book is to refuse a conflation of representation with realist figuration and to articulate other visual modes of showing up that Asian American and Asian diasporic visual artists actively produce, rescript, and evade. We can find the visual trope of the vanishing point on the horizon line, and then the proliferation of points in abstracting perceptions of reality, throughout feminist and queer Asian diasporic visual and performance practices. I shift here from the vanishing point of Uyehara's solo performance to a consideration of artists Kimsooja, Yayoi Kusama, Barbara Takenaga, and Jess X. Snow for their formal use of dots and points in their work. I consider Uyehara's theatrical vanishing point of orgasm alongside Kimsooja's clay ball installation and Kusama's dot-based visual works to show how, whether or not the "point" is visualized in a field of points or gestured to in its negative space, the dot in its plurality is a notable motif in Asian/American visual practice that constitutes racial aesthetics of abstraction.

I visited *Archive of Mind*, Kimsooja's exhibition of a meditative field of clay balls, at the Peabody Essex Museum in Salem, Massachusetts, in the summer of 2019.[45] My first visit to the Salem art museum found me in a brightly lit atrium on an 80-degree summer day, with brick walls and a ceiling of glass and metal frames. I walked down the lobby hallway, past the café to the right, and toward a dark gallery space where two gallery attendants stood in black aprons, ready to greet visitors. The walls were a soothing gray, and overhead spotlights brought focus to a large oval wooden table on which countless balls of clay lay, all roughly palm sized (see figure 1.4). The table stood on top of light hardwood floors and was encircled with wooden stools spaced evenly around. To the side was a clay table with three large bricks of clay, each a different tone of grayish brown. I noticed wall text that described the fifteen-minute loop of soundscape, with the artist gurgling water and the sound of dried clay balls rolling around and sometimes colliding into one other.[46]

The three options of clay for visitors to use sat with big scoops taken out of them, like thick blocks of ice cream emptied out from rectangular cartons. I looked to the table and noticed that the clay spheres were colored almost like skin tones, and one of the docents later informed me that the color lightens as the clay dries. I took a chunk of clay and began rolling it between my two palms as I approached and sat at the table. The cool and dark room invited

FIGURE 1.4. Kimsooja, *Archive of Mind*, 2017. Photograph by Jean-Pierre Gabriel. Courtesy of Axel Vervoordt Gallery and Kimsooja Studio.

quiet and reflection, a meditative pause while feeling the subtle stick of the clay balling up between my hands. I enjoyed the clay balling as a kind of hand massage, rolling over pulse points and tense nerves, noting, too, the light markings my handprints would make on the ball of clay. I wondered about the moisture of the clay as well, and the exchange of moisture and dryness between the clay ball and my hands—later to be met with wet wipes provided by the gallery. A couple of pairs and groups of people sat around the table with me, talking to one another as their hands moved, some having removed their rings and placed them down on the table in front of them.

I noticed the two gallery attendants walking around and removing some of the dried balls of clay. When I asked them about this practice, they said that they were in week 4 of a seven-month-long exhibition and, to make space for more of the visitors' clay balls, they were tasked to remove some of the balls according to their clay color (and, I assume, age). When I asked the attendant whether visitors behave in surprising ways, she mentioned that many people seem compelled to stand out with an individualist drive that suggests that they struggle with or resist the communal vision of Kimsooja's piece. The balls, she explained, are made to be among other balls—each is individual for the fact of being made by different people at different times, but collectively they are part of the same project. She gave an example of a visitor creating a snowman that stood out in the sea of orbs. She pointed out that no one would think to disrespect a Georgia O'Keeffe painting, but that when it comes to Kimsooja's installation, people felt like her invitation to participate somehow invited authorship and intervention over the vision of the work. The gallery attendant also spoke of the artist's instruction for the balls to stay on one level on the table: no piles. Kimsooja's installation emphasized tactile feeling in the exchange of skin on clay as well as the meditative reflection to be had in focusing on the movement and sensation of clay between hands.

At the art museum, I thought of Kimsooja's reference to the formal shape of the clay ball as like that of a planet or atom, how scale then becomes something else and open to imagination through the figure of the sphere. As the Peabody Essex Museum's curator of the present tense, Trevor Smith, notes in the museum's press release: "This work is physically simple, yet overflowing with associations—from the microscopic perspective of atoms and molecules to the planetary and intergalactic; from the use of a material that has such deep associations with the earth to invoking immaterial practices of meditation. It has a calming and introspective effect on everyone who participates."[47] The artist's and the curator's words recall Barbara Takenaga's cosmic dots or Kusama's infinity dots, and how the scope of the point is also what allows its elastic potential; each dot can be an atom with its own smaller parts, a universe with its own planets; but so too can it be a constellation to other dots without exclusivity, as a line connecting two specific dots would suggest.[48]

A focus on racial abstraction in visual art expands our sense of Asiatic form and representation, one that veers toward other modes of sensing that are not premised on realist appearance. Kimsooja's installation recalls Yayoi Kusama's visual worlds, in a muted palette. Thinking with Kusama, in turn, invites us to consider other visual modes of resistance, including Sarah Stefana Smith's concept of camouflage. Smith invokes Kusama's work as a productive abstraction of woman-of-color interiority and sociality, furthering her study of "feminist practitioners [who] have mobilized camouflage—tactics of perceptivity and imperceptibility—to contemplate the performative qualities of race, sexuality, and gender."[49] Kusama notes her use of polka dots: "*A polka-dot has the form of the sun, which is a symbol of the energy of the whole world and our living life, and also the form of the moon, which is calm. Round, soft, colourful, senseless and unknowing. Polka dots can't stay alone; like the communicative life of people, two or three polka dots become movement. . . . Polka-dots are a way to infinity.*"[50] I am compelled by Kusama's formulation of the polka dot as "unknowing" because it resonates with my interest in formal points that perform a pointlessness, that is, a multiplicity of points as a possible orientation in the world. The multiplicity of points, as ideas and as figural forms, conjures a capacious worldview that makes space for the complex forms of perception that may well deviate from the strictures of the norm.

Not dissimilarly, we may note Barbara Takenaga's cosmic paintings of organic shapes and swirling universes, which began to engage with a horizon line in her work post-2010. In 2018 I walked through *Nebraska*, Takenaga's installation at the Massachusetts Museum of Contemporary Art (MASS MoCA) in western Massachusetts, featuring a one-hundred-foot wall of beaded lines of white, black, yellow, blue, green, and pink: a recurring pattern where lines converge and ping in angled vectors, and circles collide or twin like conjoined planets (see figure 1.5). The painting presents a horizon line with not-quite-parallel perspectival lines, in wavering and uneven relation, gravitating and sometimes meeting at the horizon line though all but rendering its linearity absolute. Notably, the title *Nebraska* references the landscapes of Takenaga's home state, giving a sense of racialized rural horizons that extend the coastal-privileging imaginaries of Asian America. We may also think to other paintings by Takenaga that employ the wavy perspectival lines and the plurality of vanishing points where the sky and ground meet over and over again and the artist can highlight selectively. Refusing the singularity of one vanishing point, Takenaga's paintings demonstrate the fact of multiple points of contact.

These artists who make use of dots, spheres, or points are of interest to me in relation to a pervasive discourse of Asian American invisibility—or what I am reframing as Asian American inscrutable visuality—because of its capacious orientation and turn away from the individual and necessary connection of how two or more points relate. In each of these visual art examples, it is not as though the person is disappeared. The dots and circles are the trace and effect of the presence of the person, a way to sense out other sensations. And the viewer or gallery visitor's role as the critic and receiver of the work—that is, the relational activation of and by the viewer—becomes more apparent. Attunement to inscrutability brings out questions that may go unnoticed if one is focused exclusively on "the point" as singular, as master, as fixed. Rather, the point always exists in relation.

The Point of Vanishing/Emergence

There is a pointlessness about horizon and vanishing points that I find generative to doing Asian Americanist critique and aesthetics. In arguing for the productive force of inscrutability, I do not intend to refute strategies

FIGURE 1.5. Barbara Takenaga, *Nebraska* (installation view at MASS MoCA), 2015.

of representation and legibility as the horizon of Asian American life. I understand that material and emotional resources depend on strategic identity politics in our present reality. On college campuses across the United States, discourses of diversity, inclusion, and belonging are often the limited ways in which to ensure and protect histories and cultures of people-of-color, Indigenous, and immigrant communities. In my work on campuses toward the institutionalization of Asian American studies and ethnic studies, representation is not the singular point of feminist and anti-racist work in higher education or elsewhere. Within minoritarian aesthetics of obfuscation, a point is necessarily a moving approximation to foster curiosity for the limits of figuration, allowing questions not only of violence and erasure but also of emergence and potentiality. What could be thought together as feminist, queer, and trans Asian Americanist critique would be attention to resource redistribution across life and knowledge forms, and attunement and curiosity for modes of being that evade dominant optics and expand forms of being in relation. Despite mainstream media stories about representation and the question of Asian Americans in racial diversity discourse, finding recognition and legibility within existing structures of visual hierarchy is not the point of Asian American politics. The multiple vanishing points, as conjured by the artworks studied here, gesture also to the meager political horizon of equal representation as attainable, that is, equality as an impoverished aspiration that presumes the equivalence and comparability of difference. The horizon refuses a singular point at the same time as the vanishing point conjures the potential emergence of thought and being with.

I conclude this chapter with *I Will Never Stop Reaching for You*, a print by filmmaker, poet, and muralist Jess X. Snow that the artist describes as "honoring migrant mothers who never stop reaching for their families across borders."[51] Snow developed what they call a "visual collaboration" in 2016 with a Honduran mother who is incarcerated with her younger son at Karnes County Detention Center after attempting to cross the US-Mexico border to reunite with their family. The horizon is obstructed by the wooden stakes of the border in Snow's print, and the stellar dots in the work are what let the viewer know that the night sky's horizon and the family members' figures are of a piece, made of the stuff of both past and futurity, or what cannot be captured and burdened with representation in the present (see figure 1.6). Snow's is not an attempt to visually document the figural truth of family separation or the racism of US immigration law; rather, what appears exceeds the limits of the figural as queer diasporic critique. The recurring motif of dots and constellations in Asian/American visual arts to me shows the expansive relevance of what constitutes Asian Americanist content, leaving connections and correlations open. This openness is not without direction but is fueled by the magnetic "reach" to be found between and among people, as social and implicated as Kusama's polka dots.

These artists play with the singularity of the point to show how it may seem both insignificant and overdetermined. Though the point standing alone may not be visible, and therefore may not come across as significant, it is also the vanishing point that offers perspective and orientation to the rest of the picture. Attention to the vanishing points of Asian/American representation, then, attunes work in comparative ethnic and American studies to how the seeming absence of Asiatic racial analysis is not only negative of Asian/American figural representation but also productive of other studies of race, migration, and indigeneity.

This chapter riffs on the productive invisibility, or vanishing point, of Asian feminist and queer forms not to reify the Orientalist romance of Asian self-sacrifice or self-erasure but to reframe the historical epistemology of Asian American visual representation as a processual and romanticized vanishing from disciplining knowledges, as a strategy against visual capture and toward alternative sensory worlds. The next chapter will think through inscrutability on a sonic register, with silence and muteness as an aesthetic counterpart to the charge of Asian American invisibility. Chapter 2 highlights noise where

FIGURE 1.6. Jess X. Snow, *I Will Never Stop Reaching for You*, 2016.

silence is named, whereas this chapter has considered other visual forms in the guise of invisibility.

I think about this horizon and these vanishing points now when I am faced with the question: Where are you really from? This is a fundamental rallying point for Asian anti-racist work, not only because it asserts a performance of what Ju Yon Kim calls "the racial mundane" for Asian Americans, subjectifying oneself as a foreigner, but also because it expands the scope of imaginative worlds of support and care, and returns us to the expansiveness of the Asian American political project, which has not been about normalizing who its proper subjects were, or pinpointing origin as something other than performative copy, but rather about naming a queer internal contradiction that produced and was produced through what Lisa Lowe decades ago identified as the racial heterogeneity, multiplicity, and hybridity of Asian America.[52] There is a privilege to being asked where we are from because, indeed, as Muñoz permits me to think, we were made for another world altogether, one that is made glimpsable in the sober reality of the present. Even the violence of this world is not totalizing; it still makes sensible, if barely, another world, a place for us, somewhere that does not evacuate a past in the turn toward a future. What we have is now, and what we need is to sense and believe in the beauty of other worlds, ones that are populated by the dead we carry with us, and by the artists and activists whose genealogies inform our other temporal becoming and potential relation, and to sense out modes of survival that persist through contemporary creative practice.

SILENCE AND PARASITIC HOSPITABILITY IN THE WORKS OF YOKO ONO, LAUREL NAKADATE, AND EMMA SULKOWICZ

To perform inscrutably is to shift expectations of sensory relation. Stealth performance may not be registered, yet that does not discount its impact on modern life. This chapter takes up the charge of silence and its liberal judgment of passivity. For Asian racialized people, we may pose the question: How are we heard when modern life depends on our silence? The first chapter of *Surface Relations* takes up the celebrated self-erasure of Asian women in the American theater and the ways in which Asian American and diasporic woman artists have refigured the vanishing point. This chapter continues this sensory gendering of Asian absence through the sonic by reframing the charge of quiet as an inscrutable mode of racial performance that signals a noisy hospitability. My turn to discourses of hospitality may be surprising. As white supremacist conventions of racial visibility eradicate the presence of Asian life except as a buttress to white conquest, the tacit expectation for Asian life to support white wealth makes service a painful and draining topic. To appear through forms that do not reproduce such hatred calls for subtle strategies that work toward minoritarian endurance and grace. It may be tempting to outright refuse Orientalist strictures and perform their perceived opposite. Inscrutable aesthetics allow us to ask: How does one create modes of responding to gendered racism that are reparative and body forth other modalities altogether?

Yoko Ono and Hospitable Performance

Miss Ono sat looking inscrutably Japanese (she is actually Japanese) while members of the audience took turns to cut off her clothes with a pair of scissors.—*Daily Telegraph and Morning Post*, September 29, 1966

Yoko Ono's oft-cited *Cut Piece* could be described as a performance of hospitality par excellence. Similar to Ono's other event scripts—as famously published in her book *Grapefruit* (1964)—the premise of *Cut Piece* is simple: "Performer sits on stage with a pair of scissors in front of him. It is announced that members of the audience may come on stage—one at a time—to cut a small piece of the performer's clothing to take with them. Performer remains motionless throughout the piece. Piece ends at the performer's option."[1] In one view, Ono's six performances of her famous event script position her as the host of the performance and her audience members as the guests she invites to the stage who leave with something "to take with them." Since premiering in Kyoto in the summer of 1964, *Cut Piece* has garnered renewed relevance and circulation in feminist art historical research and (re)performance of Ono's event script, including the artist's own performance in September 2003 in Paris. From Julia Bryan-Wilson's 2003 essay on *Cut Piece* as a "ritual of remembrance" to Jack Halberstam's chapter on radical passivity in *The Queer Art of Failure*, *Cut Piece* is convincingly presented as the epitome of protofeminist performance art.[2] In the first section of this chapter, I pick up these discourses of feminist performance art and jostle them against a discourse of hospitality in order to theorize Ono's lifeworks as Asian feminist performances of hospitality. Surveying critical reception of *Cut Piece*, much of which enfolds Ono into racist and misogynistic ideologies, I suggest that Ono's own rhetoric of unconditional giving, as embodied in *Cut Piece*, circumvents persistent Western discourses that conjoin hospitality with female sacrifice and Asian docility. I will then turn to Jacques Derrida's meditation on hospitality to consider how Ono and Derrida challenge and extend one another and, in doing so, contrast figurations of Asian femininity beside an abstract universalized subject.

Reading the event script for *Cut Piece*, one may be struck by the performer's open invitation to the audience, who "may come on stage," "cut," and "take" from the performer. One may also note the script's focus on the performer as grammatical subject. Since it is imagined that the event script would only ever be initiated by the performer, as an abstract experiment for the imagination, as with arguably any of Ono's event scripts, the emphasis is on the performer's experience of the piece and how such an exercise might expand and enact the performer's world. This emphasis on the performer, however, is largely lost upon performance—or rather, in inviting audience participation, the performer's challenge is to receive not only the participant's physical cut but also the epistemes that would frame such an encounter.

I should mention that, as with other event scripts, the subject of the performance is universalized to include performers other than Ono herself. The unmarked social status of the performer and audience members of the script might be expected to welcome a similarly unmarked interpretation of the performance within a genealogy of participatory art from the sixties.[3] Ono's six performances of the piece, however, evidence the perlocutionary effects of her particular body performing the piece (see figure 2.1). That is, as critical reception of her performances demonstrates, Ono's *Cut Piece* circulates alongside tropes of Asian femininity as submissive and passive, as something to be seen but not heard. Note, for example, the ways Alexandra Munroe describes the "doing" of Ono's body as "traditional Japanese feminine" and "masklike": "In London, as in Kyoto, Tokyo, and New York, where she had previously presented this work, Ono sat motionless on stage in traditional Japanese feminine position—knees folded beneath her—and invited members of the audience to cut a piece of her clothing away until, nearly forty minutes later, she was left all but naked, her face masklike throughout."[4]

Even when Ono's Japaneseness is not explicitly named, the exotic and inscrutable aura of the East is conjured. In the opening essay accompanying Ono's retrospective at the Japan Society, Munroe writes, "*Cut Piece* expresses an anguished interiority while offering a social commentary on the quiet violence that binds individuals and society, the self and gender, alienation and connectedness."[5] Kristine Stiles asserts, "*Cut Piece* acquires an even more tragic and metaphysical tone and implication as it becomes

FIGURE 2.1. Yoko Ono, *Cut Piece.* Carnegie Recital Hall, New York, March 21, 1965. Photograph by Minoru Niizuma.

a representation of the translation of mental concepts into corporeal and spiritual deliberations on the problem of ethical human interaction."[6] Ono's *Cut Piece*, which here includes not only her physical performance but also the participation in and ongoing reception of the work, invites us to ask: Why is it that "an anguished interiority" and a "tragic and metaphysical tone and implication" can so repeatedly be figured in the performing body of Yoko Ono? As Bryan-Wilson asks, "Does *Cut Piece*, with its dual faces of passivity and exhibitionism, exemplify a collective fantasy about the contradictory status of the silent but signifying Japanese female artist?"[7]

In Ono's work, something beckons for recognition. Something invites our attention, a something that harks back to Claire Bishop's formulation of a "relational antagonism" that "would be predicated not on social harmony, but on exposing that which is repressed in sustaining the semblance of this harmony."[8] In this vein, Ono's work exposes an awkward relationship between aesthetics of Asian femininity and a discourse of harmonious hospitality. Ono's rhetoric of unconditional giving finds an interlocutor in poststructural theory. For instance, we can turn to *Of Hospitality*, a book composed of side-by-side texts by Jacques Derrida and Anne Dufourmantelle. (The format of the book, subtitled *Anne Dufourmantelle Invites Jacques Derrida to Respond*, suggests a structure for hospitality, one that juxtaposes Dufourmantelle's "Invitation" on the left-hand pages and Derrida's two lectures "Foreigner Question" and "Step of Hospitality / No Hospitality" on the right. Provokingly, both texts begin on the same longitudinal place on their first page, but, for the remainder of the 155 pages, Dufourmantelle's text is italicized and paired with substantial blank space beside Derrida's pages of full text. For now, I simply wish to gesture to this visual experience that structures the reading of *Of Hospitality* and assure the reader that we will return to this negative space, this noise, later in the chapter.) Returning us to the conceptual query of hospitality, Derrida conjures the image of a door and invites: "Let us say yes *to who or what turns up*, before any determination, before any anticipation, before any *identification*, whether or not it has to do with a foreigner, an immigrant, an invited guest, or an unexpected visitor, whether or not the new arrival is the citizen of another country, a human, animal, or divine creature, a living or dead thing, male or female."[9] Let us say yes. Derrida proposes an indiscriminate welcoming of another through the threshold, in a manner that is not so different from Ono's performance of saying yes. Regardless of who approaches her, Ono remains seated and more or less "motionless" on the stage as the participant cuts away her clothing. Ono's overall stillness makes all the more noticeable, for example, her arm's movement to her chest when an audience member cuts across her bra straps. Even then, in the famous performance document filmed by the Maysles brothers, Ono does not speak or end the performance. Rather, the camera captures her resolve in enduring the performance.

Although Ono could be said to invite participants "before any determination, before any anticipation, before any *identification*" of who or what they are, the audience anticipates Ono's presence. Derrida's formulation of the law of hospitality grants open parameters for the "who or what [that] turns up." The particulars of who the "us" in the position of saying yes is, however, are not addressed. Derrida's request for unconditional giving is seductive when the subject is universalized and abstract. However, as audience reception instructs, we marked subjects do not socially experience ourselves as such. Saying yes presupposes the possibility of saying otherwise, presumes the person inside the door has a choice. Historically, this acknowledgment is discriminately dispensed.

Derrida nods to the problematic social logics of hospitality toward the end of his second lecture, calling the model of hospitality "paternal and phallogocentric," a "conjugal model" in which the father "represents [the laws of hospitality] and submits to them to submit the others to them in this violence of the power of hospitality."[10] The philosopher's concluding images in *Of Hospitality* are of two moments when, as demonstrations of hospitality, two patriarchs in the Old Testament surrender their virgin daughters to foreign guests. Without further analysis, Derrida aligns host with patriarch and leaves room for readers to problematize the anti-woman and colonial staging of hospitality.

This relationship between hospitality and ownership calls for an intersectional analysis that critiques the position of women, children, and people of color as property. As Maurice Hamington writes in *Feminism and Hospitality*, "Women and children are historically included in the category of property and therefore become part [of] what can be offered to the guest."[11] An intersectional feminist approach might further trouble the racialized and transnational dimensions of property that are offered to guests in the name of hospitality. Maureen Sander-Staudt notes the use of military sex slaves, so-called comfort women, in the Japanese Imperial Army, for example, to argue for the ways in which certain (predominantly Korean) bodies are feminized, sexualized, and objectified as both sacrificial gifts and collateral damage for an ethnically pure (Japanese) nation.[12] The euphemism of comfort here signals the historical asymmetry of which bodies receive comfort and which bodies are objectified in the name of providing comfort.

This chapter is a study of the possibilities of and in saying yes, especially for women and trans people in the contemporary United States. The imperialist equation of certain bodies, land, and culture feminized these zones of the other as exploitable resources. The bodies of Asian women are overdetermined by xenophobic and colonial methods of conquest, where the feminized body is aligned with land and natural resources, as part of the fulfillment of Manifest Destiny. The metaphorical and material practice of penetration (of body, land, and culture) becomes not a discourse about permission to enter (presuming a code of hospitality that precedes the encounter) but rather of manifest entitlement, patriarchal benevolence, and missions to civilize. Meanwhile, women historically have been exempt from receiving hospitality, including access to naturalization or citizenship as with gendered exclusions from the United States such as the Page Law of 1875 (which effectively barred the immigration of Chinese and Japanese women, arguing all were prostitutes and therefore threatening to the moral purity of the nation).[13]

Who has possession of the door, the synecdoche of the domicile? And who is seen alongside that door as another possession, as a necessary prop in the scene of hospitality? In her consideration of the gendered division of public and private space in the Old Testament scenes, Sander-Staudt argues that a feminist approach to hospitality necessitates considerations of safety and home. She writes, "Whereas men are shown to be in need of hospitality because of the dangers of the world outside of the home, women are shown to have refuge nowhere, without condemnation."[14] Indeed, the entities created to mitigate "dangers of the world outside of the home" are often the same entities that ensure danger for women. For example, we may observe how US military campaigns around the Pacific Ocean for more than the past century figure Asian women as, simultaneously, in need of protection and, with the boom of tourist economies (sexual and otherwise) at those bases, available for purchase. Asian women, whose underacknowledged labor is the "constitutive absence" in nationalist and transnational discourses, have been conscripted to give and grant (sexual, emotional, cultural) access.[15] To be clear, my intention here is not to shame or antagonize people who work in the sex or hospitality industries. Rather, I point to the disciplinary formation of "Asian woman" as an effect of not only a conceptual discursive tradition but also the militarized and capitalist manifestations of paternal hospitality.

Discourses that promote hospitality (as with Derrida's unconditional giving) without acknowledging the historic power differentials that accompany their circulation risk once more putting the burden of "saying yes" on women of color most of all. I am critical of this hegemonic mandate for women and people of color to give (and labor) unconditionally. I desire a disidentificatory discourse of hospitality, one that does not vacate or concede the pleasures of giving or saying yes. I am moved by the scholarship of Celine Parreñas Shimizu and Nguyen Tan Hoang, who innovate gender and sexuality studies and Asian Americanist critique with their respective formulations of the "productive perversity" of Asian female hypersexuality and the bottomy methodology of gay male Asian culture.[16] If Asian women are produced as hospitable thresholds, then which relationships are possible (and desirable) between Asian femininity and hospitality? What can we do with this Western ethical imperative to say yes? Can performances of hospitality in fact constitute a practice of feminist becoming and world-making?

Though Ono does not explicitly use the language of ethics or hospitality, she has described *Cut Piece* as a gift experiment. Ono explains Buddha's travel narrative as "a form of total giving as opposed to reasonable giving like 'logically you deserve this' or 'I think this is good, therefore I am giving this to you.'"[17] Ono tells the story of the Buddha's practice of giving to contextualize her decision to perform *Cut Piece* wearing the best outfit available in her wardrobe, suggesting that to do otherwise would be against the spirit of saying yes.

In her solo performance, Ono powerfully plays with this expectation of Asian hospitality in her publicized insistence on peace and saying yes. As Hamington writes, "In hospitality, Derrida finds a fundamental tension of morality—an impossibility or *aporia*—that humanity must struggle with. Hospitality calls us to give of ourselves. In its pure form, or unconditional hospitality, absolute giving is demanded but one can no longer be the host or the giver, if all is given away."[18] Though Ono's project of total giving is in the spirit of Derrida's law of hospitality to an extent, it runs up against the problem of temporality and duration. The risk of total giving as self-sacrifice becomes prominent when the perceived host is not an unmarked and universalized body but one that traffics in historic tropes of hypersexuality and romanticized self-harm. Notably, Ono has offered a Buddhist hermeneutic that would allow for something other than an interpretation of female self-sacrifice, as historically fetishized in high Western art. With the decision to wear her best suit at the first performance of *Cut Piece*, Ono has described the Buddha as an inspiration, as one who operates in an economy of gift, of total giving. In this sense, Ono gestures to alternative genealogies that contextualize hospitable practices of Asian femininity in order to disrupt a capitalist and imperialist economy and temporality.

I invite a pause here to recognize the availability of such a reading.

Despite such possibility, a tradition of interpreting Asian female performance in a Judeo-Christian logic of hospitality emerges in reception of Ono's work. If, as Derrida suggests, the host is also always a hostage, then Ono, as the host of the performance, is also hostage to Orientalist discourse of gendered Asian racialization.[19] In other words, a performer has what some might term agency in creating the performance, but she is subject and subjected to audience reception. As Karen Shimakawa writes, "Asian American performers never walk onto an empty stage" as "that space is always already densely populated with phantasms of orientalness through and against which an Asian American performer must struggle to be seen."[20] This "struggle to be seen" is exemplified by Ono's appearance in popular art historical discourses. Ono's work is often discussed, if at all, in conversations in which her social identity serves as a foil for a white, Western, masculine subject.[21] Think of the ways in which the sign of Ono is perhaps most famous in collaboration with John Lennon or in relation to the largely white and European Fluxus crowd. As Midori Yoshimoto writes, "After 1967, Ono became so closely associated with John Lennon that her earlier avant-garde activities were forgotten or seen merely as eccentric by the public."[22] More damningly, Bryan-Wilson writes, "After [Ono's] marriage to John Lennon, she became the embodiment of the 'yellow peril' itself, a controlling Asian dragon lady, depicted in the most racist terms imaginable."[23] Despite (or perhaps because of) Ono's ethos of total giving, she cannot control how her work is received or taken up by others. A universal (in theory) and feminized and racialized (in practice) discourse of saying yes creates a mandate for minoritized womxn to offer generosity to xenophobic systems that would normalize their labor of giving as complicity or aspirational assimilation. A hegemonic discourse of hospitality, then, continues to tether the benefactor of paternal hospitality (through figures of white masculinity) to Asian femininity, defining itself by these imperialist dynamics. Can Asian femininity exist beside white masculinity without bodying forth a posture of sacrificial host? Can a hospitable posture, embodied by an Asian woman, be interpreted otherwise?

Though hospitality is a fraught topic for discussions of Asianness and femininity, I pursue it with the hope that performances of Asian femininity may model and create new epistemologies for hospitality and the "complex personhood" theorized by Avery Gordon and furthered in Kandice Chuh's work on Asian Americanist critique.[24] This chapter is my experiment in how to possibly grapple with Asian femininity and its overburdened sexual connotations, with interest not so much in narrating or defending why or what Asian femininity is, and more—sounding a familiar bell in performance studies—in what performances of Asian femininity can do for those of us craving more capacious practices of feminist sociality.

If hospitality as unconditional giving soon reinforces a tidy dichotomy between East and West, female and male, and reinscribes exhausting power differentials, then which forms of welcome, invitation, and saying yes can Asian women perform? To clarify, I write with the condition that giving and saying yes can be pleasurable social modes—pleasures that are not uninformed by a colonial hierarchy of identity production but that are also not wholly coterminous with their means. My intellectual pursuits of these pleasures are inspired by the work of queer scholars, including Elizabeth Freeman, Juana María Rodríguez, and adrienne maree brown, who create conceptual space and gesture to the lived experience of pleasure in and between bodies as important historiographic work.[25] Ono's work elegantly asserts that a discourse of hospitality historically constructs, and is constructed by, discourses of Asian femininity. It also poses questions: What does this mean for the purposive performance of hospitality by Asian women? How do these performances in turn challenge the legibility of hospitality, and also what is legible as Asian femininity?

Laurel Nakadate and Parasitic Femininity

There's always a gaping hole in the center of Nakadate's world, something that echoes the disaster of prescribed sexual roles.—JERRY SALTZ, "Whatever Laurel Wants"

In one of Laurel Nakadate's first video works, *Happy Birthday* (2000), the contemporary Brooklyn-based artist asks three men to celebrate her birthday in three one-on-one settings. These were invitations to participate in suspended disbelief; the day was not her birthday and the guests were not her friends. They met when each man separately approached Nakadate in public. Anecdotally, the three scenes follow a series of similar exchanges: he asked her out in a public space, and she asked if he would make a video with her. As Nakadate describes, "I showed up at their houses in a party dress with a birthday cake and I asked them to pretend that it was my birthday and to celebrate my birthday with me. I'd have this birthday cake and I'd set it down on their kitchen table and ask them to sing to me. So they sang 'Happy Birthday' a cappella and we had cake together."[26]

The resulting videos are often shown in a three-channel installation (see figure 2.2). In the left monitor, for example, Nakadate and a man are seated around a table in an eat-in kitchen. Behind them, opened French doors reveal a mattress on the floor. The man facing the camera has long black hair, a moustache, and glasses, and he is dressed in a white T-shirt and jeans. Beside him, on the viewer's right, Nakadate's chair is angled toward the man, her feet bare on what appears to be a red Oriental rug. She wears a black skirt with a pink sleeveless floral button-down, and her wavy hair runs down her back. She lights the cake candles and then places her hands in her lap. The man begins to warble out the familiar anniversary tune. In the middle monitor, a seated man in a collared shirt grins and looks on while Nakadate leans over the square wooden table, poised to blow out the cake's birthday candles

FIGURE 2.2. Laurel Nakadate, *Happy Birthday.* © Laurel Nakadate, courtesy of Leslie Tonkonow Artworks + Projects, New York.

(see figure 2.3). The fridge and counters behind them suggest a crowded kitchen. The man's bare feet are seen, crossed at the ankle, and beside them sit two small bowls possibly for a pet in the bottom left corner of the shot. Two white plates on the table anticipate slices of cake, while a long knife is placed as though a linear extension of the man's right arm. Behind them, a closed door's latch hangs unsecured. In the right monitor, Nakadate sits on a red couch with her feet tucked under her skirt, and she turns away from the camera to slice the cake at the center of the frame. Her sneaker-wearing costar smiles and holds out a plate while seated in a yellow armchair. In each of the scenes, Nakadate's hair is long and her feet are bare. Seen together, the monitors play out domestic scenes of uncanny birthday party convention.

The mood of the scene is unclear; neither attendee seems particularly joyful or sure of their role. Yet, when she occasionally and briefly looks straight into the camera, Nakadate seems to wink at the viewer as if to reassure us that she knows what she is doing. Perhaps unsurprisingly, Nakadate has faced criticism for exploiting her video costars, whose private spaces and, to an extent, desires are made vulnerable to her camera. The men want something

FIGURE 2.3. Laurel Nakadate, *Happy Birthday*. © Laurel Nakadate, courtesy of Leslie Tonkonow Artworks + Projects, New York.

from her that is inseparable, it would seem, from their racialized and gendered conceptions of her, and some critics suggest Nakadate takes advantage of their desires. The artist insists that the men consent to making videos with her and that some have even become her friends and repeat collaborators. She has also commented: "After hundreds of years of art history, a young half-Asian girl meets older white men, and *she's* the predator? Suddenly no one can take it?"[27]

In Nakadate's work, with the discourse of exploitation, I sense a related and perhaps parallel experiment with hospitality to Ono's. To exploit can mean to take advantage of another's hospitality, to respond to another's gift inappropriately. This would seem to reverse the racial and gender designations of host and guest as previously imagined, where Asian women are seemingly ineligible as guests but rather thresholds for the condition of hospitality. In *Happy Birthday*, the proverbial sound at the door does not make obvious who is on the inside or outside. Approached by white male strangers in parking lots and other public spaces in New Haven, Nakadate is hailed as a guest, in one formulation. She then responds from the position of impertinence, inviting the additional guest of her camera. She shows up at the men's homes, but, just as well, she could be seen to host: bringing cake, elevating the dress code, preparing activities, lighting the candles, cutting the cake.

Yet Nakadate's design of the performance suggests that she is not exactly a host. The space is pointedly not hers. Nakadate is clear to film the encounters in the men's private homes. She has said: "For me one of the primary motivations at the beginning of this work was going out into the world and meeting strangers. And whether I was meant to be part of their world or not, I just wanted to spend more time there."[28] Nakadate is a visitor, an oxymoronic invited imposer spending time in a world that may not be "meant to be" hers. Though Nakadate could be and has been interpreted as an irreverent, rude, or exploitative guest, I suggest that the language of guest and host is wrong altogether when it comes to her work.

Nakadate nominates herself as host in another's home but also as the guest of honor to be celebrated. At the same time, there is no indication of disappointment or altered expectations for the men. If Nakadate is a solicitor or an opportunist, so, too, are the men. Nakadate's video art suggests that aesthetics of Asian femininity can disrupt the dialectic of guest/host. As with Ono in *Cut Piece*, Nakadate is simultaneously host of her performance and hostage to Orientalist discourse. Nakadate's role as director of *Happy Birthday*'s video documentation, however, extends the reach of her artistic direction and blurs the dualistic focus. I now shift from the framework of hospitality to that of parasitism, with an interest in how Nakadate's performance of parasitism in turn differently shapes Asian feminist sociality.

The figure of the parasite differently sounds the knock at the door. In the preface of Michel Serres's book *The Parasite*, translator Lawrence R. Schehr clarifies that "in French, the word [*parasite*] has three meanings: a biological parasite, a social parasite, and static."[29] This static does not identify the knock of a guest or host at the threshold but announces a parasite, gnawing at the dialectic of host/guest (*hôte/hôte*). Serres's example par excellence may be instructive: his main stars are not people but rats, beginning with a city rat who invites a country rat over for leftovers at the tax farmer's table, only to be scared away by a noise at the door.[30] Eschewing a model of host and guest, Serres identifies each of the players as a parasite in its own right: the tax farmer, the city rat, the country rat, and the noise: "Strictly speaking," he writes, "they all interrupt."[31] The egalitarian rule of the parasite: it is a potential position for all. The reader may already intuit my turning to Serres's parasite in examining Nakadate's work, since roles in a domestic scene, traditionally in a rhetoric of hospitality, are Nakadate's playthings.

Serres writes that the parasite "is social technique and knows how to play at the mastery of men and at their domestication."[32] Both Nakadate and her costars rather willingly submit to the staged "domestication" of the men for the duration of the videos. Serres adds that the parasite "is the relation and not fixed in the essence, that he is not fixed in a station but is in the functioning of the relations in his being part of the warp and woof, that he is relational and thus that he is multiple and collective."[33] We note the gendering of the parasite here as well as the parasite's entitlement when Serres writes that "man is the universal parasite, that everything and everyone around him is a hospitable space."[34] What intervention would a feminist rendering of the parasite make? In thinking with Nakadate's video work, I draw upon Anna Watkins Fisher's work on feminist parasitism as a "tactical feminist remapping of the structural dynamics of gendered territoriality as the parasite comes to overwhelm the terrain of its host."[35] Recuperating Serres's parasite into a feminist rhetoric, Fisher emphasizes the shift away from a default "liberal autonomous individual" and toward "notions of the minor, the derivative, the relational."[36]

I welcome this turn and draw inspiration from Fisher's feminist intervention on parasitism as "an experimental art practice as well as a performance model for contemporary feminist politics."[37] In her work, Fisher identifies a gendered history of "the feminized parasite and her masculinized host" and studies conceptual work by artists including Sophie Calle, Chris Kraus, Roisin Byrne, and Ann Liv Young.[38] Fisher asks: "How have long-held anxieties within feminist theory over the notion of the parasite—a historically feminized metaphor for an intruder that is overly dependent, ungracious, and unwelcome—emerged as a tactical model for reinvesting contemporary feminism?"[39]

I wish to build upon this question to ask: What about the ethnic, migrant, and transnational parasite, who is already familiar with discourses of being received as "overly dependent, ungracious, and unwelcome"? How have long-held anxieties around hospitality in gender and Asian Americanist discourses given rise to a tactical model for making parasitic conventions of hospitality? This consideration allows me to wonder about the imposition of hospitality on Asian women, for whom the descriptor "ungracious" fits uneasily. As we see with descriptions of Yoko Ono's work, Asian women are often expected to be docile, submissive, and eager to serve even as they simultaneously must reassert their right to personhood, citizenship, and safety. As Leslie Bow reminds us, Asian female sexuality functions as an implicit stage for social, cultural, and political allegiance, such that Asian women are never immune to charges of betrayal from one affiliation or another.[40] In this view, "ungracious" is the paradoxical other side to subjectivization via hospitality.

We may note Asian biracial parasitism as a weaponization of this feminine threat as well. Nakadate's work is proximal to the racializing matrix of the art market and, more broadly, circuits of US sociality. Though Nakadate does not necessarily identify her work as Asian American, it is worth noting the gendered language in critical reception of her work, as well as her biraciality, as mentioned earlier in this chapter. At times the language is more nuanced, describing her as an "enigmatic, Mona Lisa beauty," "a fit and attractive woman in her mid-30s," "sporting cute clothing that's just slightly tacky, and natural hair and makeup."[41] Other language is overtly sexualized, describing Nakadate as "a baby doll [who turns] into an avenging angel and a wolf in baby doll's clothing," one who exudes a "slutty, back-alley exoticism" that "blends naïve schoolgirl with the dominatrix."[42] The racialized dimension of these sexualized tropes is further clarified in reviews like this for an artist who was born, raised, and maintains residence in the United States: "Nakadate is a half-Japanese, half-American photographer living in New York."[43] Without using the language of race and gender, the artist has stated: "It's always a problem—you've got to figure out a place to put your body."[44]

Perhaps critical comment on Nakadate's biraciality invites us to further theorize the parasite's coupling of intimacy and difference.[45] Fisher positions parasitism "as a corrosive queering move that challenges recent work in queer theory and performance studies that has privileged, under the opaque appellation 'negativity,' moves of cynical distancing, pure refusal, exit, and escape to argue instead for maneuvers of overintimacy, exaggerated mimicry, and excessive appropriation for feminist theory."[46] Thinking with queer-of-color critique and scholarship in queer diaspora that embrace and extend negativity, I suggest that it is precisely the queer parasitism of Asian femininity that challenges the logic of "instead" between "cynical distancing" and "overintimacy."[47] That is, through viewing Nakadate's work as well as Ono's, I feel the brightening sense that the queer work therein is the holding together of distance and intimacy, one that names the particular crux of Asian and feminine becoming, one that cannot entirely refuse the language of hospitality in the register of the real, but that is also not wholly delimited by such a discourse.

Yet I agree with Fisher in the sense that "negativity" is also not exactly appropriate to describe the Asian feminist practices that I argue Ono and Nakadate both perform: their silent art of giving complicates the language of negativity, not the least because their gifts are materially productive, whether in the fabric scraps of *Cut Piece*, the cake of *Happy Birthday*, Nakadate's relationships with her costars, or the performance documentation of both artworks. Neither could their performances be described as affectively negative in a straightforward sense. Studied together, alongside rhetorics of gendered hospitality, the works of Ono and Nakadate open questions about Asian negativity as a contradiction in terms.

Whether within or beside conversations of the negative, I prefer the idiom of inscrutability to reserve conceptual space for the curious relationality between Nakadate and the costarring men, one that allows for possible intimacy and exploitation, for critique and friendship. My theory of inscrutability does not foreclose intimacy but gestures to the racialized and gendered systems of knowledge used to cognize sociality as such. Nakadate parasitically stages "the minor, the derivative, the relational" by saying yes to men's invitations and in turn inviting them to participate, all the while maintaining distance in the space that the camera and imagined viewer occupy. As Serres writes, "The best relation would be no relation. By definition it does not exist, if it exists, it is not observable."[48]

Just as Nakadate's parasitic play blurs her role in the encounter, the disruption of the host and guest dialectic destabilizes what we viewers think we know about these men. Their relation to one another is not clear, but it is made observable. I wish to note, too, that Serres's "no relation" is in fact not an absence or lack in Nakadate's staging but something in excess of observation under normative optics. In this sense, parasitic relation is not antirelational or necessarily along a project of self-shattering negativity. Rather, Asian performance of feminist parasitism insists on relationality by performing it, allowing for the distance necessary for such relationality to take shape. The impossibility of its observation highlights the interruptive work of viewing. Looking at their performances of hospitality side by side, I suggest that, with Ono and Nakadate, the viewer's involvement holds the viewer accountable for the staged encounter as well and welcomes the possibility for spectatorial resistance.

The parasite needs the host/guest in some sense, but it should not be forgotten that the host/guest needs the parasite for evidence of its own existence. More, the host/guest is also always already a parasite, in the position to interrupt. If you have a parasite, you are a part of history, you are witnessed, as these men are witnessed in the video archive because of Nakadate's work. They need her to appear, just as she needs them to make her work. The parasite changes the rules, knocks on something—not to ask for permission, for permission is not in the vocabulary of the parasite. Rather, the sound rings in a new epistemology, one where the relation generates something new. We viewers might question: On which side of the door do we stand? Suddenly, we realize we have been in it, too. Nakadate's gaze into her own camera interrupts not only the domestic scene of birthday ritual but also the viewer's practice of unremarkable voyeurism.

What Is Almost Inaudible

I want to think that this noise I constantly hear at the door is produced by a being whom I would like to know.—MICHEL SERRES, *The Parasite*

Inscrutability takes different forms, or it may be more accurate to say that the judgment of something as inscrutable alerts us to the dawning articulation of a new form. Without collapsing the one into the other, I continue by juxtaposing inscrutability with Serres's formulation of parasitic static to show how hospitable sociality depends on not only sensory interruptions but also interruptions of our interpretations of sensory interruptions.

For example, in a literal understanding of static noise, it may be worth pointing out that both *Cut Piece* and *Happy Birthday* feature speechless artists. Both Ono and Nakadate sit quietly in their surroundings, communicating nonverbally. Videos of *Cut Piece* as well as *Happy Birthday* instead rely on the participants to create the soundtrack and to interpret the noise. Their deliberate silence, I suggest, positions them as observers. Serres writes that the "observer always makes less noise than the observed. He is thus unobservable by the observed."[49] Yet by emphasizing their own roles as artists and silent observers, Ono and Nakadate interrupt this dichotomous relationship with the presence of the viewer as a fellow observer and draw attention to their performance of social relation through silence.

Static and sounds of fumbling permeate the length of the Maysles brothers' film of *Cut Piece*. The camera primarily returns to Ono's face, zooming in and out to show the state of her dress, including a black cardigan and mesh stockings. The camera pans sometimes to the unlit house, from which coughs, laughter, and applause occasionally erupt. The wooden stage amplifies the heeled steps of approaching audience members, the metal weight of the scissors put down. As participants move toward Ono and cut, most often they are also speechless, perhaps uncomfortable, perhaps focused on making careful cuts. As viewers, we can speculate as to the participants' silence, though Ono's own silence sets a tone. This unspoken invitation to share in silence is not reliably heard or heeded by others. "Very delicate, it might take some time," the white-bloused man chortles to the audience before kneeling at Ono's side. He cheats out to the audience he makes a cut directly down the center line of her undershirt. Studying the shirt's exposed wing, he then snips the left shoulder strap, at which point Ono looks down to see the damage done. When Anne Dufourmantelle suggests that "we must learn to perceive what is almost inaudible," readers may question how it is that those who do not seek to perceive or listen may do so.[50] By necessitating the involvement of audience members as performers of *Cut Piece*, Ono stages a social situation that highlights their participation and responsibility.

In fact, two voices by the camera's microphone giggle, and one remarks: "Look at the expression on her face!" The other replies, "He's getting carried away." The participant onstage boasts, "I'll make a piece for *Playboy* with it." Meanwhile, Ono's eyes and neck move around, silently searching the man's face, seemingly with no returned look. He stands behind her, pulling and cutting the shirt away, and struts as he cuts the shoulders of her bra straps. From the audience shouts a voice: "For God's sake, stop being such a creep!"

Ono's disciplined silence in contrast amplifies the sounds in her audience and draws attention to the uncontrolled nature of audience members' reactions to her and to one another. No such live group audience is present in Nakadate's video world. Though Nakadate is also silent throughout her performance, the men have a score to work with and we viewers have an expectation of a song to hear. Notably, Nakadate invites and conducts the noise without making any sound herself. The audio of *Happy Birthday* highlights the convention that structures their encounter. The eponymous celebratory greeting gives us a speech act, or an Austinian total speech situation, one that could not be complete without the world's most famous tune. Though Nakadate and her costars perform the requisite conventions, with props and songs and perhaps even sincerities, there is an overriding feeling of wrongness. The strict familiarity of a birthday song makes more palpable the interruptive sense of misfire or abuse. We note the flatness of the left-monitor man's closing phrase of the song, while the man in the middle monitor leaves out the second line of the song altogether. It may be tempting to suggest that the birthday scenario is failed, and yet the fact of its doing returns to the question of *why* the two people are together and, ultimately, what it does for viewers' sense of social possibility. On these fronts, Nakadate's persistent silence through the three scenes produces a complementary sense of inscrutability. The artist avoids eye contact even when the men joke with her, as the man in the right monitor does, voicing a self-conscious refrain ("I'll have to throw my scale out!") at the sight of cake. Nakadate's muteness, juxtaposed with the men's amateur croons, plays into a facade of girlish inscrutability at the same time as it compels the men to fill the silence. They are made to provide the narrative and the entertainment. Her performance of inscrutability presents the noise, and the men are made to respond.

This note on muteness and parasitic performances of Asian femininity is not my effort to reinforce stereotypes of Asian and feminine reticence but to highlight Ono's and Nakadate's artistic use of this trope.[51] Their silence invites and commands the participants to offer the labor of talking and interpreting their actions. Their silence—reverberating against one another when read together, creating a duet over time and space—withholds readymade meaning of their work, allowing an existence in transformational noise. Their silence, too, welcomes an interest in what is there, constellating the inscrutable, the parasitic, and Sianne Ngai's writing on the aesthetic judgment of the interesting. As Ngai describes, "Regardless of the particular objects and situations to which it is ascribed, the judgment always seems underpinned by a calm, if not necessarily weak, affective intensity whose minimalism is somehow understood to secure its link to ratiocinative cognition and to lubricate the formation of social ties."[52] Like the aesthetic of the interesting, I suggest, the inscrutable has "the capacity to produce new knowledge."[53] Unlike the aesthetic of the interesting, however, the inscrutable gestures to the Orientalist abjection of the Asian, the feminine, and the silent by quietly contorting its moves to uncertain social effects. Rather than refuse a stereotype of mute Asian femininity, Ono and Nakadate perform its technical restraint, in what Shimakawa might call an abject mime, and effectively shift focus to the noisy happenings that such inscrutable performance permits.

Perhaps here I may circle back to or pull through Dufourmantelle, who has been silently waiting to appear in this chapter, as the one who invited Derrida to remark on hospitality and who comments on Derrida's "poetic hospitality" as that which in significant ways eludes "the day, the visible, and memory."[54] Dufourmantelle's language of the night, and her text's visual reliance on blank space, is sympathetic to my interest in inscrutability, feminized silence, and Serres's noise. Dufourmantelle describes her attempt "to come close to a silence around which discourse is ordered, and that a poem sometimes discovers, but always pulls itself back from unveiling in the very movement of speech or writing."[55] We may note Dufourmantelle's rhetoric of silence and unveiling as interestingly constitutive of philosophy's racializing and gendered aesthetics. One of this chapter's explorations has been to identify the silent construction of Asian woman in Western discourses of hospitality; and, through that effort, to engage the work of Ono and Nakadate as two contemporary Asian/American female artists who pointedly reconstruct and trouble the terms of their legibility as such through participant-based performance. If at moments I have struggled to do so with more clarity, consistent with my own capacity for failure, I also wonder if it is the discursive construction of Asian femininity that in fact resists straight narration. This queer ephemerality is also what returns Asian femininity once more to its ontology as performance, as that which is lived out in material bodies and takes meaning through discursive spectatorship, "always pull[ing] itself back from unveiling in the very movement of speech or writing."

Emma Sulkowicz and the Potential to Be Offered

There are qualitative distinctions between being silent and being *silenced.* Similarly, as I have suggested, it is a quite different process to be silent than it is to be unheard.—PATTI DUNCAN, *Tell This Silence*

How might these formulations of parasitic femininity and strategic Asian silence bear on Emma Sulkowicz's famed *Mattress Performance (Carry That Weight)* of the 2014–15 school year (see figure 2.4)? The durational performance by the then Columbia University undergraduate student artist may ring familiar to readers given its recent and wide coverage. Sulkowicz created an arts thesis project that made visible and material the toll of carrying the emotional, psychic, and material weight of sexual violence and inadequate institutional response. With the commitment to continue the performance until either they or their attacker, fellow student Paul Nungesser, officially left Columbia University, Sulkowicz and their performance brought urgent issues of campus safety, sexual assault and rape, and institutional responses to "private" grievance to major headlines. The performance concluded upon Sulkowicz's and Nungesser's graduation, as the institution did not expel Nungesser, nor did he leave of his own volition. Comparisons of *Mattress Performance (Carry That Weight)* have been made to Ana Mendieta's *Untitled (Rape Scene)* (1973) and Suzanne Lacy and Leslie Liebowitz's *Three Weeks in May* (1977), and we may be reminded of Ono's film *Rape* (1969) as well.[56]

The "rules of engagement" were written on the walls of Sulkowicz's art studio at Columbia, and described in a performance document on the artist's website:

1   Whenever I am on Columbia University (CU) property, I must have the mattress with me. This area includes the campus, all the buildings on campus, and any Columbia-owned buildings off-campus.

FIGURE 2.4. Emma Sulkowicz, left, with Gabriela Pelsinger, *Mattress Performance (Carry That Weight)*. Photograph by Jennifer S. Altman for the *New York Times*.

2 When I am inside a CU-owned building, the mattress must be inside the building as well. However, it *can* be in a different room.

3 I may not seek help carrying the mattress. However, if someone offers either to help me carry the mattress or carry it for me on their own accord, I can accept their aid.

4 When heading from a location owned by CU to a location that isn't owned by CU, I must leave the mattress in a safe place on campus.

5 When heading from a location not owned by CU to a location owned by CU, I must first collect the mattress from wherever I left it previously.

6 I must notify all my professors about the performance before classes begin. They may deny me a spot in their classes at their own discretion.[57]

The emphasis on the mattress as central performance prop/costar shows the overdetermined epistemology of the mattress as a metaphor for the weight of the experience and memory of sexual violence. When the press rushed to conflate the performance as legible protest, Sulkowicz critiqued, "In the news, people have been calling my piece a protest, and just ignoring the fact it is not really a protest but a performance-art piece."[58] Implications as to Sulkowicz's personal character quickly echo those of Ono's and Nakadate's reception. Writes *Elle Magazine*, "Reactions to the piece, [Sulkowicz] says, range from extreme adoration—'Emma's a goddess and angel'—to extreme hatred—'Emma's a slut and a liar who's trying to grab attention.'"[59] What might it mean, then, not to consider *Mattress Performance* as a clearly legible message and call for direct justice but instead to interpret *Mattress Performance* through aesthetics of inscrutability as they work to discipline and variously invisibilize and hypervisibilize Asian American women and nonbinary people?

The "weight" referenced within the artwork's parenthetical title may be understood not only as a simple synecdoche of the weight of rape but also the weight of insisting on consensual intimacy, and the burden of practicing this feminist ethic of consent while waiting for justice—a form of legal justice that must be demanded under neoliberalism, even if its recognition (of expelling Nungesser, for instance) would not address the greater social problems of misogyny and rape culture. The burden to do the most while one's own needs are not being tended to is an extension of what I've articulated here as parasitic femininity, where Sulkowicz contorts the burden of liveness they as an alleged rape survivor are made to bear, in performing testimony and performing perfect survivorship (further explored in their subsequent artwork, the video *Ceci N'est Pas Un Viol*). Rather than outright "saying yes" to those institutionalized avenues and scripts of redress, Sulkowicz creates a performance piece that invites practices of consent with others, including with strangers, and thereby reveals the burdens of its disappointments (see figure 2.5).

Rule number 3 delineates that the artist's relationship to the mattress can invite an expansive sociality to their task of carrying it, however asymmetrical that request for help may be. As Sulkowicz shares in an early video circulated by *Columbia Spectator*, "One of the rules of the piece is that I am not allowed to ask for help in carrying the mattress, but others are allowed to give help if they come up and offer it."[60] With this rule, the artist conjures an audience and configures the viewing public as always already in the position to (1) help and (2) offer help. Sulkowicz shows how to watch and be in their presence is already to be involved and to offer help is to respond to a preexisting responsibility. *Mattress Performance*, then, is an invitation to be involved, to take part, to engage, and to carry the weight of another as an extension of one's own. Sulkowicz directs the audience as those with the possibility of helping, and the artist's role is to consider accepting or saying yes—with no promise or need to do so. Rule 3 reminds us that it is the artist's prerogative

FIGURE 2.5. Emma Sulkowicz, *Mattress Performance (Carry That Weight)*.
Photograph by Andrew Burton/Getty Images.

to say yes, and so, too, it is the bystander's role to reach out and offer help. In this chapter, I have tried to complicate the seeming clarity of saying yes, the troubling deferral to positivist language, even or perhaps especially as college campuses today promote discourses of affirmative sexual consent of "yes means yes." Though I am not interested in speaking against those efforts, I do wish to identify racialized problems of consent, particularly with Sulkowicz's visibility as a young assigned female at birth (AFAB) gender nonconforming survivor of sexual assault simultaneous with their racial invisibility as an Asian American biracial artist. Here, it is relevant to state that Sulkowicz, since the publicity around *Mattress Performance* as an undergraduate student artist, uses "they/them" pronouns. As Sulkowicz writes, "Being the victim of assault helped me realize that I was gender non-conforming" and "'they' evokes my slippage between man and woman, but it also evokes the way that I see the slippage between human and object."[61] The slipperiness of gender in relation to body ontology, new materialist study, and sexual violence will continue in the next chapter in thinking with contemporary novels featuring transfeminist aesthetics.

I wish to make explicit how Derrida's meditation on universal hospitality and the exhortation to say yes resonates with contemporary discourses of affirmative sexual consent and rampant sexual assault. Though Ono's works are sometimes understood as activist art, as is *Mattress Performance*, it is worth recognizing the blurriness of those categories of activism and art as commonly rendered distinct from one another. Though a discourse of feminist art rose with second-wave feminist politics around the 1970s, feminist scholars and artists of color such as Coco Fusco have offered an alternative historiography wherein the embodied practices of women of color—whether under the genre of slavery, freak show, military conquest, or colonial object—have in fact been the pioneers of revolutionary body art that is personal, aesthetic, and political.[62] We may understand the works of Ono, Nakadate, and Sulkowicz, then, to variously evidence how feminist performance upsets a dichotomous relation often drawn between art and activism. To take *Mattress Performance* seriously as performance art is to attune ourselves to the multifarious effects it may have in the world, ones that exceed the bounds of legal recognition and presentist epistemology.

Strikingly, Sulkowicz's biraciality is rarely addressed in media coverage of their work. Though *Mattress Performance* is frequently if briefly contextualized in a performance art tradition, and sometimes a feminist performance art tradition, rarely is it discussed alongside Asian American or multiracial aesthetics. Rather than read this as colorblindness on the part of the press, I consider this lack of specificity as an example of Asian racial inscrutability on a national stage, particularly when it does not rehearse familiar tropes of Asian submissive respectability. Grappling with Sulkowicz's racialized gender in relation to their response to alleged sexual assault, however, enriches interpretations of their performance piece. To study *Mattress Performance* as a racialized performance of inscrutability is to consider Sulkowicz's performance as a then-college student, a gender nonconforming person, an artist, and a biracial Asian person whose gendered racialization was rendered unremarkable and thereby erased in public discourse. Rather than praise the lack of focus on race as post-racial white universalism, paralleling Derrida's embrace of hospitality, I propose that the unremarked-upon racialization and gendering of Sulkowicz cuts out a rich genealogy and futurity of their work. When I embed Sulkowicz within a genealogy of Asian and Asian American feminist art, I do not do so simply by deferring to a biography of the artist as of Chinese and Polish ancestry. Rather, I ask us to engage Sulkowicz's work with deference to an ample tradition of radical aesthetics that is the privileged domain of people of color, women, and gender nonconforming people.

Inscrutability indexes a raw vulnerability that pulsates beside any critical interpretation. In a panel discussion at Williams College in the spring of 2015, Sulkowicz critiqued the desires of others who nominate them to the position of martyr, comparing their mattress carry to Christ's walk with the cross on his back. What I heard implicit in their words was others' desires for them to represent strength and heroism, bravery and solidity, to serve as a poster child for redemption. Instead, Sulkowicz emphasized their feelings of powerlessness and vulnerability, describing the ways in which the performance (and its subsequent audience reception) further bound them to the educational institution and to the person who attacked them. In my reading, what is mesmerizing about Sulkowicz's performance is precisely this insistent vulnerability of asking others to ask for consent, especially in the face of trespass.

At an event for Sulkowicz at Williams College organized by Anjuli Fatima Raza Kolb, I discussed their work's position of generosity and feminist pedagogy in making it known that they can accept help with the mattress in the rules of engagement. In my readings of their work, I wanted to recognize the inexplicability of the performance, one that is not entirely delimited by the facts of sexual assault and institutional neglect but expands the possible social relations with vulnerability and receptivity. I was struck when Sulkowicz kindly corrected me, agreeing that the performance's terms sought out consent from participants of the work but that in practice strangers regularly grabbed onto the mattress without receiving an explicit "yes" from the artist. The actual performance and dismissal of Sulkowicz's rules of engagement, then, shed light on the sense of entitlement people had—presumably to help out, but also in ways that disappoint and trespass their boundaries.

The participant's presumption of offering help orients *Mattress Performance* in a different light, one that shows the limits of identity positions that cohere as victim or survivor. One interpretation is that people often assume that Sulkowicz needs help and believe that their shared carrying of the mattress will help the artist. I understand their performance as extending my study of Laurel Nakadate's parasitic performance. Sulkowicz is a host of sorts, where the mattress is a metonymy for a domicile or private space. In a sense, the mattress externalizes the hospitable site that an Asian woman's or femme's body is already made to bear. People who approach Sulkowicz and take on the mattress without their agreement presume to know what it is that the artist wants. The gender and racial inscrutability of Sulkowicz's body underscores the external mandates imposed on their performance work as well as the long-standing institutions that prescribe readings of their body and authority. The audience-participant's presumption to know what they want and what they mean by the performance once more betrays the anxiety of waiting for an answer, the anxiety of approaching an uncharted, though broadly reiterated, relationality.

There is a risk to each of these performances by Ono, Nakadate, and Sulkowicz that is a refusal to give up the social, to conform to a narrative of isolating self-victimization, where the only recourse is to respond in masculinist logics of aggressive reaction. It is a refusal to resign oneself to exploitation and abuse by retracting an outreached hand. It is through embodied performance that the authority of Asian women as artists compels us to problematize a persistent alignment of Asianness, femininity, and powerlessness. I locate *Mattress Performance* in this genealogy of feminist art not to essentialize or reinforce a reading where Asian women, trans, and gender nonconforming people are inevitably vulnerable and submissive, as though they are without agency to ask for help. Rather, I want to look again at Sulkowicz's third rule and align it as a feminist and Asian strategy to expand the submissive position, to position oneself to accept and receive, to risk the optic of submissiveness, and to politicize that embrace. This work by queer and feminist scholars and artists not only has the effect of problematizing a normative racial and gender discourse. These performances also have the effect of insisting on oneself as a source of desire, as social critic, as social practitioner.

I hold in mind the countless conversations between and among Asian women and gender nonconforming people, and other womxn of color in the United States and abroad, who are exhausted from the expectation to literally and figuratively "say yes" to daily mandates of sexism and racism. The stakes of my exploration in this chapter, then, include the ability for Asian people who identify as women, or who are identified as women, to manage our production as those who run the world materially and symbolically as care and service laborers, including bodying forth alternative epistemologies of care, inviting relationality by staging participatory encounter, and sometimes interrupting expectations by pointedly performing them. Though inscrutability has been racialized and gendered as threatening, I think with Ono's, Nakadate's, and Sulkowicz's participatory performances to argue that inscrutability is also the condition for hope in unknowable sociality. This unknown content and form—the "warp and woof"—of the inscrutable is also the queer horizon that, following José Esteban Muñoz, so many of us yearn for and feel pulled by. This saying yes, then, would be saying yes toward something that, like the indistinguishable sound at the door, imaginatively opens up social futures and refuses a teleology of the inevitable.

IM/PENETRABILITY, TRANS FIGURATION, AND UNRELIABLE SURFACING

Asian forms are often discussed as spectacular surfaces with mysterious interiors to penetrate or cut into, including silence, concisely heterofeminizing Asian form. This book now moves from the relational noise of silence to the tropes of the inscrutable other as both impenetrable and penetrable, at once sexually and materially penetrable *and* psychically and narratively impenetrable. I explore other mappings of penetration in this chapter, in ways that move away from a compulsory heterosexual reading that disciplines a gender binary based on genital skin. Could penetration be about something other than colonial seizure and a reconsolidation of a gender binary? Pursuing this question could change the surfacing of Asiatic form. The larger stakes of this chapter are to extend the conversation around the sexualization of Asian women and the feminization of Asian men, as historic tropes of Asianness reinforce a gender episteme that is binarized according to sexuality (hyper or hypo), ultimately reinforcing a (white) colonial masculinist perspective.

If impenetrability, as a synonym for inscrutability, also registers sexual and military application, let us ask further about the role of desire and violence on the subject formation of those racialized as impenetrable. I suggest that we consider the role of a certain kind of penetration of skin, but not one that is generally understood as sexual, though of course edgeplay, knife kinks, and piquerism would tell otherwise.[1] The language of cutting will lead us through the language of castration and its psychoanalytic treatment as lack. We will also ask: What if cutting is not subtractive, is not toward suicide or self-negation, or at least not in a straightforward way? What if cutting is regenerative? Eva Hayward writes, "The cut is not so much an opening of the body, but a generative effort to pull the body back through itself in order to feel mending, to feel the growth of new margins."[2]

The novels I now turn to grapple with the cut body in some way that does something for the characters' sense of self, which, within the greater context of the stories, are structured by their gendered racialization in time and space. I hope that analyzing these novels will enrich our understandings of what "impenetrable" means and does for Asian diasporic racial formation, and how it potentiates a transformation of racialized gender. The following pages will include readings of literary passages that involve cutting, hate speech that is racist and transphobic, and self-injury. I do not wish to treat cutting as a figurative symbol removed from the practice of cutting, and the often difficult feelings that come with it. Studies show that women, queers, and trans people are more likely to engage with self-injury, and within the category of self-injury, transfeminine-identifying trans people are more likely to cut.[3] By observing this pattern in contemporary literature, I hope to be able to engage with it and allow a more complex reading and conversation about cutting as a negotiation of surfacing through racist and patriarchal structures, especially as it is relevant to queer and trans people of color.

In the final pages of Kai Cheng Thom's debut mixed-format novel, *Fierce Femmes and Notorious Liars: A Dangerous Trans Girl's Confabulous Memoir* (2016) (see figure 3.1), the unnamed protagonist writes a letter to her younger sister Charity before signing off. She instructs, "Take care of yourself. I'm enclosing a pearl-handled switchblade with this letter. Don't use it unless you have to."[4] By this point in the novel, the reader understands the gifted switch-blade to be the "little silver fang-friend" that accompanies the protagonist on

FIGURE 3.1. Cover of Kai Cheng Thom's *Fierce Femmes and Notorious Liars*. Design and artwork by Samantha Garritano.

the book's many fantastical journeys, which include running away from the town of Gloom to the City of Smoke and Lights and joining a trans girl gang called the Lipstick Lacerators, who collectively avenge trans woman victims of police brutality.[5] The letter to Charity continues, "I will tell you everything—the truth, the whole truth, nothing but the truth—someday soon, I promise. I'm still just figuring out what exactly the truth is, you know?"[6] These parting epistolary words at the end of the self-proclaimed memoir (though, recalling notorious literary histories of women-of-color literatures, including Maxine Hong Kingston's *The Woman Warrior*, Thom classifies the book as a novel) present two entwined themes explored in this chapter: the power to cut as a temporary feminist form that can empower as opposed to victimize, and reliable truth telling as an aspirational process whose impossibility creates a future. Thom's pairing of skin cutting and unreliable narration constellates *Fierce Femmes and Notorious Liars* within a genealogy of Asian American literature that challenges historic dualisms of Asian gendered racialization as (physically) *penetrable* and (psychically) *impenetrable*. By analyzing these scenes of cutting and trans narration, this chapter makes an argument for inscrutable aesthetics of trans, queer, and feminist Asian sociality in Thom's novel as well as two other contemporary novels for, borrowing from Zairong Xiang, their transdualist "either . . . and . . ." approach to impenetrability.[7]

I center my analysis on transfeminist narratives to consider the gendered and sexualized racialization of impenetrability and to better understand how inscrutability functions as a feminist Asian racial aesthetic across forms. To be impenetrable is to present an obstacle to physical, emotional, and/or psychic access.[8] As *Surface Relations* studies, the gendered racial construction of an inscrutable other depends on and forms a perpetual foreigner whose "nature" or "meaning" cannot be satisfyingly entered or inhabited, and therefore whose gender, sexuality, and race cannot be unilaterally manipulated for the purposes of white imperialist nation building. In the previous chapter, Ono's, Nakadate's, and Sulkowicz's use of exploitative silence and parasitic hospitality demonstrate how the management of masculinist anxiety on the bodies of those assigned female at birth reproduces yet another facet of Asian inscrutability. Simultaneous to a history of the racial construction of an impenetrable racial psyche are various military and political campaigns where Asian geopolitical spaces, cultures, and bodies are in practice the site of such penetrative "entry" and "inhabitation"—think, here, of the female sex slave or "comfort woman," military base sex worker, domestic worker, war bride, wartime adoptee, and trafficked child—many of whom are written out or rescripted flatly as victims in tales of Western rescue and colonial maternalism. This sexualized Asian dialectic of impenetrability (utterly alien and inaccessible in its own terms) and penetrability (readily accessible by force) is a modern racial paradox studied in this chapter through analysis of queer and transfeminine narrative and figuration.

The threatening racial form of Asian gender fluidity that I think through here as *unreliable surfacing* also names the particular threat of transgender identities and embodiments to cis-heteropatriarchal and colonial expectations of female and "Eastern" embodiment as available, symbolically and materially manifested through a penetrable orifice. The meaning of bodies racialized as Asian has historically relied on a colonial and misogynist logic premised on a biologically deterministic gender binary. The threat and potential of inscrutable surfaces pervade trans studies. As Susan Stryker writes, "Transgender people who problematize the assumed correlation of a particular biological sex with a particular social gender are often considered to make false representations of an underlying material truth, through the willful distortion of surface appearance. Their gender presentation is seen as a lie rather than as an expression of a deep, essential truth."[9] The dangerous "lie" of trans embodiment is also Asian inscrutability's threat to Western-centric and ocular-centric notions of truth. As Mel Chen shows, the gendered threat of Asian racialization is inseparable from the threat of transgender epistemologies. In their analysis of the queer animality of Fu Manchu's inscrutability, Chen indexes the historic emasculation of male Asian racialization and the hypersexuality of Asian female subjectification to posit that "the Asian transgender body becomes both eminently possible as the logical (if socially disallowed) consequence of a significatory overreach, while at the same time, the Asian transgender body survives as an impossible spectacle."[10] Both "eminently possible" and spectacularly impossible, embodying the hyper and the hypo, the Asian transgender body becomes il/legible through matrices of Asian inscrutability and cis-heteronationalism. How, then, does the social transgression of trans and gender nonconforming "surface appearance" interface with Asian inscrutable surface, charged as "false representations of an underlying material truth"? And how do narratives of surface unreliability reroute the force of aesthetic inscrutability?

To pursue these questions, I suggest that the treatment, touch, and penetration of epidermal skin in three contemporary novels—namely, Monique Truong's *The Book of Salt* (2003), Kim Fu's *For Today I Am a Boy* (2014), and Kai Cheng Thom's *Fierce Femmes and Notorious Liars* (2016)—dislocate genital skin as the primary site of receptivity, generosity, power, and violence. I study the protagonists to consider how a desire to be penetrated, to have one's epidermal surface be pierced (and by oneself) might articulate other modes of being and relating that upend body ontologies of femininity and Asianness that rely on a cis-masculinist dialectic of a phallic other. By using the language of penetration and femininity to consider Asian racial form, I walk a fine line here because I acknowledge painful histories of trans-exclusionary radical feminism and anti-Asian misandry. I wish to think through the symbolics of femininity, and their assigned material forms, that bear effects of violence and risk as well as queer pleasure and sisterhood. My proposal here is to think in the tradition of a queer feminism that embraces and welcomes trans epistemologies, to pose questions of gender away from the phallus bias, androcentrism, gender binarism, and compulsory heterosexuality; and to think alongside trans studies scholars who trouble epistemes of embodiment.[11] Asian American and queer diasporic aesthetics of inscrutability rescript Orientalist preoccupations with colonial penetration by privileging the role of the skinbearer as one who may be the penetrator as well as the penetrated. If liberal mandates of self-testimony and transparency discipline discursive and visual legibility for citizenship, then how might strategic impenetrability, surface play, and tactile embodiment trouble the mandate to have skin attest to the truth of oneself?

Skin as Hardened Racial Surface

A primary historic alibi for Asian diasporic unbelonging has been suspicious gender presentation to a non-Asian gaze. Skin has been a primary analytic for understanding the threat of racial and gender difference. Modern Asian epidermalization might be thought of as a kind of genital surfacing, as always already too porous by virtue of being yellow. Scholarship across gender and sexuality studies teaches us that to reduce gender to genitalia is a biopolitical strategy that secures power/knowledges endemic to giving meaning to the body. How might we otherwise think of skin as actant of racialized gender knowledge? To turn to skin as fleshly organ of knowing, relating, and theorizing of potential sociality is to turn to Black cultural theorists and queer-of-color literary theorists, such as Sara Ahmed, Anne Anlin Cheng, Frantz Fanon, Amber Jamilla Musser, José Esteban Muñoz, and Hortense Spillers, who have offered surface reading as an alternative method to rigor. Racialized surface can signal threat to a majoritarian gaze, revealing the pulses of a minoritarian strategy. As Uri McMillan writes, "Surface is viewed with suspicion: as superficial, or as deceptive, or as unable to hold up to rigorous scrutiny."[12] Suspicion of the surface conjures specific stakes for Asian racialization; the threat of Asian surface is both in its inability "to hold up to rigorous scrutiny" as object of cultural critique, as flaccid or weak yellowness, and, with histories that conflate Asian with spy and perpetual foreigner, in its duplicitous and uncanny ability to withstand attempts of repeated penetration and function as durable, inscrutable surface. Asian bodies have been understood as robotic surfaces that are seen to perform so well as to seem impenetrable, disrupting distinctions between fake and authentic, performing a self-sufficiency that never leaks interiority. Such thought also betrays the idea that exteriority is self-evident or simpler than an interiority whose complexity is granted. I attend to Asian gendered racialization and surface aesthetics to distort and amplify McMillan's question: "How have we failed to perceive the liminal, luscious, and dark points of possibility summoned by the surface?"

Feminist and anti-racist scholars turn time and again to skin not only for its material and symbolic power but also specifically for its materiality as a social process. Sara Ahmed and Jackie Stacey hail a "skin-tight politics" that considers "inter-embodiment, on the mode of being-with and being-for, where one touches and is touched by others."[13] Elsewhere, Ahmed argues that "norms surface *as* the surfaces of bodies; norms are a matter of impressions, of how bodies are 'impressed upon' by the world, as a world made up of others."[14] Skin as surface occasions sociality and "being-with" at the same time as it submits itself to normalizing impressions. To be surface is to be impressionable. Michelle Ann Stephens's *Skin Acts* studies the performance of skin in the construction of Black masculinity and asserts that "the skin serves here as a threshold, a point of contact, a site of intersubjective encounter, between the inner and outer self and between the self and the other."[15] Skin as "threshold, a point of contact" functions as a social membrane that renders the body vulnerable and susceptible to otherness, porous and open to what could count as "self." Further, Stephens writes: "The skin is differentiated as belonging to different genders based on the shape of the sexual organs, genital skin; the skin is differentiated as marking different races based on the body's color, epidermal skin."[16] I find Stephens's provisional distinction of "genital skin" and "epidermal skin" helpful in order to appreciate how genital skin has been and is racialized (as with racial stereotypes of penis size), and how epidermal skin has been gendered (as with the gendering of skin according to hair density). Stephens's concept of skin acknowledges a similarity in matter and permits me to study the shift between the racializing of *epidermal skin* and the gendering of *genital skin*, back again to racializing of genital skin and the gendering of epidermal skin for queer and trans Asian diasporic characters in contemporary fiction. By playing with the twists of gendered racialization and its staging on embodied skin, this chapter analyzes the functions of touch and cutting as a transgressive gendering of epidermal skin, both to negotiate assigned manhood and to resignify racialized femininities that can "touch themselves."

In what follows, I direct our attention to quotidian scenes of skin penetration enacted by the protagonists themselves, juxtaposed with scenes of racialized and gendered violence enacted by others. I am not interested in pathologizing or romanticizing cutting as a habit, though I will engage social scientific discourses of self-harm. Rather, in a mode of surface reading put forth by Stephen Best and Sharon Marcus, I observe cutting as a literary pattern with as-yet-undetermined material stakes worthy of attention.[17] I note the correlation between the self-punctured surface of the Asian diasporic body while tracking historic racial tropes of impenetrability. Focusing on the Asian, trans, and feminized self, then, as not only the object but also the subject of skin surfacing and piercing, I ask: Which narrative and embodied forms are made possible through cutting in literature?

Yellow as Flaccid: The Gendering of Yellow Skin

Impenetrability as a trope of Asian inscrutability illuminates the racial, gender, and sexual dynamics inherited and reiterated by a colonial symbolic order. The modern fetish of hard bodily integrity exoticizes Woman and the Orient as penetrable forms and exalts Western masculinity as penetrator. Let us note how a rhetoric of penetration often conjures images of cis-heteronormative sexual intercourse, exemplified in the equation of penis-in-vagina (P/V) sex as "real" (read: hetero-reproductive) sex. Such a discourse of penetrability constructs a binaristic logic of gender and sexuality, with tidy colonial columns grouping penetrating position as masculine and active, and penetrated position as feminine and passive. Observing an Orientalist logic of heterosexism and gender conformity that maintains such an image of penetration lets us index the racialized signifying chain of femininity, passivity, and Asianness and the unmarked masculinity, active position, and whiteness. Inscrutability's supposed passivity (conveyed through modes of silence, distance, withholding, flatness, and surface) enacts a way of knowing that is not only dialectical to liberal tenets of sovereignty but simultaneously in fact operates beside such a dialectic.

It is not only the vulva or penis that reads as genital skin to anxious others. Epidermal skin—judged in relation to universalized white skin—names the reinscription of colonial gender norms and, as such, marks the failure of Asian masculinity in an imperial visual schema. "Thin" yellow skin describes a racist optic of failed masculinity that aligns yellowness with impotence, as we find in Monique Truong's beloved novel *The Book of Salt*, which tells the first-person narrative of a Vietnamese diasporic man called Bình, who works as the chef in Gertrude Stein and Alice B. Toklas's Parisian home. Truong's narration weaves Bình's memories of family and homosexual trysts in Vietnam and France, and while traveling across the ocean, into a lyrical valentine to the real-life Indochinese chefs who fed modernism's most famous lesbians. Stein, the employer, "merrily mispronounce[es]" Bình's name with the rhyme "Thin Bin," claiming to describe the protagonist's "most distinctive feature" without translating the English words for him.[18] Thinness can reference a narrowness in bodily silhouette, sometimes associated with weakness or fragility when describing men, but I would reframe it to say that thinness names a conflation of surface and depth. Stein's judgment of Bình as thin also points to his colonial invisibility within nationally framed economies. As Stephens writes, "Over the course of the Enlightenment, the skin and the body both began to harden, to be seen as less and less permeable," citing the "specific history of the skin's growing impermeability" as necessary for addressing the relationships among skin, race, and difference.[19] These Enlightenment values were borne by the theft and enslavement of colonized peoples, enforcing a powerful distinction between human bodies and exploitable flesh through the transatlantic slave trade.[20] Such fleshly hardness would come to hierarchize bodies according to ability, race, and gender in the name of modern civilization. Discourses of cross-cultural contact, of intercultural contamination, of miscegenation, coincide with a discursive thickening of the skin such that the skin provides a hardened protective barrier for the ego. The hardened exterior of the laboring body conceals the (racialized) effort and toil that modernity has required. Ahmed and Stacey cite Anne McClintock in their critique of how "the imperative of consumption is to work towards smooth and shiny surfaces that conceal the signs of labor as well as time."[21] Stein's assessment of Bình as "thin" dismisses his labor as well as the empires that structure their relation.

Where literary inscrutability elevates Stein to modern genius, the colonial construction of Bình's inscrutability upon his skin is interpreted as inferiority. Not only does thinness suggest less substance, but what Stein does not explicitly name is the yellowness of his skin. Bình, however, notices how his skin "marks [him], announces [his] weakness, displays it as yellow skin."[22] The yellowness of Bình's skin and his exiled immigrant status announce his subordination to French (white) corporeality. While he is another colonial worker in Paris, Bình is rendered "the *asiatique*, the sideshow freak" to Stein and Toklas's lesbian alterity in the French countryside.[23] When working in Stein and Toklas's summer home in Bilignin, Bình faces not only Toklas's infantilizing nickname of "her little Indochinese" but also the locals' imperial interrogation. Truong specifies three questions asked by farmers: "Did you know how to use a fork and a knife before coming to France?" "Will you marry three or four *asiatique* wives?" and "Are you circumcised?"[24]

Bình's yellow skin throws into question his masculinity based on consumption etiquette, property of women, and sexual discipline of the body. Note how these questions coalesce around the power of cutting: the dining knife and the foreskin's loss both speak to the blade's masculinizing force. The subtext of the farmers' questions seems to be an either/or formulation: Do you wield your power to cut or are you cut? Bình's thinness of skin also maps onto a propensity to be cut, a thin membrane vulnerable to penetration, the permeability to imperial hardness. The question about wives, moreover, betrays a miscegenation anxiety, placing his heterodisciplined masculinity within a colonial order according to whom and how many he is penetrating (i.e., multiple Asian women, not white women). Cutting in this scene is the threshold of power, the means for asserting mastery over another, whether the dead animal on your plate or the uncircumcised phallus (i.e., excessive genital skin that may prove feminizing). Cutting comes to symbolize power in this exchange. The imposition of these gender norms of masculinity shames Bình for his expected gender failure as a subordinate Indochinese laborer. These questions are a form of castration for this queer man; they engage with his penis through a provisional masculinity, one that is disciplined in relation to cutting and penetrating women and animals.

Though inscrutability and impenetrability are often associated with cool masculinity—where masculinity functions reductively as that which penetrates and is not penetrated—Asian and Asian American masculinities disrupt this unidirectional phallic imagery, as powerfully put forth in David L. Eng's theory of racial castration. Through a white and Western imaginary, Eng argues that there is a reverse racial fetishism at play in the emasculation of Asian men: not seeing the (Asian) penis that *is* there as a different application of the Freudian scenario where the (white) boy, for example, displaces the unseen, "castrated" penis of the mother onto an object or fetish.[25] Richard Fung's canonical critique of an Orientalist conflation of Asian with anus shows how Asian/American men not only are racially castrated but also are sexualized and feminized as penetrable.[26] Such psychoanalytic engagement within Asian American studies importantly questions a symbolic alignment of men, masculinity, penis, and impenetrability, disrupting a smooth colonial linkage. As Eng, Fung, Nguyen Tan Hoang, and other masculinity scholars teach us, it is not only the vagina that is the privileged site of phallic penetration. US American gender-exclusive immigration, trade, and miscegenation laws conditioned migrant "bachelor" or predominantly male communities in early Asian American history, thus giving shape to Chinese fraternal spaces. The concentration of immigrant working men, in turn, became fodder for anti-Asian sentiments in early modern America in the shape of mainstream cultural depictions of asexual, aggressive, and/or effeminate Asian men. But let us be clear about the misogynist, cis-sexist, and homophobic logic here: the white nation-building project produced an ontology of masculinity premised on penetrating (who would be scripted in this act as) women and colonial others. Such a reiterative performance of proper manhood was therefore threatened by the possibility that a man could be ontologically sound without penetrating markers of difference, and threatened by the possibility of being penetrated himself, let alone enjoying it.

Fung and other feminist scholars have skewered Asian American cultural nationalist efforts to "re-masculinize" Asian America by critiquing the logic of failed Asian masculinity in its pleasurable penetrability as too aesthetically close to a feminine posture. As Nguyen's work on Asian and gay male bottomhood suggests, the conflation of Asian as not only racial but also gender descriptor based on postures and practices of receptivity can be refused and criticized for its stereotypical scope as well as embraced and worked for its feminist, queer, and trans potentials. In a special issue of *TSQ: Transgender Studies Quarterly*, "Trans-in-Asia, Asia-in-Trans," Zairong Xiang writes that "the porous body [in the *I Ching*] is understood through its open orifices, in which the penis is nothing more than an orifice, undifferentiated from the vagina."[27] With Xiang, we may consider the decolonial and trans critique of "hard" or impenetrable bodily autonomy as critical to Asian diasporic feminist studies through attunement to im/penetrable racial form. Following King-Kok Cheung and fellow Asian American feminist scholars, we can ask: Rather than uphold an anti-woman ontology of "Asia" premised on forceful penetration, might we not, instead, consider the transfeminist potential for Asian diasporic people, including Asian American cis men, to have privileged insight into imperial misogyny's penetrative toxicity?[28] As part of this, what would it mean to not fear an epistemological proximity between Asian cis men and Asian trans women? This transfeminist view would not be focused around genital skin but would be a critique of a necessary relation to penetration (of body, of narrative). I suggest a reading practice of bodily surface that recognizes the porosity and intercorporeality of life. Such susceptibility should not be confused for knowability or mastery, however. What might offering curiosity for bodily orifices, interpenetration, and gender construction beside a colonial gender binary do for our study of Asian inscrutability?

Transfeminine Surfacing

For transfeminine literary characters, the masculine failure of yellow skin cuts differently—but that does not render it safe. Rather, the misogyny and transphobia that undergird racial castration are pronounced. Where Bình's "thin" yellow skin jeopardizes his manhood and can be compensated by his avowals of penetrating women and animals, thin skin on a yellow trans woman threatens to be penetrated with violence in Kai Cheng Thom's *Fierce Femmes and Notorious Liars*. In this novel, to be a trans woman is to have one's surface be consumed by risk. The novel opens with the protagonist's escape from the City of Gloom, where the neglect of her immigrant Chinese parents is attributed to their poverty and weariness from factory labor. The protagonist informs her sister Charity of her imminent departure and boards a bus to the City of Smoke and Lights. Soon, the protagonist takes note of "a man on this bus who keeps looking at [her] like [she's] a piece of meat," "like he's considering eating [her]."[29] Thom makes clear that the stranger's stare is perilous because it is gendered: "I know this guy can tell I'm trans. Trans and travelling alone on a bus in the middle of Nowhere at 3 a.m."[30] Here we may recall Bình's compulsory cutting relation to meat as one that masculinizes his yellow skin. Thom's protagonist, on the other hand, is the meat in relation to whom others negotiate their masculine power, such as this man who harasses and attacks her. Her visit to a notorious but affordable plastic surgeon in a later scene brings similar rhetoric of visual consumption when Thom describes Dr. Crocodile as "eating [the protagonist] with his eyes, his unwavering smile."[31] To be looked at as trans and yellow is to be threatened with penetration. To look and be clocked renders one vulnerable to physical violence, and in this sense epidermal skin can serve as a surface for gender-based violence.

This embodied threat does not stop at the surface of the epidermal skin of trans women. Kimaya is the first trans woman the protagonist meets in the City of Smoke and Lights, and she becomes confidante and mentor to the protagonist. Kimaya is the director of the Femme Alliance Building (FAB), a health and social services center that offers resources to trans women and sex workers, and she takes the protagonist under her wing. Kimaya tells the origin legend of the Street of Miracles, the avenue where the femmes and sex workers hang out and work: "over seventy years ago, when a femme was beaten to death by a would-be john in front of a dozen bystanders."[32] Soon after the protagonist arrives in town, a trans sister named Soraya is murdered, and the Lipstick Lacerators form to avenge her death. One night a group of men retaliate against the Lipstick Lacerators. Thom writes, "One of the men, the biggest and nastiest looking, sneers, 'We're gonna fuck you up good, ya buncha faggots. How about we cut your dicks off for ya?"[33] Extending phallic pressure in *The Book of Salt* with a difference, the bigot tries to shame the trans women as failed men, where that notion of "successful" masculinity is distinguished from faggotry and a relationship to genital skin that can read as "dick."[34] The homophobic and transmisogynist threat performs a relation where the speaker positions himself as one who can cut, and the women as the bodies to be penetrated and with something to lose. The threat of violent penetration also presumes to center the penis as the site most worthy of protection, where being cut holds the greatest stakes. Too, the sexual language of "we're gonna fuck you up good" belies the erotic and violent desires toward trans women.

In Kim Fu's bildungsroman *For Today I Am a Boy*, these fetishistic white normative standards of masculinity brandish enhanced humiliation for the gender nonconforming protagonist and reveal the cis-heterosexist logic of yellow degeneracy. Written in vignette-like chapters, *For Today I Am a Boy* is a coming-of-age story that takes the first-person perspective of a young second-generation Chinese Canadian who grows up with her parents and three sisters. For the duration of the novel, the protagonist moves through the world with the assigned name of Peter Huang. It is not until the final word of the novel that the reader learns of Audrey's chosen name and acceptance as one of four sisters.[35] Assigned Asian male markers at birth, Audrey's transforming relationship to her body and identity is brought into troubling if productive tension once she meets an older white woman named Margie. Audrey is drawn toward her peer's mother despite her blatant fetishization and misrecognition of the protagonist as "a little Chinese boy," calling her "little Peter Huang, little Huang, little wang" in a tidy conflation of ethnicity, gender, and genitals.[36] When faced with this naming, Audrey has the social consciousness to know she ought to respond with abhorrence. Fu writes, "Someone calls you little China boy and you rage, you lecture, you gook, you chink, you traitor."[37] Instead of lashing out at Margie, however, Audrey absorbs the hatred and chastises herself with racist slurs. This moment can be interpreted as an expression of self-loathing (of racial humiliation and gender discipline) that also, ironically, makes space for gendered recognition. In Fu's striking formulation, despite the running racist commentary in her mind, Audrey feels her desire for Margie fueled because she both hates and loves this racialized emasculation. The previous passage is immediately followed with "I wanted the way you looked at me, into me, pushed inside of me." This passage bespeaks a pleasurable feminized surfacing as well as a desired penetration of being "pushed inside" of and "into": a gendered surface created not through genital skin but through being "looked at" as a racialized other. Despite the wrong fit of "boy" onto Audrey's identity, there is something about Margie's penetrating look that feels surprisingly right.

As their sexual relationship develops, Margie enjoys humiliating and at times harming Audrey in forms that depend on white misogyny. Fu writes: "[Margie] liked to sit on my face, not requiring me to do much—it was the idea of suffocating me that appealed to her. She made me wear a brocade hat with a braid built into it from a novelty store; she made me fake an accent, a cruel mimicry of my father."[38] Fu's sentence construction here, with Audrey as the object of Margie's whims, connotes minimal action on the protagonist's part ("not requiring me to do much"), such that the terms of their play are not clear to the reader. Margie takes sadistic pleasure in what she believes to be the protagonist's humiliated masculinity and Chinese stereotype. When Margie "force[s the protagonist] to wear her panties and stocking," however, Audrey has to tamp down her delight for fear Margie will change her mind: "I was careful not to ruin it by seeming too eager."[39] What Margie misses, and what the protagonist takes pangs to conceal, is Audrey's desire for femme presentation and, implicitly, for Margie's (white and cis) femininity to reflect, accept, and mentor her (Chinese and trans) femininity. Here, Audrey's inscrutability shields her from Margie's transphobic gaze and opens up their sexual practice that can, to a limited degree, speak to her gender identification and offer her pleasure.

Through scenes of erotic imaging, Audrey's epidermal skin is the navigator that can both pass as the Oriental boy Margie wants and ignite the protagonist's body in pleasure through contact with Margie's folds of genital skin. Audrey is thrilled by their erotic play in moments of layered surfacing, most notably when Margie lies on top of the protagonist, face-up, and Audrey feels her bodily surface as though it were her own: "I rubbed her and could almost feel it myself."[40] Audrey's delight in touching Margie can be understood as a transfeminine phenomenology and pleasure, where the folds of her skin become an extension of her surface. At the same time, Audrey's delight in gender play cannot be extricated from Margie's unabashed Orientalism and desire to humiliate Audrey as a little China boy. Fu's scenes between Audrey and Margie show how the symbolic alignment of Asian racialization with feminization can feel both heavenly and humiliating to a transfeminine Asian person. Audrey and the reader know what Margie refuses to understand: Audrey does not take pleasure from the racist masochism so much as she takes pleasure in her gender recognition and layered bodily surfacing. Ultimately, though, Audrey cannot be held by Margie since her Orientalist fetish relies on transphobic ideology.

Audrey's pleasure disrupts the humiliation that Margie's sadism is premised on, and soon they arrive at their limits. In their penultimate scene together, after Bonnie shames Margie for her racial fetish, Margie says to Audrey, "I knew you guys [Chinese men] were, you know, shy and effeminate. I didn't know you don't even fuck."[41] Indignant and desperate for her intimacy, the protagonist responds, "They do" and, in doing so, admits "that I wasn't one of them, what she wanted me to be. Her yellow man."[42] In this passage, Margie betrays her misunderstanding of Audrey's disdain for her penis as the failure of Asian masculinity, implying that phallic penetration is the foundational requirement (to "even fuck" even if "shy and effeminate"). What she does not recognize is Audrey's counteridentification with masculinity, and, therefore, her failure to humiliate the protagonist as not manly enough. Margie locates the protagonist's penis as a simple site of cis-masculine failure, as opposed to the penis as a purposefully neglected site of betrayed surfacing. Instead, we might note how Audrey's penis becomes the screen for Margie's failure to wield cis-heteronormative white supremacy as effective sex play. While Margie shames Audrey's refusal to penetrate Margie with her genitals as racialized masculine insufficiency, the reader may interpret the protagonist's refusal of genital penetration as feminist self-affirmation and trans quest for other skin tactilities.

This reading, however, does not readily present itself as Audrey faces violence for her trans surfacing and pleasuring. In the protagonist's slipped "they" moment, Margie may sense Audrey's insubordination against her binary-gender-based power play. In the following scene, the protagonist wakes up to find "the thing" between her legs forced into Margie's genitals.[43] In this sequence, Fu shows how racialized gender affirmations such as Audrey's can be met with violence on the body in the form of forced penetration. I read this rape as Margie's retaliation against the protagonist for not playing the tidy stereotype of emasculated and embarrassed Chinese man to her powerful, sexually liberated white woman. This scene is important for its literary demonstration of sexual assault and rape against a gender-questioning, femme character, which speaks against transphobic views that question the potential for people with penises to be raped. As critiqued in Fu's novel, P/V and M/F binary ideologies normalize an idea of rape as a man with a penis penetrating a woman with a vagina without her consent. In Fu's novel, instead, the act of rape is not so much premised on Audrey being entered into physically but about nonconsensual genital skin contact. *For Today I Am a Boy* illustrates the urgency in disentangling fetish of penetration as power, as violence, and as always equating penis with aggressor. Such binary thought renders the experiences, risks, and choices of trans women illegible.

Gender discipline takes the form of homophobia and phallic control, as though anything other than penis idolatry is extra, femininity out-of-bounds, and threatening to manhood. I point this out because undergirding these literary moments is a logic where femininity (and faggotry) is put on or excessive, and masculinity and heterosexism are skin normative. What I mean by *skin normative* is the regulation of genital skin to uphold norms of gender, race, and sexuality, such that genitals betray the privileging of white, masculine, and cis phallic power because they isolate the biological from the social. To enact the body otherwise, to view genital skin as comparable to epidermal skin—whose meaning and intelligibility are socially constructed— is to threaten the normative hierarchy of skin, and to become vulnerable to retaliatory violence.

Inscrutable Skin

At the same time as the protagonists suffer from misogynist and transphobic violence, multiple scenes in the novels suggest that the trans protagonists are inscrutable in ways that present privileges and challenges specific to Asian trans women. The passability of some Asian trans women would seem to present a clear advantage for navigating public space safely. The cultural mythos that East Asian people have less body hair and have smaller features than other races suggests that transfeminine East Asians are less likely to be clocked and targeted in public. The novels evidence moments of these intersections of East Asian and trans being. During a consultation for a boob job in *Fierce Femmes and Notorious Liars*, Dr. Crocodile says to the fierce femme, "You Asians are always the best treatment subjects for this sort of thing."[44] On the next page, Kimaya calls the protagonist "fish," explaining the privileges of being fishy, including the following: "*Fish* means being able to walk in the daylight, as far as you please from the Street of Miracles, without fear of being chased and beat up by somebody or arrested by the cops."[45] The protagonist considers the weight of Kimaya's words, the racialized privilege of passing as a woman, and the ways in which "fish" also indexes the comparisons and competitiveness between trans women, as another form of racialized misogyny and homophobia. The possible visual passability of Asian trans women (in the protagonist's case at least, according to Kimaya) brings forth another form of inscrutability: the inscrutability of Asian gender in the focus on gender physicality, including skin, size, shape, and silhouette.

This Asian trans inscrutability can operate as power, as a privilege in skin hegemonic society. At the same time, Asian trans inscrutability also challenges the protagonist to feel acceptance in her trans-of-color community, especially when she has internalized hatred to confront, and her experience as a trans woman is illegible or erased on a public scale. As Blas Radi writes, in relation to Latin American and Asian communities, "The race binary [in the United States] can be as oppressive as the gender one, and it sometimes constitutes more of an obstacle than a useful analytical tool to understand oppression. In practice, it can have a deleterious effect, since it distorts critique and contributes to (and even justifies) the marginalization of non-afrodescendent people of color."[46] Such considerations of race also speak to the studies of enslavement, colonialism, militarism, and surveillance within trans-of-color critique. These novels give us a sense, then, not only of power systems outside trans communities but also of how trans communities are not immune to or protected from racism, colorism, classism, and xenophobia. Rather, queer and trans socialities are also hostage to the racist, xenophobic, and misogynist environments that occasion their creation.

Cutting as Surfacing, Remembering, and Embodying Femininities

I move us from other people's racialized anxiety over a protagonist's genital skin in these scenes to the focus on punctured racialized and gendered epidermal skin in these recent novels. How might we readers make sense of the literary pattern of cutting in these Asian American novels that feature trans and queer protagonists? Given the misogynist, homophobic, and transphobic violent surfacing of skin as visual object, what do we do with self-wielded forms of penetration and cutting?

In the novels by Thom, Truong, and Fu, cutting functions as a vitalizing stopgap, as a temporary coping strategy in the face of structural injury and collective pain. Cutting is not the end of the story; rather, cutting can be thought of as an embodied spatial corollary to waiting. Within such a search for a liberatory future, whether patiently or desperately, whatever creates more time, more possibility for trans survival can be embraced as a form of queer futurity. Cutting may be thought of not as a self-shattering but as an effort to endure a present for an imaginable future that is premised on embodiment, feeling, and movement.

These novels demonstrate how the violent treatment of skin as visual object does not itself stop at the surface. In the chapter "The Lesson of the Bees" in *Fierce Femmes and Notorious Liars*, Thom writes of killer bees that swarmed "into every orifice" of the protagonist as a child and "drank up all the nectar they could hold."[47] An orifice in this sense can be thought of as a surface lacuna, troubling the expansiveness of the bees' damage. "Some of them stayed," Thom writes. The anecdote of the bees, first attacking and then colonizing the body, needs to be foregrounded in order to contextualize the book's odes to the "knife-friend." Though Thom leaves it for the reader to interpret the significance of the bees, the swarm seems to signal some trauma borne by the body, a form of childhood violence that has structured the protagonist's relationship to her body.

A series of poems syncopate the pages of *Fierce Femmes and Notorious Liars* under the headline "from my notebook—song of the pocket knife," cohered around the protagonist's "knife-friend." In these poems, in visual and generic breaks from the running narrative, the speaker writes of her "small silver friend" who is "reliable" and "always tells the truth."[48] One of these poems alludes to cutting as a response to the swarming insects: "when there are too many insects—/ angry—alive—wriggling—under my skin, / i take a pocket knife and / open up mouths in my skin / to try / and let them / out."[49] Here the killer bees are a penetrating force that lingers, occupying and making themselves at home "under [her] skin." Notably in this passage, cutting is a form of "open[ing] up mouths in [her] skin," where the opened mouth becomes another labial possibility, invoking folds of self-touching as well as stomatous openings for expression. Here I am reminded of Susan Stryker's formative words: "The shape of my flesh was a barrier that estranged me from my desire. Like a body without a mouth, I was starving in the midst of plenty."[50] Stryker offers a foundation for thinking about the dermal surfacing of transfeminisms: the "shape of flesh" that can serve as a barrier to desire, flesh that desires "a mouth."

The epidermal skin's cut mouths are not understood as sites for penetration (and the imagery of a foreign object going *in*) so much as they are sites for escape, to "let" something "out" in *Fierce Femmes*. As opposed to the voracious and dangerous looks of the aforementioned aggressors, the knife's penetrating cut is willed and wielded by the protagonist, and functions as an outlet for the removal of the occupiers at the same time as it is to create a relationality to another—the companion of the knife, animated as a "knife-friend." In a sense, cutting one's skin *does* one's body, shaping it, giving it folds, and making space to let go of what is doing internal damage. This release of the insects buried within is not only a momentary outlet for embodied trauma but also a sculptural creation that posits embodiment anew. Thom's turns to poetry within the novel cannot be understood simply as expressions or evidence of pain or suffering. They are also attempts "to try / and let them / out." Her turn to poetry is also the turn to the knife, drawing a connection between the writing implement and a blade as both with the potential to give form to expression. The switchblade is both the instrument that contours the protagonist's body with little mouths as well as the weapon she will give to Charity for self-protection at the book's end. The lines of the poem, moreover, are cut with each line break to shape the body of the poem, whether through enjambment and negative space on the page or, as quoted here, through "/" marks like scars from a healed cut. The object of the switchblade can be understood as an instrument that folds within itself at the same time as it creates dermal folds, enacting skin folds as a transfeminine form.

While cutting continues to be categorized under the umbrella of self-injury in psychological studies, the function of cutting in *Fierce Femmes and Notorious Liars* suggests that the knife's puncture of skin can simultaneously occasion deep comfort and recognition. These scenes need not be pathologized or strictly intentional, either, to offer readings of transgender becoming. Social scientific research offers context for the theme of cutting in the literary worlds studied in this chapter, as discourses that inflect one another. Cutting is not only an internalized, self-inflicted pathology of societal violence against woman-identified, queer, and gender nonconforming people of color. Cutting also emerges as an accessible strategy to cope with structures of societal violence and the desperate isolation that can come from feeling inscrutable.

Let us note the significance of studies of self-harm that center the impacts of Asian racialization. The inscrutable other is not conjured out of concern for their well-being; perceived threat lies in their capacity to infect and harm others with their duplicity. We recall David Eng and Shinhee Han's work on racial melancholia and racial dissociation, to consider why it is that cutting and self-injury can go unnoticed or unthinkable within Asian communities. How do discourses of threatening impenetrability impact and shape Asian American self-making?

Social scientists research cutting (often described as self-injury) in relation to specific social demographics, including Asian Americans, queers, trans people, and women, but through epistemes that render some inscrutable, including Asia diasporic gender nonconforming people. For instance, in one social science study, Hyeouk Chris Hahm and her coauthors write that "among [their] participants [of self-harming Asian American women], cutting was the most frequent method used to inflict self-harm, an act that was often viewed by participants as a way to regain or assert control . . . whether as an act of rebellion or self-punishment."[51] Notably, the authors of this study do not clarify whether trans and gender nonconforming people were invited to participate in conversations around self-injury and the experience of Asian American women. As such, implicit binary structures within studies can render trans experiences inscrutable.

A 2016 study undertaken by the American Association of Suicidology found that "one quarter of all transgender youth have attempted suicide, and over one third have engaged in self-injurious behaviors."[52] These statistics offer a striking account of the serious wounds of transphobic systems on health outcomes. These studies may risk eliding, however, the distinctions between suicide and self-injury, and treating trans individuals as victims as opposed to agentive subjects who live within toxic institutions. Similarly, in *The Tender Cut,* Patricia A. Adler and Peter Adler interview "practitioners" of self-injury to find that "nearly all of these people regarded this behavior as a coping strategy, perhaps one they wished they did not need (and might someday be able to quit), but one that functioned to fill needs for them nevertheless. Several referred to it as a form of 'self-therapy,' noting that when things are rough and they had nowhere else to turn, a brief interlude helped them to pull themselves together."[53] In a separate coauthored article, Elizabeth McDermott, Katrina Roen, and Anna Piela focus on queer youth and find that "the difficulties of negotiating stigmatized identities and navigating sexual and gendered norms, at a young age, can be distressing. Here, self-harm is produced as a way of coping with distress."[54] These findings make space for cutting to be understood as a form of "coping" not as a lifelong fix but as a "brief interlude," as an ephemeral practice to create possible futurities of being embodied, of enduring within one's body while creating a live relationship to it. In this sense, I wonder if we may consider cutting within not only a spectrum of self-harm but also a spectrum of gender-affirming surgery. To reframe cutting as a practice that holds potential to empower oneself in one's own terms is not to romanticize or idealize the risks of such a bloody practice. In the study "'Attempting to Dull the Dysphoria,'" researchers use the language of harm reduction and suggest that their subjects reframe nonsuicidal self-injury "as a means to reduce or otherwise distract themselves from gender dysphoria in differing capacities" and "to identify with their bodies."[55] It is to contextualize cutting as a bodily violence that cannot be thought separate from so many intersected forms of institutional violence, whether understood as material or symbolic. As Trystan T. Cotten writes, "Redrawing the body's sex contours affirms the feminist mantra that biology is not destiny."[56]

The reclamatory rhetoric of coping, control, therapy, and rebellion, available within social science research, invites other interpretations of cutting tangential to the discourse of injury. Cutting can be empowering and alluring even if it can also be harmful. As one option of embodied expression, cutting is a part of a story, something to be done when it is not clear what can be done. Environmental conditions of gender, race, and sexuality-based violence must be part of the story of cutting. The Adlers' stated interest is to consider the perspectives of practitioners, yet they are careful not to glamorize self-injury and note, "Without wanting to pathologize it, we acknowledge that self-injury falls within the realm of a social problem."[57] This chapter's engagement with queer and trans literature wishes to offer another avenue for broaching these questions outside a medical or pathological gaze. Rather, violence is a nuanced effect of gender and racial construction in these novels, and it takes multiple forms of embodiment, directed both from outside the protagonist and from the protagonist them/herself. I want to center what Susan Stryker and Talia M. Bettcher write as "the question of transgender agency—that is, of trans people making conscious, informed choices about the best way to live their own embodied lives."[58]

Cutting as Resurfacing One's Story

One could read *The Book of Salt* and never pick up on Bình's "habit" of cutting the surface of his skin, first mentioned in the novel's seventh chapter. Truong's allusions to Bình's habit are more elliptical than descriptive. She writes, "I never do it for them [his employers]. I would never waste myself in such a way. It is only a few minutes out of my day, usually in the late evening hours when all the real work has been done. The extreme cold or the usual bouts of loneliness will trigger it."[59] Cutting is a form of heat and contact that the protagonist can control, relational touch that won't lead to exile or betrayal. Truong implies that Bình cuts himself *for himself* ("never do it for them"). This unarticulated habit of cutting plunges him into a visceral feeling, opening himself up to forms of memory and desire.

Piercing his skin brings Bình back to maternal spaces of homeland and his mother's kitchen.[60] Here, it is not so much desire for another man that renders him queer; rather, this queer relationship to his skin, a willed violence and tenderness enacted on the skin, elicits poignant memories of his beloved and faraway mother. Truong conveys this spatial and temporal transport fluidly with her words. Bình's habit transports his body to the first memory of cutting himself with a knife (as opposed to, for example, being cut or circumcised by another): in his childhood kitchen with Má. Bình's hold on the knife slips when he is mesmerized by his mother humming in the kitchen. Recounting the first time silver "thread[s his] skin," Truong describes his wounded skin as "a landscape that would become as familiar to me as the way home."[61] This positive association—being entranced by his mother's song, together making food in his mother's kitchen in the homeland—disrupts any simple pathological reading of his habit of breaking skin and "wasting" himself. This rupture of his body is also a pulsing reminder of his body in connection and humanity: "Blood makes me a man. No one can take that away from me, I thought."[62] The open reading of "man" could index a presence of the human, a status Bình cannot take for granted in colonial France or in his homophobic father's house. Too, this excerpt could be interpreted as a moment of self-empowerment through a susceptible masculinization.

In *The Book of Salt*, readers may imagine how cutting is not only a violent separation of skin; it also necessitates and sets forth the skin's intention to come together and mend through finding itself again. As Truong describes, "That part that [Bình] savor[s] most" is "the throbbing of flesh compromised, meeting and mending."[63] Here, the "meeting and mending" of flesh speaks to an intimacy of skin with skin, one of encounter, of contact, meeting the same as the other. The character's relish may be understood not necessarily in the violence but in the occasion of skin-on-skin intimacy and healing. Skin cutting reasserts not only Bình's humanity but also the legacy of his mother. Truong writes that "sometimes when it [the cut] is deep enough, there is an ache that fools my heart. Tricks it into a false memory of love lost to a wide, open sea. I say to myself, 'Ah, this reminds me of you.'"[64] This passage, following the sequence of his first cut in the kitchen with Má, leaves ambiguous who the "you" refers to: to his mother, to a place of home, and to "myself." His mother's blood is his embodied inheritance, one that Bình holds dear as a touchstone of home while he lives in homosexual exile. Epidermal skin, as opposed to genital skin, is not usually understood as matter proper to the feminine. Truong's creation of a mother-loving queer diasporic character in Bình significantly indexes the refusal by a feminized Asian man to turn away from the feminine and queer, and to embrace it and call them home. Cutting is not a simple self-negation or act of self-harm but also gestures toward something else: a bloody porosity, a negotiation with gendered vulnerability, and the decolonial and transfeminist pursuit and practice of body autonomy.

Inherited Hurt and Femme Healing Practices on Skin

Identifying the body's matter as feminine is a feminist and gender noncon-forming practice in these novels, identifying the body as a maternal or sisterly site of connection, instead of reinforcing a feminine-masculine cis-gender binary. What Audrey longs for is to become one among several sisters, particularly her idolized oldest sister, Adele. Sisterhood offers its own pedagogy not only in femininity but also in feminism. In *Fierce Femmes and Notorious Liars*, Thom's protagonist's relationship to her sisters, both bio and chosen sisters, teaches her about the relationship to knife cutting and transfemi-nisms. In one of the knife-friend poems, Thom anthropomorphizes the knife as a loving friend, such that its "slic[es]" are "sharp true kisses," touching the protagonist in intimate "places / no one can see," including her arms and thighs.[65] The protagonist's relationship to the knife-friend long precedes her participation and belonging in the girl gang. The knife-friend is the compan-ion, the confidant, the one the protagonist can be emotionally and physi-cally porous with, the one to anticipate the femme relationality that is as yet unfulfilled. The physical and emotional access granted to the knife-friend bespeaks the protagonist's trust for the knife, another entity with which to share touch. The knife, with its "sweet razor smile," is also an extension of the protagonist's hurt: her capacity both to hurt and to be hurt.[66]

Through trans sisterhood, the protagonist is confronted with the opportu-nity to test her emotional and physical vulnerability with other women. This sisterhood brings a self-confrontation and self-learning in transfeminist soci-ality that brings light to the protagonist's existing relationship to the knife. In part 6 of *Fierce Femmes and Notorious Liars*, Thom constructs a love poem to the knife-friend that is also a break-up poem. She writes: "after all this time, / it isn't you, it's me, / little silver pocket knife, / sweet razor smile / with your sharp true kisses, / you didn't let me down, / you've never failed me, / it's not your fault, / you couldn't cleanse me, / cure me, / forgive me, / love me, / i have to do those things / on my own."[67] In a twist of a conventional "it's not you, it's me" rejection, Thom suggests that the protagonist cannot merely counteract the gendered violence that she experiences by inflicting hurt on her own body or those of other people. When harm is wielded by the self, the knife still mediates as a weapon. The knife is a tool that does not cleanse, cure, forgive, or love, but it may be a part of the process for these actions. Thom writes, "i have to do those things / on my own," meaning that forgiveness, love, and healing must be found also without the knife. The knife cannot be a proxy for an other or for the self.

This personal pain, however, is depathologized and socially contextualized by Kimaya as not individual but collective crisis: "Honey, you hurt yourself," she says, "because everybody around you hurts people and is hurting and that's just the story you were given. You can't get stuck in that. Don't get stuck in any one story, not even your own."[68] Kimaya continues: "Hunger is a story you get stuck in. Love's the story that takes you somewhere new."[69] Hurt and pain caused and circulated by systemic sexism and racism—understood in this novel through participants in white-supremacist cis-heteronormative patriarchy as, for example, police officers—are formulated as inherited stories, transmitted and transmittable across bodies and storytellers. Thom shows how trans women are also not immune to perpetrating that pain and cycle of violence onto community members and others, since the protagonist needs to contend with the hurt within the Lipstick Lacerators gang she has contributed to. In part 4 of the book, titled simply "Forgiveness," Alzena the Witch offers the protagonist a cup of crying tea and gifts one of the truisms of the novel: "You will be able to stop hurting people when you can stop hurting yourself."[70]

A self-reflective critique of inherited structures of violence becomes femme pedagogy. This story—not only of hurt but also of fighting patterns of hurt and practicing forgiveness—is also transmitted, from Alzena to the protagonist, from the protagonist to her sister Charity. Echoing Alzena, the protagonist later advises her sister in a letter: "You can only stop hurting when you stop hurting yourself."[71] She writes, "I live in a dangerous world. So do you. . . . I wanted to protect you, but I'm starting to think that the best thing you can do for people is teach them how to protect themselves."[72]

Though this chapter studies literary themes and works for the most part within the literary, conceptual, and symbolic realm, the relevance of the material, physical, and emotional stakes of cutting in queer, trans, and Asian American discourses is an interdisciplinary topic that should be taken seriously for its real-world implications and manifestations—without collapsing fiction into social science or vice versa. This self-willed penetrability of the body is not merely figurative language but can be language that figures and enfigures. The causal factors for cutting and self-harm are myriad in scholarly studies but often do involve family and cultural sources in the framework of the research. However, these novels frame the broader social dynamics of misogyny, heteronormativity, anti-immigrant violence, model minoritarianism, transphobia, capitalism, and homophobia that simultaneously shape public life, the "private" family sphere, and personal identification. That is, one of the lessons across *The Book of Salt, Fierce Femmes and Notorious Liars*, and *For Today I Am a Boy* is how there is no singular cultural family alibi to hide behind. Rather, violence rooted in interpretations of gender, race, and sexuality (as interwoven with nationality, class, religion, and ability) are structured into everyday experience, including of intimate family life, cultural practice, and self-embodiment.

Surfacing Pleasures through Touch

Although scenes of violence in *For Today I Am a Boy* can threaten and materialize dermal violence, they can also potentiate dermal pleasure and recognition by granting contact that is not dependent on p/v penetration or a misogynist gaze. Moments of nominally masculine bonding, moreover, can allow for feminine recognition. Consider, for example, Audrey's workout sessions with high school classmate Ollie. When the protagonist admires the toned body of a woman on a gym poster, Ollie "didn't seem to think there was anything strange about [Audrey's] wanting to look like her—like it was as legitimate as his desire to be hulking and large. Another thing [Ollie and Audrey] had in common: [they] wanted different bodies than [their] own."[73] Similarly, in the restaurant kitchen where she works as a dishwasher, Audrey "loved the way the cooks at the restaurant talked about sex. Mapping out women's bodies for one another like explorers who've returned home. Their jokes with animals, old women, and babies as the punch lines. It was over-the-top enough, absurd enough, that it didn't feel real."[74] The non-real feeling of what otherwise would be described as misogynist locker-room talk suggests that Audrey's preoccupation with bodies has less to do with sex than it is about an imaginative, perhaps "absurd," relationship to her own body.

How, then, does Audrey explore her capacity for bodily pleasure? This happens in the shift from skin as necessarily discursively significant to that as initially and primarily about touch. Audrey explores her gender identity through imagining sexual possibilities not only by experimenting with Margie's layered surfacing but also in hearing of other examples of trans sexuality. Audrey later learns the vital lesson that a woman with a penis can still be desirable and sexually legible regardless of identity. Misogynist sexual banter becomes monotonous in the workplace kitchen until Chef mentions one day that he once "fucked a guy in Montreal."[75] Chef describes how "she lay down on the bed on her stomach, pulled her kimono up, and told [him] to fuck her in the ass."[76] When coworker Simon interjects, "Her hairy *man* ass," Chef corrects him: "Nope. Smooth as a baby's. Greased up. Like perfect, firm pillows and round as peaches."[77] In this moment, locker-room talk turns from a normalized heterosexual objectification of women's bodies to the body of one described both as "a guy" and as "she," making explicit the reality that someone with a penis could also be feminine and have a smooth ass. Further, Chef's description of the paramour's rump is more descriptive of tactility: "smooth," "greased up," "firm," where touch is primary. While Simon guesses, "And he leaped up afterward and waved his cock in your face," Chef corrects him again, saying, "No, she rolled over to yell at me for getting cum on her kimono, and I realized something was off."[78] Chef pointedly uses "she" and "her" pronouns as a corrective to Simon's insistent male pronoun usage and fixation on the emergence of the penis at this point of his story. Simon, the picture of masculinist anxiety in this scene, betrays a homophobic disdain for another person's "cock," as though a penis should not be sexually objectified unless it is one's own. Enthralled but afraid, Audrey asks what Chef did afterward, and Chef replies: "What do you mean? Nothing to do. A good fuck's a good fuck. Didn't change that."[79] The gendered significance of what (visually) emerges when a lover rolls over, then, does not need to inform the (haptic) "good fuck" itself. This scene is important for the protagonist's sense of sexual possibility through her gender identification, where the sexual possibility of two bodies is premised not on the look (and related social significance) of skin but rather on the touch, pleasure, and erotics of surfacing together.

As in this story of fucking, the body, objectified through sighted skin, has other capacities than being seen. Where Chef's penetrative sexual encounter with his lover amounts to what he describes as a good fuck, we might be interested in modes of touch that could not be simplistically judged as "good." The complex sensations of penetration and other forms of touch, however, do not need to limit our curiosity for them, especially as they may extend feminist investments in self-empowered embodiment.

The habit of cutting in these novels becomes a way for readers to consider not only how skin reads visually but also how it is felt by the protagonists subjectively. Bình, for example, describes a feeling of safety coming from a visual anonymity. Truong describes how the lack of exceptionalism and spectacle makes him feel safe.[80] Forms of pleasure are not disconnected from forms of violence, as we see with Audrey and Margie. The protagonist of *Fierce Femmes and Notorious Liars* has a long-standing sensual relationship with a character named Ghost Friend. When they first meet through touch, Thom writes how the protagonist "whirled around, grabbing frantically for the pocket knife [she] always kept in [her] jeans, but of course [she] saw no one there."[81] Notably, it is the knife-friend who can help the protagonist protect herself, her surface. We note how Ghost Friend's invisible presence destabilizes the visual field as a primary sense of sexuality. Ghost Friend's immateriality also renders them protected from the protagonist's instinct to physically fight back. Rather, the protagonist learns she can receive Ghost Friend's touch and respond through orgasm. The touching of skin, then, is a mode of relating and sensing, of pleasuring and rewiring associations between touch and trauma. The protagonist of *Fierce Femmes and Notorious Liars* experiences sexual pleasure and orgasm with a figure who has no body or voice. Thom writes, "Ghost Friend wasn't at all threatening. I could tell right away, even though they're invisible and mute. There was just something about the way they touched me—gentle, tentative, almost apologetic."[82] Here, when touch can awaken experience with trauma in the body, the invisible Ghost Friend has a touch that is nonthreatening.

This theory can prove useful even when people or characters involved do not identify as trans or women; rather, what I'm suggesting these novels gesture toward is a radical reformation of what sexual encounter consists of, one adaptive to different forms and combinations of epidermal skin. As Truong describes in *The Book of Salt*, "I climbed down from my bunk and stood before his. I took his hands, warmer than the South China Sea, and I showed him how to form a cleft in between my legs that disappeared into my inner thighs. In the dark, I again heard him moan. This time for me, I told myself."[83] This elliptical scene locates a sexual encounter between migrant workers Bình and Bảo aboard the ship the *Niobe* and centers the encounter around a "cleft in between [Bình's] legs that disappeared into [his] inner thighs."[84] This creation of a cleft or cleaving is a receptive gesture that is more about a queer and feminist epidermal formation for sexual encounter than it is about identifying with femininity or pursuing penetration per se. I wish to make clear I do not wish to suggest that clefts, mouths, or vaginas are the sole domain of the feminine, as though to suggest that any of myriad other skin formations would disqualify a body from feminine identity. Rather, I wish to note literary imagery of folds, clefts, lips, and cuts that depict more of a surface relationship between skin and skin than one based on penetration or entrance. Through this lens, even normative P/V sex could be interpreted as skin surfacing. Considering Asian feminine embodiment and feminist sexuality through a layering of surfaces, through the touch and rub of skin, instead, becomes of interest to both queer aesthetic and erotic theory. This queer and feminist surfacing in a sense extends Nguyen Tan Hoang's formulation of Asian gay male bottomhood away from penetration of skin and toward rubbing, bringing us once more to the question of epidermal skin as matter with feminist and queer potential.

This tactile surfacing of skin shifts womanly determination away from genital skin and toward maternal and sisterly para-embodiment as a form of trans and queer feminist Asian becoming. As such, although theories of Asian anality as queer and feminist practice are important in articulating Asian feminist receptivity and vulnerability, a continued focus on penetration within Asian American sexuality studies conflates femininity with penetrability, betraying a reliance and reproduction of cis heteronormative structures of knowledge. Let us theorize, name, and hail wider practices of sexual intimacy and gender embodiment that are in conversation with transfeminist and queer women-loving politics, ones that do not normalize violence on the body but acknowledge and articulate its gendered and racialized forms, and destabilize the privileging of the phallus as the central motif of sexual life. One such practice of skin surfacing as transfeminist method emerges in this literary motif of self-cutting that swerves away from an Orientalist fetish of Asian female self-harm and toward queer and transfeminist self-determination.

I theorize unreliable surfacing as either impenetrable *and* penetrable to put pressure on the ways in which Orientalism has shaped contemporary discourses of sex that are lived out on the bodies of Asian diasporic people. In this chapter, I have attempted to show how performances of inscrutability (as unknowability, inaccessibility, impenetrability) are strategic responses to the violence that can come from being rendered Asian, woman, trans, queer, and yellow. These identifiers are effected on the skin and absorbed within, with the possibility of emerging if not anew then with a transfeminist difference. There is a way to think about cutting as part of a love (for a processual self, sister, mother, or collective) that takes one elsewhere than the transphobic and misogynist present. As a coping response, there is no question that cutting is risky. These novels demonstrate how cutting can bring focus, presence, and imagined futurity in the body at the same time as it can transport one out of the constraints of the embodied present. In this sense, cutting as a method of unreliable bodily surfacing contributes to the signification of skin as a site of gender and racial aesthetic practices that may render the subject externally illegible outside a rhetoric of pathology at the same time as it performs a vital labor of queer and trans endurance.

Unreliable Narration, or Cutting Us Out

Let us return to the protagonist's promise to Charity: "I will tell you everything—the truth, the whole truth, nothing but the truth—someday soon, I promise. I'm still just figuring out what exactly the truth is, you know?"[85] *Fierce Femmes and Notorious Liars* disappoints the happily-ever-after ending: although the protagonist meets and moves in with a cute academic trans man, she leaves him after a comical meditation on toilet paper ply count. Recalling Kimaya's advice about not getting stuck in anyone's story, the protagonist moves on to continue pursuing her own narrative, whatever that may be. Ultimately, by the final page of the novel, the reader does not know what will happen in the protagonist's life, and that kind of withholding and disruption of conventional narrative plot resounds in *The Book of Salt* and *For Today I Am a Boy* as well.

Self-narration, like cutting, is a viable way to play with the aesthetic form and constraints of reality. Writing one's story is a way of moving on, a way of enacting a future story. Experimental form (in bodily and literary form) can trouble and expand aspirations for truthfulness in the novel/memoir mixed genre. In *Fierce Femmes and Notorious Liars*, Thom suggests that storytelling is doing something other than truth telling, that is, not the penetrative act of demanding truth, demanding depth and access, but of a creative surfacing that momentarily rearranges the body. This sculpting is imaginable not only as damage to the body but also as permission for it to do something else, a kind of rupture for one's own self, not for another. Storytelling is performative: "Because maybe what really matters isn't whether something is true or false, maybe what matters is the story itself: what kinds of doors it opens, what kinds of dreams it brings."[86] In contrast to Foucault's famous formulation of knowledge as a cutting, these characters show us that they are not in fact trying to be known, that they are strategically subverting a will to (gender, racial, sexual) truth—and simultaneously producing a different mode of becoming and being in the world that cannot be precisely encapsulated through a rhetoric of knowledge. In this sense, the physical unreliability and porosity of trans embodiment and cutting are mirrored by the formal and diegetic stability within each narrative.

One way in which this inscrutability as a formal aesthetic emerges is through the unreliability of the protagonists' names in each of the three novels. As mentioned, the protagonist of *Fierce Femmes and Notorious Liars* is never named. In the first-person narration of *For Today I Am a Boy*, it is not until the last pages of the novel that the protagonist is asked: "You okay with being called Peter?" to which the protagonist responds: "What else would you call me?"[87] The word is not the point, but it allows the story to continue. In the last chapter of the book, focused on Audrey's relationship with a group of (white) queers, the protagonist instead longs for others through "the comfort of being only partly understood."[88] The "comfort of being only partly

Im/penetrability, Trans Figuration   101

understood" is a poignant provocation for thinking about queer, trans, and Asian inscrutability, one that is a marked disidentification from mainstream unidimensional identity discourse and also an abject mime of Asian foreignness. Here, the effect of these first-person fictitious accounts is irreverence to significatory stability, since the meaning of language (and bodies) can, and indeed does, change.

Truong's rapturous storytelling of Bình's life makes all the more startling the narrator's revealed unreliability toward the end of the novel, when we learn that—contrary to what we as readers have been led to believe—Bình is not in fact the character's "real" name. Truong writes, "I never meant to deceive, but real names are never exchanged."[89] By allusion we learn that the protagonist's given name is Bão, a Vietnamese word for "storm," an organic fluid that surfaces and disrupts, like blood. Truong implements a number of literary devices to trouble the stability of the speaker: the unreliability of names (and, with them, identities), and a framing device that structures the novel in relation to a potentially unpublished book by Gertrude Stein, a metanarrative that is effected through the name of the book. Moving through the world as Bình, the protagonist is called other names by most every other character. Stein refers to him as the aforementioned Thin Bin, Marcus Lattimore refers to him as "Bee" (reminding us of Bình's relationship to his "honey" mother), and the man on the bridge calls him *bạn* or "friend."[90]

As Truong writes, "The more impenetrable the language, the more unpronounceable it is, the easier life becomes for a man like me."[91] Not dissimilarly, for all of Bình/Bão's erotic longing and reminiscing, Truong withholds describing sex scenes in the novel, instead offering: "There is no narrative in sex, in good sex that is. There is no beginning and there is no end, just the rub, the sting, the tickle, the white light of the here and now. That is why it is so addictive, so worth the risk. That is why men like me brave ourselves for it. It is a gamble worth taking."[92] This description of sex (the haptic "rub, the sting, the tickle" and the clarion "here and now") mirrors Truong's language for Bão's cutting practice, as something that brings him into the present moment, as a reminder of his living, fleshly state.

Truong's repeated gesture to that which Bão is not telling us, not interested in sharing, or that place where language does not go or transport us to teaches me about the work of impenetrability as an aesthetic mode and literary device that refuses the confessional mandates of queer liberalism. Bão regularly condones ignorance as "best for someone like [him]."[93] I understand this ignorance to be not the opposite of intelligence but relief from the racialized burdens of knowability. Being known by another through the skin carries with it not only pleasures and chance of recognition but also imbrications of power and violence, specifically for gender, sexual, and racial others. Cultivating curiosity for a desirable self-form creates a futurity. Knowledge of the body's meaning, then, is not an end in itself but bespeaks the desire to have a relationship to one's emotions, sensations, and material body. A desire to be recognized, however, must be understood as a simultaneous desire to be free to change and abandon the given, shifting terms of one's legibility.

4

FLATNESS, INDUSTRIOUSNESS, AND LABORIOUS FLEXIBILITY

To be inscrutable is to upset the perceived order of things, and so to be abstracted into illegibility. The political act of abstracting and nullifying racial experience is not innocent but bespeaks a maintenance of power through the exploitation of gendered racial labor. To survive through these hurdles of political viability conditions a certain choreography that this book understands through modes of inscrutability. The book shifts now from a study of im/penetrable fleshy surface of Asian bodies to the flat flexibility of racial discourses in the twentieth century that solidify in furniture design and the production of exteriority. If the Asiatic body and its labor have been rendered as a silent vanishing point in the political landscape of the United States, then this racial form of nonappearance also produces and is influenced by environmental design rhetorics, ones that contemporary Asian American artists strategically take up for creative ends.

In the spring of 2012, the Seattle Art Museum hosted Mika Tajima's solo exhibition *After the Martini Shot* in a second-floor gallery space of the downtown Seattle building that had housed Washington Mutual before JPMorgan Chase absorbed the bank in 2009. As the artist and assistant curator separately pointed out to me, these empty offices loomed over Tajima's exhibition as a relevant backdrop of precarity to the contemporary mixed-media artist's work. In conjunction with the ghosts of the 2008 economic recession and the workers who were not at work, the exhibition's eponymous "martini shot"—a phrase referring to the day's final take on a film set—enhanced a feeling of uncertain futurity in Tajima's exhibition space. The show's title provoked timely questions: After production is ostensibly wrapped, what becomes of its remaining parts and structures? What happens after?

With focus on an aesthetic mode of inscrutability I identify as *flatness*, this chapter juxtaposes modern office design, globalization, and the Asiatic laborer to articulate contemporary racial forms for what industrial designer Robert Propst describes as the "economic health of people and organizations."[1] I reconsider the persistent binarized racial tropes of Asian workers as either domestic model minority worker or yellow peril of cheap and encroaching foreign labor by analyzing Tajima's contemporary visual art practice through 1960s discourses of the Herman Miller Research Corporation's Action Office furniture series, the model minority myth, and British psychoanalyst D. W. Winnicott's theory of transitional phenomena. This chapter examines the overlapping aesthetics of modular office furniture and model minority racialization as flat and flexible by asking what it would mean to play with model minority discourse as a racial transitional object for Asian American subject formation. I position the model minority trope, alongside modular cubicle structures, as a transitional object through which one can create a "good-enough environment" and experiment with alternative forms of grappling with difference. Tajima's contemporary art practice inspires this foray into the relevance of office furniture and model minority discourses in articulating and imagining Asian American subjective becoming. Positioning discourse as an object, I argue that model minority discourse is a racial form constructive of one's social environment. By comprehending discourses of Asiatic labor and laborers as social architecture, I examine Tajima's repurposing of modern design elements to make space for creative doings that restructure everyday racial performatives.

When I write of the flatness and flexibility of Asiatic racial form, imagined within the geopolitical space of the United States and beyond, I write of how Asianness has become part of a social environment as setting, as context, as backdrop. A rhetoric of "flatness" here is useful for my purposes because of its theatrical invocation as in stage flats, or wooden architectural planes, that can create a sense of interior or exterior space, just as easily conjuring a living room as a landscape expanse on stage. "Flat" also conjures something lifeless, as in flat soda or flat affect, which alludes to a general absence of demonstrable emotion. These associations, of architectural scene in the style of trompe l'oeil and dull personality, thought together give a sense of material artifice and emptiness that I have put forth as the queer surface aesthetics of Asiatic form. Flat has become entwined with flexible in the modern age, for things may be flattened to aid their flexible movement, as with IKEA furniture.

When I think about Asiatic racial form as flat and flexible in this chapter, I follow the work of Colleen Lye, whose *America's Asia* identified Asiatic racial form in terms of economic efficiency. While the "authentic" representation of Asian American people continues to be a liberal project in mainstream television and film, we could just as well argue that Asianness and the literal if abstracted touch of Asian people is already everywhere, as with the computer keyboard typing this book or the ink on its pages. Observing the "putatively unusual capacity for economic modernity" associated with America's Asia, Lye shows how the "international context of Asian American racialization" is instrumental in having any sense of America's racial forms.[2] In this chapter, I think through the affective and aesthetic modes of Asiatic labor as flat and flexible. By analyzing the visual and performance practice of contemporary artist Mika Tajima, particularly her use of modular office furniture and her attunement to the relationship between object design and human bodies, I hope to show how flatness is not a politically neutral modality but can allow readers a way to think through the formation of Asian labor as unremarkable background—as modular furniture that epitomizes modernism, as it were. How does the ornamental exteriorization of Asianness, rather than draw attention to a spectacular sculptural racial form, instead objectify Asian labor as political backdrop and social furniture?

Los Angeles–born and Brooklyn-based Tajima is a contemporary visual artist and founding member of the performance collaborative New Humans, whose work could be described as flexible labor. A former Creative Time Global Resident, Tajima has exhibited her site-specific work internationally and domestically, including in the Asia Society's 2006–8 traveling show *One Way or Another: Asian American Art Now*, the 2008 Whitney Biennial, The

Kitchen in New York City, the San Francisco Museum of Modern Art, and the South London Gallery. Actively cross-disciplinary, Tajima's artworks have featured collaborators such as performance artist Vito Acconci, scholar Judith Butler, video artist Charles Atlas, and violinist C. Spencer Yeh. Reliable themes of Tajima's work include her blurring of relational boundaries between visual culture and performance, between viewing the art object and participating in it, between the object in and of itself and the production of the object. As the catalog of the Whitney Biennial describes, "Tajima's projects slip from foreground sculptures to background props, staging markers, and function structures, their status in continual transition and production."[3] By working the intense flexibility of readymade objects, Tajima's aesthetic play of object relations offers an embodied model for troubling long-standing racial metonymies.

The "slip" and "continual transition and production" of Tajima's work resonates with the play of positionalities offered by Margo Machida's foundational framework for Asian American visual studies, thought through here in terms of flat flexibility.[4] Particularly useful is Machida's articulation of "a continually evolving play of positions" to contextualize the work of artists of Asian heritage who "conceptualize the world and position themselves as cultural and historical subjects through the symbolic languages and media of visual art."[5] Tajima's work performs such a flexible materialization of the world by using the universalist language of modular office furniture. Tajima's artist biography on the Creative Time residency website remarks on her exploration of "how the performing subject (e.g., speaker, dancer, designer, factory worker, musician, filmmaker) is constructed in spaces in which material objects outline action and engagement."[6] I note this repeated discursive emphasis on positions, production, and the performing subject with an interest in thinking about the flexibility in time and space, in history and geopolitics, that Tajima's work both performs and critiques. My efforts here are to explore racial aesthetics not by essentializing Asian American art practice as biographically dependent but by reframing model minority and other racial discourses of Asiatic economic efficiency as an aestheticizing discourse with psychic ramifications for Asian American subject formation.

After the Martini Shot

Tajima's solo exhibition *After the Martini Shot* took place in a rectangular white gallery space with two entrances on the second level of the Seattle Art Museum.[7] Upon approach, the museum visitor was confronted with a room of freestanding and mounted sculptures composed with plywood, paints of primary colors, and spray-painted Plexiglas on the gallery walls. Toward the middle of the gallery space were two sculptures transformed from cubicle wall panels by the Herman Miller Research Corporation introduced in 1964. Tajima reclaimed original pieces of Herman Miller Action Office Furniture from a bankrupt New Jersey warehouse and stretched new canvases on their frames for a cubicle-inspired series. These Action Office originals became the readymade objects that Tajima built upon for works such as *Disassociate* (2007) and *A Facility Based on Change* (2010–11), as featured in *After the Martini Shot*. For *Living Room Eyes* (2007), Tajima created a monochrome by painting one side of the cubicle wall panel coral and, using black tacks and binder clips, attaching a poster for New Humans, cofounded in 2003 with Howie Chen (see figure 4.1). On the other side of the wall panel was a mirror that was positioned at an acute angle to the gallery wall such that, at my height of 5′4″, I could see my body reflected up to my shoulders, leaving the visual identification of the face withheld.

I understand flatness at work in Tajima's exhibition through the walled-off panels of cubicle furniture as well as the smooth consistency of the monochrome coral. Monochrome is flat here, as in a plane of two-dimensional consistency, that then conjures rhetorics of wholeness, purity, homogeneity. Tajima incorporated the work of geometric abstractionists (e.g., Josef Albers) and pop artists (e.g., Andy Warhol) in her paint-rack sculpture, borrowing from the museum's permanent collection. Her seemingly casual play with canonized modern artists commented on the materials of production themselves, the fact and act of painting, canvas stretching, and composition, of the artist's labor and its circulation within an institutionalized art market.

The paneled sculptures initially created something of an alienating space, with minimalist starkness and bold geometry that refused figuration. The use of mirrors throughout the exhibition, however, visualized my body in the gallery as an epistemological necessity. Though I was suddenly placed in the exhibition as a visual object, it was notably not the identificatory metonym of my face that was reflected. Tajima's decision to create a mirrored panel and to place the furniture piece at that height and angle to the wall simultaneously located and disoriented my sense of self in the space. Self-conscious, I circled around the sculptures and returned to find my legs looking back at me. I was not alone in my interaction with the mirrored panel. Though my time in the gallery was mostly solitary on my first visit, two people caught my attention when they engaged with the mirror by hiding and reappearing on different sides of its structure. Tajima's use of the mirror is worth remark because of a

FIGURE 4.1. Mika Tajima, *Living Room Eyes* (installed in *After the Martini Shot*), 2012. Photograph by the author.

mirror's material flatness simultaneous to its illusion of visual depth, much like a theater flat.

Creating the Modern and Modular Work Environment

If not for the exhibition's accompanying texts, it would not be obvious that the sculptures were made from cubicle paneling. What the use of Action Office cubicle parts offers, however, is a framework through which to consider Tajima's art environment alongside modern discourses of office furniture and, by extension, living labor. The design of the Herman Miller Research Corporation, the initial Action Office furniture series of 1964 and progenitor of the now-ubiquitous cubicle, revolutionized modern aesthetics of office space. The Herman Miller cubicle materially manifested universalist rhetoric with American individualist values. A modular and therefore customizable system, the Action Office series shaped office space with its right angles, neutral hues, and invitation for personalization to each company's needs. The underlying premise was that, with the Action line's common foundation of select shapes, materials, and colors, any worker could create a workable space to call their own. With these universal panels and parts, people could create a sense of privacy and personality within the workplace. The cubicle's continued proliferation today speaks to its offered sense of personal space to employees, boosting worker morale and cultivation of good feeling in the workplace.[8]

A Foucauldian precept would argue that the Herman Miller furniture line served to offer a sense of agency and personalization at the same time as it disciplined and surveilled its worker population. Though workers may have felt more personal identification with their designated space, they were after all confined to predetermined uses of the furniture as a means to maximize their productivity. The cubicle design effectively limits privacy, for example in its open-air form exposing sounds and smells not enclosed by the cubicle's walls. With the wall height below eye level, the cubicle design permits scrutiny from above in the form of visual technologies like surveillance cameras as well as the wandering gaze of other workers. Executives maintained private offices, complete with doors and floor-to-ceiling walls. In this sense, the cubicle design promoted certain forms of surveillance while reserving a greater sense of privacy for the middle management worker. Certainly, those working in a cubicle would be familiar with the games of compliance one might play regarding what can be displayed, which phone calls taken, or which websites visited behind its porous walls. These perlocutionary effects of spatial management and control, including self-surveillance, are supported by the furniture line's modularity.

With the cubicle panels determining vertical optics, the standing worker's head is often visible from across the room, the rest of the body concealed behind the panel's wall. As demonstrated by the two exhibition visitors I observed, from some angles, the cubicle panel in *After the Martini Shot* still functioned as a site of permissive obfuscation. However, Tajima's transformed cubicle mirror flipped expectations by refusing facial recognition and making visible one's own body below. Walking around the mirrored cubicle wall in the gallery, I was made conscious of the ways in which the furniture fragmented my perception of my body, disrupting the relationship to my own reflection. A mirrored reflection, of course, is a different but not entirely inconsonant sort of visual obfuscation from an otherwise canvassed cubicle wall. Notably, a mirror is a visual demand for self-reflexivity, something that modern designs such as the Action Office furniture line purport to accomplish even as they abstract the specificities of the self. A mirrored cubicle becomes something of a paradox, then: an appropriate fulfillment of the Action Office's tenets of personalization even as the mirrored environment, in its visual dynamism, may prove distracting from the office work at hand.[9]

In the 2006 catalog for the touring group exhibition *One Way or Another: Asian American Art Now*, Reena Jana articulates Tajima's artistic project as "reveal[ing] possibilities within a system of contradictions."[10] An object is not a static entity in Tajima's hands. For her cubicle series, as mentioned previously, Tajima painted the canvases in bright monochromes and, in the style of geometric abstractionists like Josef Albers, transformed the wall units into two-dimensional objects of visual art.[11] The wall partition–turned-painting also stood as bulletin boards, as Tajima tacked on screen-printed posters; then, an acoustic panel when she stretched another canvas on the frame's backside and filled the panel with wool; and then, once more, as a set piece when Tajima installed wheels on its base and filmed its surroundings, as evidenced in the New Humans' short film *Holding Your Breath (Taking the Long Way)* (2008) (see figure 4.2). The Seattle Art Museum also commissioned Tajima's collaboration with fashion designer Mary Ping, resulting in a photo shoot titled *Deep Focus*, in which converted wall panels served as backdrop and stage prop. I argue that Tajima's transformations of the cubicle pieces are an ironic extension of the Herman Miller fascination with modularity and modern aesthetics. If the designers of Action Office furniture sought to improve the economic health of companies by reimagining the building

FIGURE 4.2. View of Mika Tajima's installation and performance *Disassociate*, featuring New Humans, Vito Acconci, and C. Spencer Yeh. Elizabeth Dee Gallery, New York, 2007. Photograph by Jenny Moore.

blocks of the work environment, then Tajima's transformations of these same building blocks trouble the foundational precepts of economic health.

Part of my curiosity about Tajima's installation to begin with was based in her vision to aggressively make the cubicle panel *work*—not the mere disciplining backdrop to others' work. Tajima reveals the cubicle panel to be an object that can do so much, and in fact has been doing so much with its flatness and modularity. Tajima's art making meant that the cubicle panel was stuffed with batting and made into a conscious acoustic panel; was rotated along a horizontal axis and spun like a giant game on *The Price Is Right*; was tacked into and made to advertise, suddenly a community board; was painted on and stored in a painting shelf; and was posed in front of and suddenly a model's backdrop. The flatness of the cubicle panel, and its original design for modularity, is what formally allows an openness to its future uses. Its flatness is its flexibility.

These rhetorics of flatness and flexibility circulate within our contemporary world as praise for global capitalism. Robert Propst and the Herman Miller designers may be progenitors of the economist champions of globalization, such as Thomas L. Friedman, whose *The World Is Flat* made the audacious statement that "hierarchies are being flattened" by globalization.[12] My interest in flatness and flexibility as aesthetic modes of inscrutability purposefully invokes Friedman's celebratory line of capitalist thought while critiquing its logic as a convenient fix for equalization—or what is actually privatized, radical wealth inequality and increasingly disparate resource accessibility between the world's rich and poor. What neoliberal economists celebrate is the linking of flatness with economic efficiency, where "flat" conjures an image of the world that is not messy or complex and therefore dismisses accountability to the imbricated structures of global economics. In this view, Tajima's use of the mirror is provocative in its seeming function to help the viewer self-reflect at the same time as that self-reflexibility is obstructed.

Where this chapter enters this conversation is in thinking about the twenty-first-century Asian laborer as an inheritor of the inscrutable other trope, as an abstract racial figure whose function is to service the flattening of the world. The decade of the 1960s, contemporary with the design of modular office furniture, saw the lifting of quotas in Asian immigration and the celebration of new pathways for Asian immigration to the United States. The Cold War politics and ideologies as well as the collective organizing of the 1960s would also set the stage for the neoliberal policies and ideological divides of the 1980s. With Tajima's visual and performance work, however, I see an intriguing engagement with materials of the 1960s, where flatness is a facet of inscrutability through which the artist critiques modernity's reliance and fetish of the flat. Tajima plays with the flat flexibility of racial capitalism both to show the production of labor and to critique global capitalism and the mandate to work that artists, including herself, are beholden to.

In this sense, I read the model minoritarian and the migrant laborer together—through the performance artist—not separate as might make sense to do in terms of class-based analysis. The model minority worker is often embodied by white-collar workers who may face a "bamboo ceiling" but who overwhelmingly are formally educated and may even be recruited and granted work visas based on their capacity to contribute intellectually and economically to the United States, in the "brain drain" of the 1970s. It is also true that work visas have been allotted for skilled as well as unskilled migrant workers, as the country depends on the exploitable work of unskilled laborers, who may have very limited opportunities for upward mobility but whose services comprise the quotidian foundation of the national economy. Reading these two class groups together may risk eliding the differences between them. I wish to think these two laboring figures together for the similar aesthetic dimensions of productive flatness that I argue have been used to racialize both groups as a function of streamlining their humanly concerns toward robotic efficiency, a specific sort of capitalist dehumanization that never successfully takes away the human but does reveal insights on the porous boundaries between human and robot.[13] While anti-Asian sentiment, like other anti-immigrant sentiment, continues to be riled up in US national politics, we should not pretend this is not internalized by Asian/Americans who may wish to see themselves as exceptional to immigrant positions. Rather than comply with this possibility of abjecting Asian foreignness in order to claim US national citizenship, this chapter thinks the Asian/American laborer as a non-monolithic yet aesthetically broad racial figure, regardless of geopolitical positioning, in terms of flat aesthetics, flexible labor, and global capitalism that troubles national boundaries at the same time that it deepens the wealth and health disparities between the Global North and Global South.

Critical Slacking

Studying aesthetics of flatness and flexibility reveals a slippage between the perception of office workers and that of office furniture. Is it that the modularity of office furniture mimes the flexibility of the human worker, or is it that the human worker must adapt to the modularity of modern furniture? The necessity of flexible fleshy forms is made explicit in one of Tajima's performance activations, as documented in a video by Art21, when Tajima hired contortionists to animate the gallery space of cubicle furniture (see figure 4.3).[14] Gallery visitors look on as one contortionist, Tony Mitchell (later to be joined by Christopher Bousquet), wearing a white-collar uniform of button-up shirt, tie, and slacks, juts out their hips and bends back to touch the floor. An ergonomic chair stands beside the artist and a cubicle wall, offering a visual mime/muse of their contorted body. Soon the video shows Mitchell and Bousquet bending and balancing off of one another, ribs on ribs and hands on ankles. In their standing upon and leaning into one another, and in turn providing balance and structure for the other, the two contortionists' bodies become foundation and scaffolding for one another. The performers' chair-like postures turn the surrounding furniture as co-performers in their mirroring of one another, as chairs among chairs. The Art21 video shows gallery visitors asking Tajima about the performers, and she makes clear that they were hired for the one-off gig through an agency for contortionists. Tajima's direction of the performance in her gallery installation, then, highlights the fact of flexible bodies performing flexible labor. Though the materiality of Mitchell's and Bousquet's bodies are not mistaken for the installation's

FIGURE 4.3. Mika Tajima, Contortionist salon event with performer Tony Mitchell. New York, 2011. Photograph by Mika Tajima.

cubicles and ergonomic chairs, neither are they wholly distinct from the office furniture.

Thinking flatness and flexibility together may seem paradoxical at first, since flat forms like the cubicle panel may appear to be not flexible but rather rigid. However, Tajima's work with the office furniture, in showing the intense flexibility of the flat objects' uses, suggests that it is the flatness of the objects that allows for its flexible labor. In this sense, my thinking of flatness and flexibility together is akin to Tajima's own phrasing of "slack" labor.

As Tajima and popular filmmaker Richard Linklater discuss in an Art21 online video interview, slacking involves a refusal and a withdrawal that is commonly conflated with laziness and apathy, and is counter to capitalism's story of progress through production.[15] Together, Tajima and Linklater trace a genealogy of the purportedly passive perpetrators through time, from US hippies in the seventies to Herman Melville's Bartleby, from Sudanese anti-imperialist protesters to US American draft dodgers. Tajima and Linklater's dialogue subtly reminds listeners how the creation of a laboring class has made possible conditions for the expansion of empire and further racial and economic oppression.[16] It is not slacking but industriousness that is popularly attributed to Asian Americans in the shape of model minority discourse. Tajima and Linklater's generative dwelling in slackerdom is provocative, particularly in the relationship drawn between art practice and slacking. What kind of method is slacking? How could art making be thought of as a kind of slack labor?

Through a discussion of Linklater's 1991 feature film *Slackers*, the two artists together trace an art historical genealogy, including the minimalist works of Agnes Martin and the durational films of Andy Warhol. I think of my keyword "flat" when Tajima describes these Structuralist works as "dry" (as a positive attribute) and offers an example in *Suprematist Composition: White on White* (1918) by Kazimir Malevich: "[It's] a very slacker painting because it's like, ugh, white on white, what kind of painting is that? But it's so conceptually rich. It's pointing to the surface; it's pointing to the structure. It's impossibly uninterpretable but also so interpretable, all the meanings in that work, and all it is is a monochrome. You can project onto it."[17]

Tellingly, Tajima's description of a slacker object, and what she later calls a "slack object," refers to an object that is not recognizable in the tradition of its medium or genre (as exemplified in the groan that precedes "what kind of painting is that?"). Instead, it calls attention to the "surface," "structure," and medium, refusing to be legible as representation. In its refusal to represent, the Malevich painting frustrates viewers who would wish for a predetermined meaning in their encounter with the art object. Tajima's impersonation of a viewer's response suggests that there is something disappointing about being met with an opaque surface. In Tajima's language, slacking becomes a mode of critique performed by an object, particularly when it looks passive. The aesthetic inscrutability of the Malevich monochrome, then, performs refusal in its determined opacity.

This aesthetic relationship between art viewer-subject and art object resembles a persistent mode of encountering and aestheticizing racial others. In this sense, social encounter operates on aesthetic convention, where the subject is the unmarked viewer and the (marked) object is the other to be seen. The discourse of inscrutable Asians in the United States, as such, reveals a viewer's need for the aestheticized object to represent its meaning faithfully and clearly. Yet, for Tajima, the inscrutable factor is "conceptually rich," both "impossibly interpretable but also so interpretable." An art object slacks when it offers a flat screen when depth was desired. Following Tajima's theory, slacking is a refusal to self-represent. Further, slacking calls into question the very possibility of self-representation, subverting any pretense of authenticity, thus recalling the previous chapter's studies of unreliable narratives and gender performance.

The perceived dullness of Malevich's "white on white" speaks to a social permutation where the blasé monotony of whiteness is almost unremarkable in its "suprematist composition"—a phrase that indexes an arts movement as well as the rhyme of "supremacist composition." Rather, Tajima and Linklater's interest in *White on White* seems to be in the marking of the regularly unremarkable whiteness of whiteness. The selection of Malevich's white painting as an epitomic slack object suggests that there is something potentially racially self-reflective about slacking. Flat objects index and potentiate racial critique. Though Tajima and Linklater do not explicitly address racial discourse in their interview, "slacker" as a derogatory epithet is more often associated with certain racialized, gendered, and classed subjects than others. In this sense, the valuation of "slacker" regulates the social borders of appropriate behavior where industriousness constitutes rewarded expectation for economic efficiency and worker compliance.

Pointedly, slacking—commonly understood as, at best, a half-hearted attempt to succeed—is rarely seen as a model minority proclivity. At the same time, affective flatness is routinely associated with Asian Americanness (as I will discuss further in the next chapter, on distance). However, in light of Tajima's conceptualization of slacking as a critique of self-representation, I bring model minority discourse into the conversation as an unspoken foil to Tajima's work. If model minority persists as a stereotype for Asian Americans, what might it mean to think of model minority discourse as a slack object, in Tajima's sense of the term? What might it mean to think of model minority figuration as a surface that outlines social success at the same time as it critiques epistemological protocol? As a figure of industriousness, model minority is inherently slack in its refusal to represent an essential racial being as truth. The flatness of model minoritarianism could be construed as a modular racial form. I wish to think through the associations between flatness and abstraction with universalism and neutrality because these linkages through political discourse have been used to orient Asianness toward white assimilation. Instead, I wish to divorce the assumed affinity between flatness and neutrality and show how flatness as an Asiatic racial and class form needs to be leveraged as political critique.

For some viewers, conceptual artworks like Malevich's bore with their dryness, implying that a lack of figuration signifies a lack of meaning. Similarly, the model minority myth depicts Asian Americans as self-sufficient and isolated, as though social abstraction justifies public neglect, disinterest, or exclusion. However, Tajima's defense of conceptual art here points to the paradox of being "impossibly uninterpretable but also so interpretable." Tajima suggests that minimalist practices are not without meaning but draw attention to the conditions of production. I understand Tajima's use of "slack" as performing a type of refusal to comply with agreed-upon structures like the temporal, affective, and social logics of capitalism. Tajima's installation work is slack in this sense, aggressively drawing attention to the surfaces of things and disrupting the notion that the successful use of an object can be determined from the outset.

Part of the brilliance of the Action Office's modularity was in its semblance of environmental personalization, while its design depended on units and premises of standardization. As Tajima has described in *Artforum*, the Herman Miller Action Office was "the first designed cubicle spaces in which work and social interaction were organized to control [and] produce life's abstractions."[18] One could just as well substitute "model minority thesis" for "cubicle spaces" in Tajima's words to suggest that the racializing myth is a form through which "work and social interaction [are] organized to control [and] produce life's abstractions." I wish to juxtapose Tajima's critique of the cubicle environment's production of laboring subjects to the racial formation of Asian Americans as model minority laborers in the 1960s and Asian gig workers under neoliberalism.

Controlling Life's Abstractions

Tajima's description of the Herman Miller designs "as controlling and productive of social abstraction" can correlate to the role of racializing discourses in the face of social and political upheaval in the mid-1960s, as evidenced in official documents like the notorious Moynihan Report and the *U.S. News and World Report*'s "Success Story of One Minority in the U.S."[19] One of the pivotal articles to develop a discourse of model minority, the *U.S. News* article lauds Chinese Americans as "an important racial minority pulling itself up from hardship and discrimination to become a model of self-respect and achievement in today's America." Tracing a population's "model" success to individual effort, the article generates a sense of exceptional self-sufficiency on the part of Chinese Americans, arguing that "Chinese-Americans are moving ahead on their own—with no help from anyone else."[20] Further, the article explicitly homogenizes "the Chinese and other Orientals" and contrasts them to "Negroes," effectively disciplining Orientals in an anti-Black triangulation from a white racial hegemony.

Responses to the model minority myth have generated a rich critical discourse within Asian American studies. Bob H. Suzuki's influential 1989 article challenges the facile deductions of model minority myth upon the release of the 1970 US census, which fueled perennial anxieties felt by dominant groups that immigrants and racial minorities were impinging on a sacred American way of life, one where white racial dominance corresponded with economic health. Suzuki explains how such interpretations from the census risked "fixating the model minority image as social reality in the minds of most Americans."[21] David Palumbo-Liu writes that "the logic of model minority discourse argues that an inward adjustment is necessary for the suture of the ethnic subject into an optimal position within the dominant culture."[22] In this formulation, it is the responsibility of the individual whether she succeeds or fails, evacuating the role of the social, the cultural, and the political in creating environmental conditions and reiterating an "inward"/outward opposition that constructs Asian American racial formation as spectacular exteriority and inscrutable interiority.

As these select texts attest, model minority discourse racializes Asians in the United States as the politically apathetic traitors to a coalitional politics for people of color, a pernicious threat to anti-racist solidarity as vital today as it was in the 1960s. The model minority as a fictional figure functions as a liberal multicultural pawn for dominant white interests in relegating perceived-minority interests to the concern of minoritarian individuals alone. At the same time, this racializing discourse is multiply productive since the model minority can create animosity across and among racial and ethnic communities, both within and without contours of Asian America.

Though Tajima nowhere points to the model minority myth in her exhibition, I enfold this racializing discourse into the mix of her modern furniture art in order to critique the ideological designs of subjectivity and space in the sixties. I reframe model minority discourse as a racial aesthetic that, like cubicle office furniture, works "to control [and] produce life's abstractions." The model minority social optic places Asian Americanness between poles of success and failure, industriousness or slackerdom. In this sense, the model minority functions as a rubric for Asian American productivity not unlike the material environment created by cubicle furniture. Racial ideology produces the terms for space, for embodied possibility, and thus a feeling of belonging. Tajima's work allows us to juxtapose the spatial units of modern industrial design and US Asian racial design.

One approach to examining the environmental impact of what José Esteban Muñoz calls a "crypto-universalist aspiration" is to consider the geopolitical stakes of its mapping.[23] As Victor Bascara writes in *Model Minority Imperialism*, model minority discourse in the sixties renamed US imperialist practices as multiculturalism and globalization. Asian American studies as a formal discipline emerged through the nation's strategic break from aspirations of empire and the redirection toward multicultural assimilation for US hegemony. Bascara articulates the double bind of colorblind politics as "the dilemma of a desire for formal abstraction, and the reality of historical markedness" for Asian American subjects.[24]

Though Herman Miller Action Office Furniture is not usually discussed along racial lines, implicit in its design goals are its "desire for formal abstraction" and the production of effective workers without accounting for "the reality of historical markedness." The bodies proper to such an office space are those of a skilled and productive worker population, no doubt including those of model minorities.[25] I analyze the modular design of Action Office furniture together with the homogenized rhetoric of the model minority myth because both move away from concerns of particularity and are instead preoccupied with standardized units for effectiveness and efficiency. Just as cubicle furniture is designed to maximize worker morale and efficiency, model minority discourse purports to celebrate the successful contributions of the Asian worker while neglecting a reflexive critique of the terms of success or economic health. Both modular office furniture and model minority discourses function as liberal multicultural racial forms.

Though one might argue that the model minority operates as a "good stereotype," when thought of as an aesthetic that buttresses white universalist bourgeois sensibilities of success while obscuring the scaffolding of empire, this trope obfuscates the internal complexity of Asian American history; flattens the solidarities among Black, Third World, and labor movements; and limits popular optics of anti-racist subject formation. A vital effect of model minority discourse is its role in producing an Asian American psyche, where one's social legibility is premised on the "inward adjustment" toward bland aesthetics of professional success, middle-class respectability, and normative white universalist hopes. The social environmental mandate to identify as a standardizable unit and to assimilate can constitute a material desire with great psychic impact.

Assimilation and Winnicottian Compliance

With certainty, how well we live and function in our offices determines the economic health of people and organizations. The degree to which we have survived in unfavorable circumstances is a tribute to human adaptability. However, *the fact that we can adapt does not mean that we do not also pay the penalties for forced fits.*—ROBERT PROPST, *The Office*

British child psychoanalyst D. W. Winnicott may be usefully reframed as a social theorist for ethnic studies, particularly for his writings on compliance, creativity, and the role of the environment in human development. While psychoanalysis as a social science is sometimes eschewed in critical ethnic and race studies for its history of pathologizing minority experience, I turn to Winnicott's theories of play and creativity specifically for his interest in a topic that psychoanalysis is notorious for neglecting: the role of the environment in subject formation. Winnicott is best known for his writings on transitional phenomena, wherein a child negotiates the precarity of objectivity and subjectivity through playing with a transitional object (e.g., security blanket, mother's breast, one's thumb). For Winnicott, play is a world-making ability. Playing does not occur internally or externally but is a performative "doing" in a "third area" that Winnicott describes as a "playground" and a "potential space" that overlaps between the world of the child and that of the object. Before subjectivity and objectivity emerge as conscious concepts, a transitional object helps the infant wean itself from both the mother and feelings of omnipotence. For Winnicott, a transitional object eases the infant's sense of anxiety and, if all goes well, will eventually lose its meaning by dispersing its use "over the whole cultural field."

Psychotherapist and theorist Adam Phillips has described the British School of object relations as translating psychoanalysis "from a theory of sexual desire into a theory of emotional nurture."[26] Winnicott's contributions to psychoanalysis, in contrast to those of Melanie Klein and Sigmund Freud, are his pointed emphases on play and its role in constructing a "good-enough" environment for the subject in formation. In his essay "The Use of an Object and Relating through Identifications," Winnicott acknowledges a prejudice against environmental considerations within psychoanalysis: "Psychoanalysis always likes to be able to eliminate all factors that are environmental, except in so far as the environment can be thought of in terms of projective mechanisms. But in examining usage there is no escape: the analyst must take into account the nature of the object, not as a projection, but as a thing in itself."[27] In contrast to what Palumbo-Liu formulates as the "inward adjustment" deemed necessary for model minorities, Winnicott's intervention in this passage emphatically distinguishes individual capacities from environmental factors.[28] The environment, though structured through the subject's attempts of destruction, is ultimately not within the subject's omnipotence and stands as "a thing in itself" to analyze. The distinction and relationship between individual and environment are significant for my study here, particularly because the operability of the model minority myth relies on a liberal understanding of self-determination and "personal responsibility" over systemic accountability. Studying the environment as "a thing in itself" makes it possible to articulate racialized discourse as constitutive of the environment. As a result, responding to racism is not just a matter of individual will or personal concern but an environmental factor that necessitates collective recognition, accountability, and dismantling. At the same time, by suggesting that Asian laboring bodies have been objectified as environmental furniture, I wish to elucidate the psychic stakes of coming into racial being as background.

Perhaps the most insidious effects of model minority discourse are in the dominant desires installed in constructions of Asian American identity. Assimilation, even in its necessary infelicity, depends on the production of desire for what is already accepted as desirable, adapting to prescribed ways of being. This ability to fit into the fantastical melting pot grants racialized others provisional passing as a modern American individual. As Robert G. Lee writes, "Ethnic assimilation is the vehicle through which the social identities of race, class, sex, and nationality can be displaced by the individual embrace of the modern."[29] It is by desiring assimilation and forgoing the particularities of race, class, sex, and nationality that one is granted access to a modern understanding of self.

As Bascara's work teaches us, the contemporary relevance of critiques of empire, racist policy, and labor exploitation can be unsavory publicity for a national project of liberal multiculturalism. The aspiration of assimilation—or what Winnicott calls "adaptation" and, more provokingly, "compliance"—carries psychic consequence that psychoanalysis helps elucidate. Winnicott describes compliance as the condition wherein "the world and its details [are] recognized but only as something to be fitted in with or demanding adaptation. Compliance carries with it a sense of futility for the individual and is associated with the idea that nothing matters and that life is not worth living. In a tantalizing way many individuals have experienced just enough of creative living to recognize that for most of their time they are living uncreatively, as if caught up in the creativity of someone else, or of a machine."[30]

Disengaging from the world, the compliant infant loses the ability to play and instead can function as another's environmental prop (e.g., as political furniture of racial liberalism). Though Winnicott is famous as a child psychoanalyst, and his case studies focus on juvenile patients, he is quick to point out that his theories of play apply to adults and children alike. Certainly, Winnicott's focus on "futility" and the sense that "nothing matters" names symptoms popularly diagnosed as depression. I wish to connect compliance to existing scholarship on the psychic dimensions of Asian racialization. Scholarship at the intersection of psychoanalysis and Asian American studies has largely orbited around racial melancholia, as developed by Anne Anlin Cheng, David L. Eng, and Shinhee Han, where racial and sexual minorities experience the loss of norms, including "whiteness, heterosexuality, [and] middle-class family values."[31] Winnicott does not articulate these societal factors as ideals to lose; rather, compliance names the child's adaptive technique to fit in. What is missing, and what therapeutic encounter aims to discover, is the ability to play.[32]

With Winnicott's formulation of compliance, I suggest that racialization names the process of producing populations as compliant for the service of others, or living "as if caught up in the creativity of someone else, or of a machine." The model minority thesis is regularly circulated as productive of compliance, where compliance is a deadening of alternative desirable ways of living. For Winnicott, a patient must be able to play to practice creative living and counter the fatal consequences of compliance. This model deviates from Kleinian reparation insofar as Winnicott's concern is for the creation of a real environment that is found to exist in and of itself.[33] If Winnicott's theories of creative living offer a third framework of modern subjectivity in addition to the model minority thesis and the modular formation of the modern office worker, then it is one premised on the subject's ability to play.

To be sure, I do not wish to equate all Asian success with compliance; it is not my aim to pathologize certain rubrics of success. Rather, I want to play with model minority discourse as an ambivalent object of Asian American studies that remains relevant for its psychic scaffolding of one's social environment and self-making. The model minority subject position functions as a scapegoat for dominant interests to justify the deregulation of anti-racist policies and practices. The prevalent templates of model minority discourse also render Asian subjectivity dependent on tropes of a limited scope of a good life, one that prioritizes "economic health" over psychic health and creative living. A main buttress to this bind, importantly, is in the model minority's adoption of dominant aesthetics of success and of protecting oneself against normative optics of failure, often to the detriment of one's own well-being.[34]

Tajima's performative practice embodies Winnicott's practice of play as a method for creative living. By building the conditions for play in her exhibition space, Tajima retools modern aesthetic discourses as transitional objects. Through her art practice, we can better consider the relationship between race and the potential for art to make a provisionally "good-enough environment." Tajima's playing with the Action Office furniture unmoors the object's meaning and resignifies its utility and mode of being in the context of the gallery space. The labor that Tajima performs with these structures, however, is not one that stabilizes the environment and reaffirms roles or positions of subjectivity and objectivity. Tajima's installations, in their destruction and construction of a good-enough environment, perform creative living and the limits of individualist minority discourses.

Tajima's art practice constantly upsets the ordered environment the Action Office panels were intended to construct. There is no premium on ends-driven work in Tajima's uses of the wall panels, no clear function for their presence. Indeed, reminding one of Iyko Day's study of Ken Lum's furniture sculptures, Tajima's furniture sculptures perform a kind of closetness. Tajima conjoins wall panels to create cubicles that lead nowhere, encasing themselves or embracing walls of the gallery and refusing access beyond. Tajima's play with these cubicle pieces transforms the performance of office environment. Originally created and marketed as products conducive for worker productivity, the Action Office wall panels under Tajima's hand better use their potential for customization. Rather than creating an environment of order and economy, Tajima's installations perform disorientation of space. The spatial order that the industrial objects are meant to create instead offer confusion and alienation, modeling a disordering of what was known. Objects that were once familiar as cubicle wall partitions disguise themselves as posters, mirrors, speakers, and questionable props. Like Malevich's slack *White on White*, they are surfaces that refuse figuration and representation in every permutation. If an Action Office space is supposed to both enrich employee feeling for the space of productivity and serve the company's goal of efficient work for a maximum profit, then Tajima's enhancements to the Action Office pieces refuse such warm liberal feeling and create a slack environment.

In Winnicott's analysis, an object is transitional not because the object itself is transitioning. Rather, "transitional" describes the condition of the subject who transitions through play. Likewise, what is immediately troubled in Tajima's installations is the inherent instability of objectivity as well as subjectivity. A gallery visitor soon realizes the dependence of her behavior on her understanding of the art object's performance. Yet there is no simple understanding to be acquired between art viewer and art object. Struggling to locate the art object's ontology, a visitor may sense her relationship to the object shifting as the object transforms in function.

The object of the cubicle panel becomes something that it always had the potential to be. By reupholstering and reassembling the mobile walls, Tajima multiplies the function of the thing and restructures the space. At the same time, her cosmetic changes to the objects reveal the potential of the object that was already there. Winnicott theorizes a parallel phenomenon as the "paradox" inherent to play and object usage: the child "creates" the object in the moment the object is "found." The child must never question this paradox so central to transitional theory. The performance of this paradox resonates with the concerns of those dubious of the facticity and evidence of race and racialization. Racialized subjects neither wholly find nor create their social identities. Rather, a negotiation occurs that complicates the notion of agency willed by the model minority myth. This paradox of play can be useful: evidently not omnipotent, an infant cannot create an entirely other environment, but she can work within the terms of her existing environment. To figure out the parameters of said environment, she must test its bounds by playing with its objects.

Though this destabilization of subject and object orientations is threatening, it is simultaneously exciting for its gesture toward an abundance of potential relationalities. Thus, what I describe as an aesthetics of inscrutability in Tajima's work is not only in the awkward feeling of uncertainty produced in her installations but also the sense that emerges in these spaces that something meaningful lies at the fringe of incoherence. Unraveling, spinning out of what could be, Tajima's environments embrace and explore the potentiality borne from giving up logics of inevitability. Further, this reparative building-up of what could be as opposed to a paranoid reduction and return to what already is refuses identity politics or racializing logics premised on coherent and stable self-making. Tajima has touched on this urgent openness to what could be in an interview referenced in the catalog for *One Way or Another: Asian American Art Now*: "I leave my work open so that there is ambiguity. Sometimes expectations and intentions don't work out the way we expected and this is what I'm looking for."[35] The incomplete work of creating a good-enough environment is an example of a slack project.

Such openness and ambiguity are necessary to generate alternative modes of being in the world, though often these modes are not acknowledged by systems that reward ends over means.

Destruction and Reality Testing

Tajima's work addresses the temporality of subject formation in Winnicott's transitional phenomena theory. Winnicott's theories of the subject risk linear narration, one that could be misread as consistent with the model minority discourse and neoconservative political pursuits of a post-racial world. Winnicott's play is not one of singular transition, however, from compliance to creative living in one straight line. As Eng and Han clarify, "The task of reality-acceptance is never complete."[36] It is in "those privileged zones of transitional space whereby the recurring burdens of reality are negotiated throughout a subject's life," including the domains of "artistic creativity."[37] I conclude this chapter by focusing on the role of destruction in Winnicott's theory and Tajima's work to explore a temporal relationship between self and world—one where destruction is productive of possibility.

I return to the back corner of the gallery space at the Seattle Art Museum where a yellow tarp served as a monochrome screen for a projected video of New Humans' short film *Dead by Third Act*. In 2008 Tajima and her performance collaborative New Humans filmed *Dead by Third Act* at the old Fiat Lingotto building in Via Nizza, Italy, which was the largest car factory in the world in 1923, switching hands officially in 1982.[38] Ubuweb describes the original Fiat Lingotto factory as "a historically complex site of industrialism, modernism, worker struggle, and Futurism" that becomes "a post-industrial disassembly line" in the New Humans performance.[39] The video reflects on its medium in Tajima's trademark use of geometric shapes and sans serif font on film surfaces. The short film, just under fifteen minutes, begins with slow pans of the famous architecture, now empty. Revolutionary for its assembly line design of vehicle manufacturing, the space is expansive and clearly built to the scale of the car rather than the human. Four minutes into the film, the camera focuses on Tajima shattering the mirrored floor with a sledgehammer. The film cuts to the procurement of a blue Fiat car in a scrap heap. At eight minutes, the car is rolled into the Lingotto building. The car is parked on one side of the mirrored stage at an angle, where fellow New Humans performer Eric Tsai marks its windows and hood with a red spray can. The camera captures Tajima's image in the mirror as she smashes the floor into shards, fragmenting her image along with the silver material. Tsai builds a skyscraper-like tower out of empty soda cans. Howie Chen crouches over the destroyed floor, his long black hair mirroring Tajima's. The artists remove the car's tires. Chen repeatedly brings down a mallet onto the car's hood with increasing rapidity, creating dents and a rhythmic beat. The car does not give easily, and the camera witnesses the mallet's blunt bounce upon each contact. Tajima, wearing a blue dress, long hair in her face, and a noticeable lack of protective gear, takes the sledgehammer to the car windows and windshield. Shortly thereafter, Tajima and Chen unhinge the driver's door and heave it at the tower of soda cans, bringing them down in a swift cascade. The video concludes with juxtapositions of close-ups of the destroyed performance objects (piles of damaged soda cans, the battered mirror floor, and the beaten body of the car) and pans of the Lingotto building.

The New Humans score the film with the use of pedals and amplifications, creating noise that sonically channels the space's industrial haunting. The resounding theme through sound, object, medium, venue, and action is destruction. This insistence on destruction contrasts with the architectural purpose of the Lingotto building. The apparent violence is hard not to notice whether through the performers' methodical mutilation of the car or Tajima's hammering the reflective floor to dust. It is in this strain of destruction in the performance of *Dead by Third Act* that I would like to bring in Winnicott's concept of destruction in his theories of play as reality testing.

Destruction is not to be pathologized in child development in Winnicott's psychology. Destruction is fundamental to establishing object use; the child attempts to destroy something in order to trust its environment. Destruction makes reality possible. As Adam Phillips writes, "For Winnicott it is the 'destructive drive that creates the quality of externality'; and it is the externality, the separate reality of the object, that makes it available for satisfaction. It is destructiveness, paradoxically, that creates reality, not reality that creates destructiveness. . . . In Winnicott's view the object was not reconstituted by the subject's reparation—as [Melanie] Klein believed—but constituted by its own survival."[40]

The subject must (attempt to) destroy the object to see if it can depend on it. The object may resist attempts of destruction. For Winnicott, the capacity for culture to exist depends on the object's resilience in the face of destruction. Destruction is not a one-time event for Winnicott that leads to a sense of wholeness for the object upon survival. The subject continually attempts to destroy its objects; the subject's ability to construct reality and negotiate its lost sense of omnipotence is contingent on the objects' survival. The subject effectively creates a sense of the real world through seeing what arises in its wake of destruction. I do not wish to romanticize destruction, although some system designs should absolutely be destroyed. I hope to thicken our understandings of harm and destruction, not as concepts or practices to disavow or fear but to name as parts of larger processes for change.

Slacking in *Dead by Third Act*

The short film's title, *Dead by Third Act*, critiques the insufficiency of a traditional three-act dramatic narrative. A familiar drama structure, a three-act story organizes a plot toward coherent conflict and resolution. Tajima and the New Humans play on the unsustainability of this structure for the promise of modernism. Whose health benefits from the three-act structure of racial form? The payoff is not materialized; not everyone makes it to the narrative resolution. To be dead by the third act points to a problem of sustainability. The linear model of setup, conflict, and resolution itself is what is unsustainable. The New Humans destroy the structure by dismantling the parts and putting them to destructive use, breaking the windshields, unhinging the door and using it as a bowling ball, and pointedly smashing a mirror.

I see this anti-teleological pulse throughout Tajima's use of the Herman Miller wall panels, this overwhelming insistence that the ends-driven uses of these modern objects have proven deadening. A different reality is required; a better good-enough environment must be created out of what already exists. The materials one can work with are already present, as with the Fiat car and the fallen tower of soda cans, but they must be used differently or destroyed. Winnicott's theory of destructive object use indexes the child's desire for a different kind of holding environment. Similarly, playing with model minority discourse as a racial transitional object might unleash a different mode of racial becoming, and different understandings of model minority as a racialized laborer.

For Winnicott, destruction is the basis of reality; "because of the survival of the object, the subject may now have started to live a life in the world of objects, and so the subject stands to gain immeasurably."[41] In this sense, destruction is essential to reality testing not only through hate but also through love. Winnicott's examples of the transitional object are of the thumb, the security blanket, or the mother's breast, but those are each sources of comfort for the child. What if the object under discussion is a racializing discourse?

The model minority thesis is an environmental container of racial particularity to contend with and as such can become a rather intimate object for subjects through identification. Winnicott's transitional object is attractive because it mitigates feelings of vulnerability endemic to sociality. Similarly, the model minority thesis is alluring as a type of racialized transitional object because it offers the abstractly racialized subject a modicum of social legibility through racial affiliation. The model minority stereotype occasions social recognition as well as an externally acceptable constellation of life choices and desires. As such, the model minority thesis offers a coherent goal to subjects in formation, regardless of how unattainable that third act of assimilated middle-class respectability may be. These parameters for success are informed by the designs of modern office furniture like the Action Office line, including gainful employment, economic security, achievement in higher education, and customizing a space to call one's own. The model minority thesis shows itself as an aspirational three-act narrative structure, as referenced in the film's title.

The ability for the Winnicottian object to survive and prove itself as "outside the area of omnipotent control" is significant since the exteriority of the object counters the internalization of model minority compliance, by recognizing that racialization belongs to the external world. It is through destruction that the subject can learn to trust her environment and be able to hold her objects accountable as outside the subject's omnipotence. This, in contrast to the model minority thesis, is a remarkable separation between what the subject is responsible for and what the environment provides for the subject.

In *Dead by Third Act*, Tajima and the New Humans enter an abandoned environment haunted by the failures of industry. The New Humans saturate each pan and each frame of the video with destruction. The sounds of the film were the only installed aural component of Tajima's solo exhibition at the Seattle Art Museum, and, as such, the metallic soundtrack of destruction permeated the space and reverberated off the acoustic panels. The performance asks: Can destruction bring about a better environment? For Winnicott, it is only through the object's survival that a subject in formation can learn to use the object. Use, as a concept that recognizes something about the object, is distinct from both exploitation and object relating here. As Winnicott clarifies, "Object-relating can be described in terms of the experience of the subject." In distinction: "Description of object-usage involves consideration of the nature of the object. I am offering for discussion the reasons why, in my opinion, a capacity to use an object is more sophisticated than a capacity to relate to objects; and relating may be to a subjective object, but usage implies that the object is part of external reality."[42] Destruction is constitutive of "external reality," allowing a subject not only to relate but also to use an object as something in and of itself. This capacity to acknowledge that the object, as a "subjective object," is both part of the shared external world and part of its own internal world makes way for a theory of love in Winnicott's transitional psychology. Reality testing is persistent, and so the subject is always destroying the object in fantasy. The development of fantasy allows that "destruction becomes the unconscious backcloth for love of a real object; that is, an object outside the area of the subject's omnipotent control."[43] Destructiveness allows the infant to use the object, meaning it is in this moment of attempted destruction that the object and the subject emerge as separate entities. Reality becomes the "positive value of destructiveness" for Winnicott.[44] In this way, if the model minority thesis is to be useful and generative for a different kind of environment and a matrix for other becomings, then it must be destroyed and acknowledged as something separate from the self.

The line between destruction and re-creation may not be a hard one, for both are methods of creative living. The role of desire distinguishes creative living from compliance. As Phillips writes, "There are those people, Winnicott implies, who recreate what they find out of their own desire, and those who comply by catering excessively to the needs of the environment."[45] Destruction, then, is not necessarily a method with an ends to fitting in or contorting to an established environment but a means of nurturing one's "own desire" and building a supportive environment.

Performing a Good-Enough Environment

I consider Tajima's artworks through Winnicottian play as a performative doing toward a desirable environment. In this sense, the environments provisionally set up and destroyed in Tajima's art practice materialize the racial performativity of model minority discourse. Tajima has spoken of the ways in which critics have misread her work as performative in the sense of addressing the artist's own movements and bodily presence inside the installations. Rather, Tajima highlights how the sculptures she creates, including the readymades she transforms, perform. In performing, these objects activate, change, and make possible new social relations in the space, thereby creating the space as it is experienced. Tajima's formulation of the object here resonates with Winnicott's concept of object usage, where the object is seen in its own right. Tajima plays with the very notion of relationality, modularity, and environment in her manipulations of the Action Office wall units.

As Eng and Han articulate, Winnicott's theory of object use is fundamentally performative: "On the one hand, Winnicott associates object relating with orthodox Freudian notions of transference, with the analyst as blank screen on whom figures from the past (mother, father, siblings) are projected. On the other hand, Winnicott argues, object use not only takes into account the question, 'Who am I representing?' but *also raises the important question, 'What am I being used to do?'*[46] In the analytic scene, the "I" reflected here is the therapist, that is, what is the therapist being used to do? In the gallery space, the object being used can be understood not only as the artist's working materials such as the Action Office pieces but also the gallery visitor. The distinction between object relating and object use is also a useful way to come to Asian American visual culture and performance, where my interest is less in establishing a relationship that assimilates everything into one interpretation. More, I find interest in the performative impulse where difference is necessary to repetition, where redeployment registers the possibility of exit. Tajima's practice of constructing a space with the cubicle furniture pieces shows one way to do this. Her work is not an effort to represent the model minority thesis—rather, this chapter attempts to do something with her work by discursively playing with it.

By analyzing Tajima's aesthetic practice with Winnicottian models for environment building, I argue that model minority discourse needs to be productive as a means to construct a good-enough environment. The discourse can be a transitional object with which to play and through which the racialized subject can think about the work of subject formation as an ongoing project. Given the stakes of compliance and depression, the destruction of bad objects becomes vital to transition with and through the redirection of failed modes of being. The model minority myth, as such an uninspired object, can be performatively retooled, commented on, and transitioned with in local scenes of site building.

Flatness is not neutrality. Flatness as material smoothness and as withheld affect is not neutral, and its non-neutrality is of racial and gender significance. Part of the study of inscrutability necessitates interrogation of neutrality and how a framework that includes the neutral presupposes certain accepted ideologies. It is from J de Leon that I learn most acutely of this reading against neutrality, specifically in their repudiation of language of "gender-neutral" whether for restrooms or clothing. Neutrality, I learn from them, suggests that gender is not constructed and that it is possible to exist in a vacuum separate from gender and the power structures through which it is enforced and carries meaning. It is not possible to take a neutral position to gender or race in the real world. Those who disagree carry the privilege of not feeling the symbolic and physical force that gender and race enact on bodies.

It is more necessary to argue against neutrality especially as minority liberals may be wooed by and/or rise to positions of power that would suggest a neutral posture is possible. What reads as neutrality is always something else. Inscrutability is not neutrality and should not be mistaken for an aspiration of neutrality. Rather, inscrutability might be thought of as a slack neutrality. Neutrality here functions as a proxy to universalism, where both erase the regulation of social difference. Neutral aesthetics do not possess a necessary politics. What can be sensed as neutrality, I argue, must be used in service of resistance. This refusal of neutrality as a given position is one that theater and certainly theaters of war make evident, with so-called bystanders or witnesses to history's genocides as agential players in the scene. In this sense, I wish to suggest that East Asians, though in recent decades provisionally enfolded into a capitalist class of elites, must repurpose their labor as those bodies that are often read as affectively flat to occasion other modes of doing and becoming, to operationalize their perceived flatness for feminist and antiracist critique. The inscrutable other has evolved into a particular kind of race-neutral and gender-neutral fictional figure—not actually race or gender neutral, to be clear, but bespeaking the anxiety of not knowing how the figure fits within familiar binaristic rubrics. That not-knowing reception, however, is not neutral, and history shows how quickly the charge of inscrutability can be weaponized as threat and suspicion of disloyal allegiance. Eluding normative epistemes of gender, sexuality, and race, the inscrutable other is and is not of this social world, read as a foil and thereby providing insight into what norms of racial and gender form pervade and structure our shared world.

My interest in flat aesthetics here will bring us to the next chapter, wherein we consider the labors of flat affect as performed by the inscrutable other, there impersonated by 1980s artist Tseng Kwong Chi. While the seeming evacuation of interiority would constitute a flattening of surface and depth, outside and inside, and would facilitate a streamlined flexibility of the worker, the following chapter articulates a theory of distance as a mode of flat affect and aesthetics that does not refuse or foreclose robust sociality and political critique. Instead, it is through the embrace of the trope of the inscrutable other as flat object-human-surface that Tseng performs long-distance relationality and queer coordination of being-with across space and time.

DISTANCE, NEGATIVITY, AND SLUTTY SOCIALITY IN TSENG KWONG CHI'S PERFORMANCE PHOTOGRAPHS

Asian racial modes of critique are entirely obfuscated by the reiterative public casting of Asian Americans as bland model minorities with no needs, creativity, or politics of their own. Yet Asian American and diasporic people nevertheless navigate political realities and make internal space to negotiate racialized feelings of loss and grief that are often publicly disavowed. From Mika Tajima's installed environments, *Surface Relations* now shifts to another artist's affectively flat and distant relationship to his environs. While Asian American communities have been repeatedly described as invisible, silent, and withdrawn, this chapter studies the ardently relational work of performing distance. These mournful and campy moods and modes attenuate

Asian American people to minoritarian life, to the cleavages between invisibility and silence that permit presence and the possibility of shared existence. These sad, mad modes of racial being—the inscrutable difference of Asiatic racialization—need to be recognized as minoritarian to create the potential for collective sharing out and building with that does not stall at a defense of Asian American legitimacy.

The Negative Personality of Asian Americans

Harvard consistently rated Asian-American applicants lower than others on traits like "positive personality," likeability, courage, kindness and being "widely respected," according to an analysis of more than 160,000 student records filed Friday by a group representing Asian-American students in a lawsuit against the university.—ANEMONA HARTOCOLLIS, "Harvard Rated Asian-American Applicants Lower on Personality Traits, Suit Says"

The 2018 Harvard College admissions lawsuit offers a prominent example of the racialization of Asian Americans as affective failures in the category of "positive personality." How might we understand the notably low rankings of Asian American personality in an elite college's admissions as reflecting national affect and racial form? The writings of Jeffrey Santa Ana, K. Hyoejin Yoon, and Sara Ahmed describe and analyze the gendering and racialization of happiness, cheer, and other positively connoted affects, the better to understand how the failure of Asianness to perform positive personalities relates to the heteropatriarchal liberal mandate of a US American brand of the pursuit of happiness. Rather than argue for or against this discourse of Asian Americans having terrible personalities, I wonder if it is not worth thinking through inscrutability as an Asian American structure of feeling. Notably, Asian American negative personality is not commonly narrated in news coverage in relation to structural policy or history. Low personality scores are not interpreted as relating to Asian American anger or harm from centuries of exclusion, war, and labor exploitation. There is no popular effort to contextualize what or how to interpret this data, if entertaining the validity of its findings. Even when Asian American affect is gauged, as in the Harvard admissions data set, there appears to be no public curiosity for what Asian American feeling might indicate for the national racial mood. But if we consider the subjective experience, of being told that your race ranks lower on personality assessments, we may better question how it is that Asian racialization is formed through affective positioning.

As the Harvard case suggests, Asian Americans, regardless of gender identity, are expected to perform model minority emotionology that, implicitly or explicitly, propagates white heteronormative happiness. Asian Americans need to fail assessments of belonging if predominantly white institutions like Harvard are to continue their racial hierarchies. As the admissions case shows, if these shortcomings are not achieved through categories of intellect or property, then white normative systems will produce Asian American failure through affect. That is, if Asian American affect is of public interest only when it is in service of white normative if not supremacist ideologies, then its gauge of positive or negative attribution can fluctuate in accordance to what affective support a dominant status quo requires.

While suffering is not a main analytic for me here, it is worth pointing out that there is little public discourse of Asian racial suffering. Consider Sara Ahmed's words, where "suffering enters not as self-consciousness—as a consciousness of one's own suffering—but as a heightening of consciousness, a world-consciousness in which the suffering of those who do not belong is allowed to disturb an atmosphere."[1] By turning to Asian affective distance in this chapter, then, as a form of racial attunement, I mean to theorize the capacious possibility of distance, not as a mode of turning away and making relationality impossible but as a queer diasporic practice of relating, widening the aperture of social possibility.

Tseng Kwong Chi as the Inscrutable Chinese

In a thirty-six-inch-square gelatin print titled *Disneyland, California, 1979*, two familiar figures stand beside one another (see figure 5.1). To the viewer's left, the Disney character Goofy poses in a cheeky stance, and to the right stands a man wearing sunglasses and a suit made notorious by Mao Zedong. In the background, striped table umbrellas and neatly manicured hedges set the stage for the eponymous amusement park in Southern California. Both Goofy and the uniformed man face the camera, though their postures are strikingly different. Goofy (performed by an anonymized actor donning a Goofy costume and character head) stands with his left knee sharply bent toward the man and his right leg extended toward the camera, revealing the sole of a cartoonishly big shoe.[2] Goofy's head is slightly downcast as if in the midst of a playful guffaw, the white glove of his left hand brought to his mouth and his right arm bent in a four-digited wave to the camera. In this meticulously rehearsed pose, the performer of Goofy appears to deliver on his namesake.

While Goofy embodies the floppy friendliness of the Disney canine, the figure beside him stands rigid with stoicism. Though this foreign-uniformed

FIGURE 5.1. Tseng Kwong Chi, *Disneyland, California, 1979.* © Muna Tseng Dance Projects Inc.

figure may not quite be a household name as Goofy, I would suggest that the costumed man in this photograph performs the role of the "inscrutable Chinese" as an instantly recognizable, if imprecise, figure in the American imaginary. Just as much a consumable and iconic character as Goofy, the inscrutable Chinese in this photograph stands tall with arms along his side, directly facing the camera as if not acknowledging Goofy's presence beside him. From the looks of his tensed body and facial expression, the inscrutable Chinese could be photographing himself with a statue or a building, as much as another sentient being. He betrays no affective regard for Goofy. The man stands with his black boots together, his mouth pressed in a line and his eyes covered by black, reflective sunglasses. A white shirt with sleeves and a collar peek out from under the man's utilitarian overshirt, where an identification badge is clipped to his left breast pocket, displaying a bespectacled headshot of him. Unlike the actor for Goofy, the performer of the inscrutable Chinese is not anonymized to the viewer, for the photograph signals to his role as the photographer. A shutter release cord connects Tseng Kwong Chi's right hand to the bottom edge of the photograph, toward the viewer.

Tseng Kwong Chi's campy performance of inscrutable Chinese in his expansive self-portraiture series from 1979 to his death at age thirty-nine, in 1990, epitomizes the queer sociality made possible through surface relations. Performing surface through facial withholding and virtuosic photography, blending conventions of self-portraiture, landscape photography, and tourist photography, Tseng embraces the abject inscrutability ascribed to Chinese and Asian people and hails queer forms of viewing that allow for promiscuous sociality even in visual solitude. Tseng's minoritarian aesthetic of distance in his prolific photography work positions his body as a kind of mirrored surface to his surrounding environments, occasioning reflection on his coordinates of time and space. This chapter thinks through the performance of distance in negotiations of Asian masculinity, where distance is less about privacy, pride/shame, or insularity and more about queer attunement to comparative (if not comparable) racial histories of violence and a visible bodying forth that memorializes rather than abets the erasure of minoritarian stories.

In this image, one of his many Disneyland photographs, Tseng's performance as the decidedly ungoofy Chinese other, in the wonderland of the Mouse House, ironizes visuality as artifice. In the amusement park, Goofy or any Disney character is expected to be outgoing and warm, actively sought out for group photos and autographs. When one asks for a photograph with Goofy, one might anticipate a certain affective response to standing by the character's side and—whether that in actuality might include delight, fright, suspicion, or humiliation—the compulsory comportment would be one of happiness. Tseng as the inscrutable Chinese, in rigid visual and affective contrast to the floppy Goofy, however, reveals no warmth in this photograph. Meanwhile, Goofy, with his predetermined facial expression, appears not to notice Tseng's serious countenance. This picture contrasts the ubiquity and enforced warmth of Disney characters like Goofy with the recognizability and inscrutability of the Chinese other in one frame. Both performers play their parts with such virtuosity that there appears to be no live dynamic between them.

Such deadpan performances of the inscrutable Chinese were the subject of Tseng's self-portraiture career, creating a persona in the "Mao suit"–donning foreigner whose authority few interlocutors appeared to question. A downtown darling of 1980s New York City, born in British-occupied Hong Kong and educated in Paris, Tseng sutured the lines between life and art with an oeuvre of more than 100,000 photographs. Using the camera as a social passport, Tseng worked as a photojournalist for glossy magazines like GQ and *Vanity Fair* and the downtown publication *Soho Weekly News*, where he documented his gallivants in photo essays, including crashing the Met Costume Gala in 1980 or photographing some of the most powerful neoconservative politicians of the Reagan administration while smirking in a seersucker suit. From 1979 to 1989, Tseng would travel around the continental United States, photographing himself with his father's Rolleiflex camera and a shutter release, and across the Atlantic and Pacific Oceans with assistant and boyfriend Kristoffer Haynes and a Hasselblad camera. Amy Brandt describes Tseng's "performance as a perpetual tourist, masquerading as a Chinese official, and a globe-trekker whose ironic presence conjures the displacement and disjunctive realities of the Asian diaspora."[3] In Christine Lombard's short film *East Meets West*, Tseng describes himself as a performance artist bodying forth "an inquisitive traveler, a witness of [his] time, and an ambiguous ambassador."

It may be misleading to call Tseng's photographs self-portraits, since Tseng's persona in these portraits troubles fidelity to the concept of self. In much of the series, as in the one with Goofy, Tseng's fisted right hand holds a shutter release, a technical device that allows him to compose, feature in, and capture the portrait. Tseng's performance of the Asian alien has inspired many scholars, including Dan Bacalzo, Iyko Day, Warren Liu, Mari Matsuda, Sean Metzger, Chandan Reddy, and Joshua Chambers-Letson. As Bacalzo observes, Tseng's portraits obscure if not refuse the concept of an authentic self. His identification badge, featuring a passport-style portrait with him donning the mirrored sunglasses, reads "Visitor/Visiteur" and "SlutForArt"—the former a nod to both his presumed foreigner status and his art training in Paris and fluency in French (a fact that surprised and impressed Yves Saint Laurent when interviewed at the Met Gala) and theorized here as Tseng's performance of distance, and the latter appellation to be discussed in this chapter as promiscuous migrant sociality.

Tseng's artful shenanigans in the first year of his ambitious series, known together as *East Meets West* and *The Expeditionary Series*, critique the racial affective norms of common sociality.[4] Tseng's photographs show how

Asian racialization disrupts social norms of belonging based on warm cap-italist aesthetics and positive affect. This chapter analyzes the portraiture of Tseng Kwong Chi to theorize distance as an aesthetic and affective mode of disidentificatory inscrutability employed by Asian American and diasporic performers. To position distance as an Asian American and diasporic affect, as a racial feeling as well as a racial form, we need look no further than the contemporary political landscape of feeling and race, and how the percep-tion of Asian Americans' lack of positive personality would structure or re-produce racial discourse in our times.

Distant Feeling, Distant Relations

Distance (between people and land, people and history) in Tseng's work is spatial—spanning coordinates across the Americas, Western Europe, and Japan—as well as temporal, the series accumulating over the ten-year period and end of the artist's life (not essential, but redundant) of AIDS-related ill-ness. Tseng's art making in the 1980s, at the height of HIV terror and state homophobia, was powered by and constitutive of a queer downtown arts lifeworld. Distance is aesthetically registered through Tseng's deliberate co-ordination of space and time over the course of this series. We sense out distance in the relationship between his figure and the background and fore-ground, distance in the viewer's relation to 1979, for example, or between where one is viewing or reading this and his travels in the Badlands of South Dakota. Distance, too, is registered as affect in Tseng's stoic performance, a campy distance that winks from behind mirrored sunglasses and withholds intentionality or context for *why* he was where he was, when he was.

Questions of belonging via distance resonate for immigrant, Asian, and queer demographics in the United States. As David L. Eng writes, "Sus-pended between departure and arrival, Asian Americans remain perma-nently disenfranchised from home, relegated to a nostalgic sense of its loss or to an optative sense of its unattainability."[5] Describing Asian America as a "siteless locale with no territorial sovereignty," Eng reminds readers that "queer entitlements to home and nation-state remain doubtful as well."[6] The materiality of distance and place are precisely what Tseng emphasizes in his travel series. The artist's biography further supports a transnational mode of being both here and there. Tseng was born in 1950 in Hong Kong; immi-grated with his family in 1966 to Vancouver, Canada, and then to Montreal; finished his art training in Paris in 1977 first as a painter, then as a photogra-pher; and moved to New York in 1978. A self-proclaimed "snow queen" who lived on three continents in his abbreviated life, Tseng strategically deploys discourses of the Asian perpetual foreigner as doing something more than recounting presiding rhetorics of unassimilability. An analysis of the visual codes in Tseng's photographs registers important social and ethical implications for Asian inscrutability.

A rhetoric of distant feeling is useful for a robust theory of Asian inscrutability because it invokes the affinities between the affective and the spatial. "Distant" describes something far away in space or time, or (of a person) not intimate; cool or reserved. Feeling distant reminds us that it is through feelings that we map our worlds. Feeling distant marks a racialized affect that looks singular and separate. Moreover, feeling distant acknowledges a separation that is spatially marked and informed by the diasporic, the migratory, and the transnational. Thus, "distant" as a concept bridges the language of geography and the language of affect. Distance signifies an abstraction that separates two or more things, without specifics of measurement. The relationship between space and feeling of course need not be correlative: one can be touching something and yet feel distant from it. Conversely, one can be continents or years away from something and feel close to it. I understand distance as bringing more texture and nuance to conversations on racialized affective life, including that on racial melancholia, isolation, loneliness, and depression. Legally, politically, and historically, this distance has been structured by policies of Asian exclusion, antimiscegenation, deportation, incarceration, labor exploitation, and other forms of social alienation.

Tseng's performance of distance through portraiture registers Asian and queer diasporic practice in the visual historical record. To feel distant is to identify a separation from the norm, to experience difference on the body and in the psyche. To feel distant is not to feel close and yet it is also to index an object from which to feel distant. In this sense, feeling distant emphasizes the relational aspect of what can feel like a solitary experience. Further, since one can feel distant to multiple things at once, and since "distance" does not privilege either location (of "here" or "there"; nation or diaspora; settler or Indigenous) as major or minor, central or marginal, I find distance a useful concept to both work against antirelational and binaristic logics and insist on a constellation of relations.[7]

Tseng's work teaches me about the relationship between Asian visuality and distance as affective comportment. As studies evidence, and as those of us working with and living as Asian American youth learn, it is difficult to feel unseen in a rhetorical landscape where visual representation is equated with existence, warm feeling with humanity. Visual reflection is desired and desirable for modern subject formation. As chapter 1 explores, omitted realist representation holds undeniable psychic effects for invisibilized minorities. What the metric of visual representation cannot perceive or track as desirable, however, are those modes of desiring, being, and becoming that are not premised on reflection but instead occasion other forms of self-making and being in time and space, other forms that may seem fractured or out of joint with a 1:1 ratio of self and image. Asian American culture evidences that realist reflection is not the only mode of becoming, self-knowing, and world-making. Distance, as a disidentification from an Asian burden of liveliness in the expression of cheer and hospitality, is another necessary and vital mode.

To be clear, I do not wish to romanticize feelings of alienation but rather to illuminate the social labors of alienation. Rather than being antirelational, feeling distant is insistently relational since it indexes a liminal space between. Feeling distant recognizes that feeling differently and feeling different are in fact forms of doing the emotional work for collective belonging—a belonging that does not depend on the warmth of American multiculturalism. This affective labor is often rendered invisible, made to be nothing, a nothingness that this book archives through its aesthetic objects and its considerations of inscrutable epistemologies.

Happiness, Racialized Masculinity, and a Capitalist Emotional Culture

Attunement to affect discourse around Asian Americans' unlikability equips readers with the ability to identify and critique a racialized affective economy operative in the United States, an affective economy that reproduces systemic values and inequities of race, gender, sexuality, immigrant status, and class. Sara Ahmed's by-now famous formulation of a "feminist killjoy" orientation within "affective economies" critiques the charge often put on women, in particular, to smile and be happy for the comfort of others. Ahmed's notion of the feminist as "affect alien" can support my idea here not only of feminists but of Asian Americans as interpellated subjects historically positioned to experience misogynist discrimination regardless of gender, and Asian Americans as affect aliens. Ahmed writes, "We cannot always close the gap between how we feel and how we think we should feel. To feel the gap might be to feel a sense of disappointment. . . . We become strangers, or affect aliens, in such moments."[8] Ahmed's discursive "gap" here between feeling and desirable feeling names the distance that radiates around and between strangers or, say, admissions counselors and Asian American college applicants. The affect alien feels the gap, and, in my reading of Tseng's photographs, performs the distance of that gap.

Tseng's performance of distance can be understood not only as an affect alien but also specifically as a communist feminist killjoy of capitalist promise. US racial affective economies, often of positive capitalist warmth, fueled by Asian American alien affect. The juxtaposition of Tseng's distant presence with the kitsch of Disneyland, then, conjures a mismatch that mines economic anxieties of Chinese foreignness. Tseng's formal dress as a Chinese dignitary interjects these associations of Chinese communism into the capitalist Western space of Disneyland. As Malini Johar Schueller writes of Tseng's *Disneyland* portraits, "The intrusion of the communist figure into Disneyland undoubtedly signifies upon the cold war origins of Disneyland as a capitalist extravaganza inaugurated in 1956, into which Khrushchev was denied entry in 1959."[9] And, to be clear, Tseng does not need to be a communist to be read as one, to be embodying the threat of communism. The so-identified "Mao suit" that Tseng found in a Montreal thrift store was, in fact, a Zhongshan suit and therefore politically adversarial to the communist sweep that threatened capitalist modernity. The readiness with which some read Tseng's as communist uniform, however, further evidences the perceived threat of Chinese bodies against capitalism. In his book *Racial Feelings*, Jeffrey Santa Ana writes that, within a "capitalist emotional culture," Asian Americans figure as both exemplary and menacing "model economic characters."[10]

The intrusion of Chinese inscrutability is not always parsed in relationship to the racialized whiteness of respectable affect. Consider how José Esteban Muñoz defines whiteness as "a cultural logic that prescribes and regulates national feelings and comportment. White is thus an affective gauge that helps us understand some modes of emotional countenance and comportment as good or bad."[11] Santa Ana identifies how "happiness in its racial liberalism context as the affective possession of the white propertied self fundamentally structures the attitudes and temperaments that Americans have about race and racial difference."[12] Following this logic, happiness is historically exclusionary and proper not only to whiteness but also to property-owning men, clarifying the misogynist constructions of the feminist killjoy, lesbian menace, and angry woman of color. What can Tseng's performance of distance teach us not only about Chinese inscrutability's foil to white masculinity but also Chinese inscrutability as a prism for queer-of-color critique?

The often unmarked affective racial coupling of happiness with whiteness helps us understand the normative expectation for Asian Americans, to gloss

Homi K. Bhabha's phrasing, as *almost but not quite white* minorities—and, we could riff, *almost but not quite happy*—to support and buttress this racialized affective economy.[13] As K. Hyoejin Yoon argues, cheer, as adjacent to others' happiness, is the prominent racial affect disciplined of Asian Americans and particularly Asian American women. Yoon writes that "in exchange for a conditional status, Asian American 'model minorities' perform cheer, dedication, and team spirit to maintain the affective economy in which dominant notions of citizenship, belonging, and identity circulate."[14] As Yoon writes, noting the "cheerful self-sacrifice" of cheerleader Kristi Yamaoka as she is rolled off the court after an injury, Asian American women are expected to perform "cheer and please regardless of [their] own condition."[15] Couching Yamaoka's performance of cheer within "a national pedagogy of affect," Yoon offers a theory of "'model minority' emotionology" that I extend and engage in a conversation about the gendered slipperiness of Asian American subjects.[16] Yoon focuses her analysis on Asian American femininity (as I do in chapter 2, on hospitality and parasitic femininity), but Tseng's photographs suggest that we consider the racialized affects of Asian and Asian American gender performativity in the construction of the masculinist nation.

As scholars such as Lisa Lowe and David Eng have written, Asian American manhood has been historically excluded from white masculine claims to citizenship, with immigration and economic policies that have meant Asian male survival in the United States has included traditionally feminized work such as laundering, cleaning, and cooking. Through immigration policy, landowning laws, and cultural representations, Asian American men have been hypo-sexualized and emasculated in comparison to white male personhood. Often, Asian/American masculinity reads simply as foreign and unintelligible, as David Eng and Alice Hom's bathroom anecdote in the introduction of *Q&A* reminds us.[17] While Asian femininity is hegemonically legible as cheerful, hospitable, and cute, if not hyper(hetero)sexualized, we might consider how Asian masculinity is often perceived as flat, unfamiliar, and distant. That distinction and distance should not be thought separate from a misogynist culture or one in which Asian masculinity does not have clear avenues for appearance or validation. That is, if Asian men have been symbolically and legally banned from national masculinity, then it would not be altogether surprising if Asian men would find distinction from Asian femininity by refusing a performance of cheer, hospitality, or cuteness. This has manifested at times in explicitly misogynist forms such as Frank Chin's notorious attacks against Asian American women writers, including Maxine Hong Kingston. But it is worth asking: How might we understand the performance of Asian or Asian American masculinity otherwise in its affective expressions, where masculinity is not the opposite of or rejection of femininity? I suggest that Tseng's campy performance of distance is one such negotiation of gendered racial affect through portrait photography.

If Asian Americans are implicitly expected to uphold racialized affective norms, relegated through a white supremacist, misogynist affective economy, then let us consider how Tseng critically engages with and challenges this charge for positive personality and its gendered implications. How do we make sense of this masculinized distance—or is distance an affront on bodies read as Asian because of this disruption of masculine affect, the chafing between Asianness and affective remove? Asian unlikability could be understood as not only a racialized but also a gendered racial failure of affect, a failure to meet the expectation for the feminized East to support and serve a masculinized West through affective accommodation.

American studies scholars need to develop the language to assess and analyze not only the stereotypes Asian Americans face but also the racial forms those stereotypes occasion, and therefore the racial aesthetics that are made playable for ends other than racial essentialism or racial legibility. Where I would extend Santa Ana's analysis is precisely into the intersections of race, sexuality, and performance studies, where, as Sedgwick reminds us, emotions are queer things: "Affects can be, and are, attached to any number of other things, including other affects. Thus, one can be excited by anger, disgusted by shame, or surprised by joy."[18] That is, theoretically at least, one need not be turned off by a lack of cheer or an expression of sadness. One may hold a promiscuous orientation to unlikability. I also wish to address the gender essentialism inherent to some discourses of Asian masculinity. By considering the racialized gendering of affective comportment, I think we may better appreciate Asian American subversions of hegemonic gender norms.

The Labor of Background

This blankness was the way in which this culture at large expected him, as an Asian man, to—to exist. So he became a kind of cipher, a smooth surface that because it was so impenetrable, this persona, it reflected everything!—BILL T. JONES, quoted in Muna Tseng and Ping Chong, *SlutForArt*

Consider *Bellows Falls, Vermont, 1983*, where Tseng and a uniformed train conductor are center stage with a train directly behind them (see figure 5.2). Tseng, on the left, stands erect in uniform, and the mirror of his sunglasses shines. His mouth draws a line, and his right hand grasps the shutter release.

FIGURE 5.2. Tseng Kwong Chi, *Bellows Falls, Vermont, 1983.* © Muna Tseng Dance Projects Inc.

The sun highlights his uniform, such that the train conductor's dark tie and suit, in contrast, almost blend into the train behind him. Instead, the conductor's white collared shirt and white beard frame his figure, complete with a conductor's hat on his head and a ticket sticking out of his chest pocket. The conductor squints, his arms behind his back and his left knee propped up to the side. As in the Disneyland portrait, both figures are in uniform. The train behind them, marked as number 1246, is in three-fourths profile and looms large, appearing to expel exhaust into the landscape visible to the right side of the image.

It is possible to view this photograph and not be attuned to its distant relative in the visual archive, another image of a US railroad that foregrounds American men and a train. I gesture, of course, to the photograph taken by Andrew J. Russell in 1869 at Promontory Point, Utah, upon the completion of the Transcontinental Railroad that would catalyze an industrial revolution. Russell's photograph documents the joining of the eastern and western sections of the railroad, a celebration that erased the historical presence of exploited "Eastern" life and labor in the endeavor of Western economic expansion and Manifest Destiny. The image of the Golden Spike Ceremony notoriously omits the Chinese laborers who not only completed the majority of the railroad's construction but also were on the frontlines of the most dangerous tasks in the effort. Despite the Chinese laborers risking life and limb, deportation and poverty, to construct the major transportation for an economic boom, exactly none is included in the iconic photograph.

With the omitted visual presence, the photograph instead tells a story of the triumph of white masculinist labor and foreshadows the series of policies that would exclude Asian claims to legal and political belonging in the coming decades. As Seulghee Lee writes, "The bigotry that fueled the Chinese Exclusion Act was not only a xenophobic codification of anti-Asian racism but a form of racialized misandry."[19] The strategic erasure of Chinese immigrant men as *the* laboring bodies that effected the railroad, then, must be understood as part of the long history of white nation building in the United States, one that has depended on the invisibilizing of US economic imperialism and its dependence on an exploited racialized and heterogendered working class. A theory of inscrutability and distance helps us grapple with the productive force of this invisibilization. If we believe that the labor of those migrant Chinese workers is not lost to the archive, then we may need to develop better intellectual and analytical tools, better sensorial practices, to attune us to these incriminating visual omissions.

Viewed together, Tseng's *Disneyland* and *Bellows Falls* photographs signal to the ideological structures of place making, and the visual composition of the uniformed Chinese man as out of place. The economic histories of these spaces, conjured through these photographs, however, is so subtle that it is Tseng's body as the performer throughout the series that allows for such a reading of the affective economies at work. Through aesthetics of inscrutability, we might reframe this understanding as the figuration of Asian bodies at the distant limit, such that the bodies of the Chinese railroad workers are flattened as the symbolic background to both the Russell and Tseng photographs, invisibilized as the necessary grounds of the occasion. While a discourse of invisibility would suggest the absence of these figures and histories, I suggest that an Asian Americanist and queer visual practice of inscrutability, of humbling ourselves to a reading position of not knowing, allows us to see Tseng's photographs as performing social distance toward different practices of historiography and embodied relation, ones that can easily be misread as apathetic, asocial, or antisocial but in fact are socially operative, socially performative.

Present Distant Witness

To further study the performative work of Asian distance in Tseng's oeuvre, let us consider two other images from Tseng's performance documents. In one, a short-haired, uniformed Tseng bends over a field of cotton blooms, cupping a boll of white fluff in the left hand, his right hand in a fist (see figure 5.3). Tseng's face angles down toward the cotton, in three-quarters profile. His mouth is closed, and the sunglasses obscure the direction of his gaze. Clipped onto his left chest pocket is the identification badge. Though its written content is illegible to the viewer, the bright reflection from his sunglasses conveys an alien-like visage. He stands with his legs together but the flurry of cotton stems obscures his feet. The field of both soft and prickly occupies roughly three-fifths of the vertical space of the photograph, with a ribbon of light gray sky illuminating the top of the image. A sloped wooden roof and two leafless trees appear in the skyline. Otherwise, the composition focuses on the tangle of cotton and the man dressed as a Chinese dignitary. The shirt appears wrinkled, perhaps from the trek to this position in the field, yet a crease down the right pant leg suggests attention to a crisp outfit. The title of the photograph, *Cotton Field, Tennessee, 1979*, locates us in a space of a historic, if generic, site of enslaved Black labor in the American South as well as a time that ramps up to neoconservative policies and neoliberalism. If, as in *Bellows Falls*, we consider Tseng's visual presence as performing his not belonging, pivoting our attention, then, to the otherwise starkly unpopulated surroundings, we note the absence of the cotton field workers who might be imagined in his place. And from there we note the invisibility of any enslaved people who worked colonial cotton plantations or sharecropped cotton fields under Jim Crow. The violent systems and visceral histories of cotton fields are not visually represented, however. Rather, Tseng, standing in a mess of sharp branches, displays a posture that suggests a sort of reverence and focus on the cotton's bright fibers.

Tseng's performance of communist drag and inscrutable witness in the American South inverts the work of visuality, of figural/tourist foreground and environmental background. An inscrutably queer viewing of his photograph

FIGURE 5.3. Tseng Kwong Chi, *Cotton Field, Tennessee, 1979.* © Muna Tseng Dance Projects Inc.

allows us to remember not only the enslaved labor of Black workers but also the relationship between Chinese migrant workers in those same cotton fields and shifting forms of racialization and racism. We may think with Gary Okihiro and Moon-Ho Jung, who write about coolies and cane, about the triangulation of white Americans, Black Americans, and Asian Americans. As Okihiro writes, "The African slave and Asian coolie were kinsmen and kinswomen in that world created by European masters."[20] Tseng's photographs refuse the instrumentalization of Asianness to reinforce a binaristic Black-white racial hierarchy.

FIGURE 5.4. Tseng Kwong Chi, *Monument Valley, Arizona, 1987*. © Muna Tseng Dance Projects Inc.

In *Monument Valley, Arizona, 1987*, a grand landscape of ancient buttes, an expansive sky of clouds, and a foreground of desert flora overwhelm the viewer in virtuosic display (see figure 5.4). The left half of the photograph features a prominent landmass of sedimented rock, reaching up as though to touch a wide cloud that floats across the photograph. Between the camera and the rock stands a leafy tree, its thick trunk the darkest concentration in the photograph, contrasting with the bright white of the clouds above. On the right side of the landmass, near the center of the image, is a protuberance of note. On the same plane as the tree, in the right half of the photograph,

Tseng stands in profile, facing up toward the landmass, wearing his uniform, sunglasses, and expressionless gaze. Behind him in the distance are other land formations, though his image is mostly framed by sky. A fluffy cloud floats above him as well, mirroring the landmass's vertical reach on a smaller scale. Here, Tseng's figure paradoxically blends in with the grand surroundings, the size and verticality of his person mirroring the land formation above; or perhaps, the land formation reflecting an elevated version of the human. The photograph suggests a reverential relationship between human figure and monumental landscape, one of recognition and splendor, and one effected by visual distance in the multiple backgrounds.

As with the *Cotton Field* photograph, a history of racial violence is all but invisibilized in Tseng's photographs of Monument Valley. Though the image's title does not make this explicit, Monument Valley is registered land of the Navajo Nation. Tseng's photograph attunes the viewer to the relationship between the foreign figure embodied by Tseng, the self-proclaimed "Visitor/Visiteur," and the site of settler colonial violence and Indigenous struggle. Monument Valley may be read as the film site of John Wayne westerns, thereby representing the West in popular culture and signaling, at once, an iconic Hollywood American West as well as the haunted and spectacularized site of the attempted genocide of First Nations people.

I understand Tseng's performance of inscrutable Chinese as embodying the distance, remove, and flatness that has historically been excluded and backgrounded. Tseng's performing body as the inscrutable Chinese, paradoxically, embodies the aestheticization of Asian male labor as backdrop. If Tseng shows how Asian male performativity functions through the embodiment of distance, then we can read his self/landscape portraiture as doing something inventive with the camping and layering of distance and visual omission. That is, the landscapes of cotton field and desert plain often serve as the iconic literal background to US national imagery. And Tseng shows, too, that the Asian male figure functions as still another kind of racialized gender backdrop that is also fundamental to US national imagery in its distance. By foregrounding his costumed body in these landscape photographs, Tseng effects a layering of invisibilized histories and modes that have served as the grounds of US nation building. This layering is also a flattening since the photograph is constrained by its two-dimensionality, and so the photographs refuse a holistic capture. Tseng's performative constellation of national backdrop enacts a queer relationship to distance, one that makes way for the negative image and occasions curiosity and intimacy between spaces. Tseng's formal relation to these racialized landscapes opens out interpretations as to how to understand the forms composed together. Distance, then, is not only a performance technique that Tseng employs in these photographs, mashing up portraiture with landscape photography; it is also a queer viewing practice that refracts our attention to what is not pictured.

Tseng's performance of queer, promiscuous distance in these photographs positions inscrutable distance as an aesthetic form and affect that opens out Asian racial performativity as vitally imbricated in comparative racial studies and queer diasporic critique. Tseng enacts promiscuous and long distance as a queer relational form that follows Summer Kim Lee's critique of the "compulsory sociability" of Asian Americans (recalling the low scores of positive personality) and performs distance on an interpersonal and disciplinary level, refusing white supremacist logics of what has been deemed appropriate racial subject matter.[21] By looking at these images side by side, as well as studying others in Tseng's prolific oeuvre, we may articulate a visual culture of inscrutability that both registers that which is invisibilized, as the violence of racial capitalism, and at the same time refuses figuration and positive comportment as the only claims to humanity and historical presence.

If we pull through the theme of the anticapitalist killjoy through Tseng's photographs that implicitly comment on histories of racial capitalism, then we better understand the disruptive affective and political economies that his photographs occasion. The performance of distance has been thought in relation to the genre of landscape. Tseng's play with tourist and landscape photography conventions allows a campy critique of how land is both monumentalized and erased of history, treated as inanimate matter untouched by time. The nonpresence of human figures is a convention of landscape photography, but one that has romanticized and ahistoricized the land. Iyko Day's exquisite analysis of Tseng's self-portraiture in iconic Canadian national parks (e.g., Banff) offers an Asian Americanist critique of settler colonialist practices of celebrated Canadian nation-building landscape photography. Her scholarship reads Tseng's work within discourses of eugenics, biopolitics, labor, and landscape photography. Day writes, "As an index of the abstract, degenerative value of nonreproductive, alien sexualities, [Tseng] highlights the eugenic spirit of white racial reproduction and regeneration projected onto the landscape."[22] Day's scholarship allows me to think through Tseng's photographs in the Americas, including the Tennessee cotton field, Monument Valley, and Puerto Rico.

Distance need not be understood as antisocial or asocial but as a critique of the terms of sociality, and a refusal of being-in-time premised on closeness of vision or warmth of affect. As Day writes, "Given that landscape art of this period was broadly concerned with honoring nature's vitality and universalizing power, the intrusion of Tseng's alien body is a sign not of life-affirming incorporation but of extravagant degeneration."[23] While some readers may interpret the alien body's "extravagant degeneration" as a kind of antirelational shattering of the abject self, I theorize distance as a form of queer diasporic relationality, within an Asian Americanist orientation that critiques the antirelational thesis within queer theory. Asian Americanness necessarily bodies forth a queer opposition to the US nation in its nationalist and nativist imaging, in a way aligned with Muñozian queer utopia. Just as brown and Black kids cannot afford a politics of "no future" in Lee Edelman's white-normative thesis, for alien, migrant, and transnational people (including children of immigrants), the future cannot be forsaken or taken for granted.[24] Neither can the terms of migrant futurity be premised on spatial or temporal assimilation or visual incorporation. Though Asian insularity within the Americas may be narrated as a kind of antirelationality, I critique the rhetoric of insularity as something that may be a cipher for desirable optics of sociality.

The Promiscuity of Long Distance

To articulate distance as a mode of feeling, sensing, and relating is to reorient a common perception of Asians as self-sufficient and insular perpetual foreigners to the nation, as gestured to in Tseng's identification as a visitor/ visiteur. My formulation of distance as a queer-of-color aesthetic mode also plays with the antinormativity of long-distance relationships and nonmonogamous relationships. I wish to hold space for these open, forms of intimacy. An external proscription of asexuality or hyposexuality onto Asian men writes these robust forms of sexuality and sociality out of possibility. However, Tseng's photographs render a kind of promiscuous and robust queer, coalitional historiosociality. One can hail the Tennessee cotton fields and Navajo land and Disneyland together in one portraiture series, connecting seemingly disparate sites as intimate and remarkable sequence, as a kind of queer coordination. These distant affiliations are not self-evident but are performed, by Tseng, through composition of his body in space and time.

These promiscuous modes of performing distant intimacy are underdiscussed even within sexuality studies, where a presumption of romantic and sexual partners as geographically and temporally close, as well as contingent on one other person, reproduce a monogamous couple form as normal.[25] Rather, Tseng's photographs show us the limited taxonomies we have for understanding relationality, all the truer when it comes to the social lives of minoritarian subjects with and among each other's histories of suffering. The world-making work of Tseng's photographs is less about romance or sex, per se, and more about affectively alien relation through promiscuous witness and ir/reverent attention.

Tseng's performance of distance can be understood as simultaneously asexual and slutty. Tseng's identification badge, as we may recall its glory, read not only "Visitor/Visiteur" but also "SlutForArt." "SlutForArt" functions as a sort of identity of Tseng's, as he also had a rubber stamp that he would use on his photo montages as well as a black T-shirt with white lettering that read "SlutForArt" in caps. "SlutForArt," on his identification badge, can be extrapolated as a form of identification, as a form of belonging and passport, how one knows oneself. But what might it mean to be a slut for art? The hedonist excess so often associated with sluttiness is not visually reflected in the series, marked as it is with Tseng's impassive demeanor. There seems to be no feeling between his figure and his surroundings, nothing close to the extravagant intimacy commonly associated with sexual promiscuity. Where I sense a distant sluttiness, however, one specific to the racialization of Chinese masculinity in the United States, is in a promiscuous hyposexual relationship with historic sites of violence and racial grief. Noting Tseng's identification as a slut for art, Dan Bacalzo writes that the "connotations of promiscuous sexuality is highly at odds with the stereotype of the Asian and/or Asian American male, who often tends to be desexualized. The ascetic and seemingly asexual persona in the photographs suddenly acquires a sexual resonance with Tseng's identity badge."[26] Here we may think with Seulghee Lee's writing on anti-Asian misandry when he writes that the "psychosexual threat of the Asiatic male covertly invading and sneakily infiltrating western civilization has been the core of white supremacy's racial-sexual abjection of Asian Americans."[27] Lee's writing toward Asian Americanist abundance as part and parcel of Black plenitude is consistent with the work that Tseng is doing in these photographs, where the distant abundance of being a slut for art twists conventional visuals of racial plentitude.

Long-distance relationality is another mode of being-with and holding on to historical being, in contrast to dominant ideals of monogamous proximity. In Tseng's photography series, long distance is a mode of queer and migrant belonging not particular so much to an individual as to a place.[28] By refusing to "let go" of these national histories of racial violence, Tseng performs a commitment to modes of relating and being-with that are not based on fixed location, disrupting romances of national belonging and community formations premised on calling the same place home. Long-distance relationality is not so much about a longing for distance as it is a longing for distance as not antithetical to sociohistorical significance or memory.

Tseng's performance of distance, as aesthetic form and racial affect, necessitates a reconsideration of tacit labors of migrant sociality, ones that take up the effort of being the visitor, of being out of place, to meet you where you are and necessitate a second or third or fourth look at a neglected body, place, or history. My sense of queer distance here is inspired by Gayatri Gopinath's articulation of queerness as a viewing and sensing practice, referencing "both the production and regulation of nonheteronormative bodies, desires, and practices, as well as alternative modes of seeing and sensing these braided histories and their imprint on bodily, psychic, and geographic landscapes. Queerness, in other words, is an optic through which we can glean the unexpected congruence that these histories engender."[29] Following Gopinath, I suggest slutty and long-distance relational modes as another aesthetic practice of queer diaspora in Tseng's work.

Nonmonogamous and long-distance relationships are forms of art in a sex-negative, heteronormative, and immigrant-phobic world. Slutty distance is in tune with Karen Tongson's notion of "remote intimacy," building on Jennifer Terry's research, to name the queer-of-color suburban subject's capacity to feel out other lifeworlds through the mediation of television, radio, and the convivial escape to be found in driving around the California sprawl.[30] Distance, too, is like its queer sibling in Martin Manalansan's formulation of queer diasporic disaffection, in his study of Filipina world-making.[31] While distance may register in normative optics as a kind of stasis, like disaffection, it may be thought as "more of a crossroad than an affective impasse or an emotional dead-end or cul-de-sac in that it suggests possibilities of movement or 'moving' . . . despite appearing to be unmoved."[32] I think with Tongson and Manalansan out of interest in Tseng's queer world-making and the ways that ambivalent or flat affects must be read as anticipating inscrutable worlds as well as inhabiting them in the present via performance. Further, Tseng's performative distance not only evidences and enacts possibilities of movement, and the conditions for moving, but also invites the viewer's possibility of being moved.

In the Distance

Tseng's costumed figure quietly spectacularizes the omission of Black, Indigenous, and migrant laboring bodies within the photographic frame. Whether or not we, like Tseng, prostrate ourselves in front of these seething sites, we are entangled in promiscuous relations across space and time. The stakes of interpreting Tseng's photographs as a form of slutty visual historiography via distance is to refuse a narrative that renders Asian Americans visible through limited optics of model minoritarian assimilation, as desiring reflection through a straight white optic, as well as to refuse a reading practice that enforces queer intimacy as necessarily about a warm and accessible homonormative couple form. If there is something queer about Asian America, it is not only the grief that pervades immigrant, refugee, labor, and war histories but also the resilient tracks and bridges that Asian Americans and other people of color have built and rebuilt to continue to hold on to what remains through those losses, the histories and lives that persist everywhere we are. Though it may seem counterintuitive, distance is another form of bridging. Though Tseng is the only visualized human figure, he does not in fact stand alone. We viewers activate and witness his images, as I attempt to do here. By standing outside the exegesis of the image, we may find ourselves hailed into the frame, into this queer affiliation of space, time, and figure. Despite ongoing histories that a/sexualize Asian bodies—in relation to an economic mandate for racial utility, utility under racial capitalism—modes of critical desire persist and are enacted by quotidian and spectacular performances of robust, distant intimacy. The distance of foreignness is not necessarily or simply prohibitive of sociality or coalition; Tseng shows it to be a vital mode of embodied context. Tseng's performance of promiscuous distance, then, is a way to both "stay in," in Kim Lee's idiom, and be out, literally outdoors and in public spaces, while also refusing the transparency or nonthreatening friendliness of normative Asian American comportment.[33]

Distance figures in a queer reading not only as cold refusal of the social but as an alternative mode of relationality, a form of intimacy that is not for the judgment of external viewers who long for welcoming looks so much as it is the expansive bridging and wide array of feelings that looking can enact. Intimacy here is less between two individuals and more, in Tseng's photographs, conjured between histories of racial capitalism, opening space for queer Indigenous, enslaved, and migrant intimacies that exist through the promiscuous presence of his body. It is his body along with the viewer's cognition that create a queer practice of looking with distance—performing as an inscrutable other who enacts a queer coalition that both practices and critiques identity politics—refusing the limited imagined visual subject of "Asian American" or "Asian diasporic" and drawing attention away from the phenotypic and toward the racial aesthetic of space, time, and belonging. The blurring of human figure and landscape is not an equivalence or reduction but a productive twinning of animate forms, animate histories, that give shape to the matter of flesh and space, that render a cotton field a synecdoche of the transatlantic slave trade and a railroad train the symbol of Chinese labor together as the invisibilized grounds of American modernity.

Through language of the close proximal and the long distance, we may better sense out some of the ways that social misfits build their lives through relating to multiple spaces and times that pulse with memory, history, and sociality. Queers of color body forth marginal histories as foreground. Interpreting these photographs and the work of Tseng's quotidian and documented performance, I think of my role as the viewer as well as his enactments of being-with. Tseng's performance documents also invite and hail a kind of slutty distant practice of witnessing his travels and art/life. "SlutForArt" is also a reading method, then, one open to engagement, open to one's desire to feel connected through thought and art.

Queer Coordinates of Distance and Proximity

In Tseng's *Tank, Puerto Rico, 1987*, the artist stands on top of what looks to be an abandoned military tank at the beach (see figure 5.5). A cloudy sky encases the square image in a bright gray, and Tseng's head forms the apex of a triangle silhouetted by his standing figure and the heavy tank. Along the edges, we see the sand and beach below and to the right of the tank; some beach flora and detritus appear at the photograph's lower left edge. There appears to be wind sweeping Tseng's crew cut into a cowlick, with his face looking up and out, above the camera, and his sunglasses reflecting clouds. The tank is immobilized and its details visually obscured in darkness. How might we interpret the artist's stance atop this military vehicle of occupation, terror, and murder? We could interpret his figure as a strange general in a powerful stance of command; but that is not right exactly. Or consider *Puerto Rico, 1987*, in which Tseng's figure is barely visible in the distance. What we see is an elaborate stone bridge or cove, one that is white and gray and textured such that its depth and dimensions are difficult to discern in the flatness of the photograph; the ocean beckons from the top half of the frame and the horizon line is punctured by the sun's wink to the camera. Near the bright white of the sun's nonimage is the backlit human figure whom we surmise is Tseng, feet together, arms behind his back; it's not clear if he's facing the camera or the sun; he is pure silhouette, the same dark gray as the landmass he stands atop in the darkened top-right quadrant of the photograph. Here we register so many distances—the camera's relationship to the stone cove,

FIGURE 5.5. Tseng Kwong Chi, *Tank, Puerto Rico, 1987*. © Muna Tseng Dance Projects Inc.

to the near ocean, to the horizon line, to the sun, to the landmass, to Tseng; and we can vicariously imagine Tseng's perspective in standing alone there, his views so different in the 360-degree turn, perhaps waving to assistant Haynes before throwing up the white flag for Haynes to take the photograph.

My formulation of aesthetic and affective distance in Tseng's photographs is in conversation with Roy Pérez's "spatial metaphor of proximity," which he frames as "a way to describe modes of queer affiliation that do not give themselves over to easy representation, but that nonetheless appear and unfold their drama in the aesthetic field."[34] While Tseng's suited figure may not appear obviously connected to the cannonballs of Puerto Rico, or the beached tank on the island, he performs the proximal/distant affiliation that refuses "easy representation" yet gestures to and arguably performs the "brown commons." Writing of Martin Wong's work within the Nuyorican art scene of the 1980s, Pérez continues:

> A theory of the proximal allows us to talk about desire as a poetics rather than as a sleuthing of the implicated subjects' interests, cathections, and sexual practices. Rather than an argument against such sleuthing or gossip, a theory of proximity is more nearly a way to make something out of the aporia created in the Latino archive by the bifurcation of race and sexuality into separate histories, and attend to the gaps and contradictions where queerness seems to be the missing conjunction but where its denotative confirmation is either ignored, inaccessible, or unspeakable.[35]

Pérez employs a phrase I adore from Muñoz's idiom that, when read in others' writing, sparks a lightbulb: "more nearly." Pérez's theory of proximity extends Muñoz's "more nearly," where the nearly is not about an arrival at a predetermined destination and not a teleological orientation to construct a judgment about being more or less near. Rather, it is about critical engagement moving one toward another, swerving into something else that is yet to be identified.

With Pérez's work on proximity and this chapter on distance, I mean to make more space within queer studies for an interest in what could be called *queer coordination*, which I understand through Tseng's prolific coordinates of space and time, all brought together through the prism of his body in the photograph. Viewing his photographs—piecemeal and through various media, including in person at the Center for Creative Photography in Tucson, Arizona; various exhibitions, including at the Grey Art Gallery, online, and in his estate holdings of artist-sister Muna Tseng's downtown New York apartment—coordinates me, puts me in formation, looking for him as a predecessor to affiliate with across great distances. Queer coordination need not depend on closeness or conventional modes of intimacy that presuppose the ability to reach out and touch, the ability to fetishize the live by grasping it. Distance refuses that grasp or contact, which registers the pain and loss of distance but also insists on the possible pleasures and poignancies of and through distance, ones that queer, diasporic, migrant, refugee, adopted, and transnational subjects are most privy to, those of us who know home not by a specific given coordinate but by a constellation of sought-out coordinates. This queer constellation—one that can be traversed and mapped not as conquest but as always standing on historic lands, in relation to histories of dispossession and exploitation but also of survival and activism, of decolonial resistance and artistic creativity—is done in the performing body, offering an alternative visual record via the technologies of photography.

Tseng's figure, posed as the inscrutable alien persona, activates these spaces and their seething presence without attempting to represent the populations historically oppressed there. Nor is he representing himself in a straightforward autobiographical gesture. The self is not fixed but is created, as with the portraiture of Cindy Sherman or Nikki S. Lee. At the same time, Tseng comments on the resonances between histories of racialization in the United States. We see a critique of the United States' violent economic and political exploits in Tseng's photographs that stir in their silence and invisibility.

Allow me to clarify my thoughts on distance and its limitations in effecting progressive politics. This critical distance may perform an other that puts inscrutability and insularity in tension, where insularity suggests closed-off self-sufficiency. By insularity, I think with Shireen Roshanravan's work articulating the coalitional potential of Asian American feminist work as part of women-of-color activism. Roshanravan makes a case for Asian American insularity as necessarily anti-Black, where blackness becomes the hypervisible non-white minority in a national visual field, and Asian Americans both benefit from the shield of that racial positioning and fall invisible to it. I am convinced by Roshanravan's thesis, which challenges me not to romanticize the "in"wardness of inscrutability and insularity. Roshanravan's warning against such an uncritical embrace of infrapolitics, especially for Asian Americans, helps me better understand the work of Tseng's photographs, which are not about an inwardness of self-discovery or autobiography but gesture outward and around to his periphery, to his surroundings, widening the question of the relationship between the artist's body and the site as historical residue, between the artist's body and the viewing subject, and then transversely, between the geopolitical site and the viewing subject. That is, though Tseng performs Asian alienness as an indistinguishable cipher, Tseng also camps up that invisibility by performing himself as hypervisible yet inscrutable: the anonymized alien in the visual field. Roshanravan's caution against insularity and infrapolitics may resonate with Joshua Chambers-Letson's reading of blankness in Tseng's photographs. As Joshua Chambers-Letson writes, "Blankness was the cost Kwong Chi was willing to pay to live in and gain access to a white world, but his friend [Bill T. Jones] still seemed to sense that his appropriation of it was an inherently disidentificatory act, transforming blankness into the grounds of insurgent critique."[36] Tseng's performed distance as the Chinese other can be interpreted as a means to gain access to a white world, but his embodiment of distance also enacts anti-racist and decolonial work within the aesthetic conventions of the white world. Asian inscrutability is one vernacular with which Asian racialization is used to binarize racial taxonomies further, but Tseng's inscrutable Chinese works to fragment this dyad. We need to think Asianness, alienness, blackness, and, in Iyko Day's words, "the contradictory logics of exclusion and elimination that condition the triangulation of Native, alien, and settler positions within settler colonialism in North America."[37]

Recent public rhetorics of disqualified Asian American personalities reveal the contradictions of Asian racialization within a racial landscape that neutralizes and universalizes whiteness. The distance I am formulating as queer Asian American and diasporic is attuned to the particular forms of solitude and ennui that are in distinction to and pointedly not assimilable into white hetero-reproductive universalism, though their performances may appear similar at times. As is argued throughout this book, what can appear to be assimilationist aspiration in Asian American aesthetics in reading as what Muñoz formulated as the "blandness" of a specific but not simply phenotypic whiteness might more constructively be thought as a pointed racial and gendered embodiment of inscrutable difference—a form of refusal that marks both the impossibility of passing as white (given its historic contradistinction from citizenship) and a gesture toward modes of being and knowing that refuse translation or understanding. Though Asian aloofness can be read as a form of racial and class privilege, and sometimes is that, it is also worth uplifting the particular forms of Asian distance that abet decolonial and queer praxis. Though distance can be insulating and isolating, Tseng's work is decidedly about taking up space and inviting the reader to look again at where he is, why those spaces, what brings us there.

Distant Social Practices

Tseng's performance of inscrutability queers these national affective economies, both miming the affective distance of the perpetual foreigner stereotype and queering the perceived alienation of this figure in stunning virtuosity. Whether or not Tseng is the singular figure in the photograph's frame, he photographs himself wearing the familiar Zhongshan suit and black boots. In *Puck Ball (The Gang's All Here)* from 1983, Tseng is socially legible in ways refused in the *East Meets West* series. The distance between himself and other is no distance at all. If anything, I as the viewer might sense the group's collective distance to me and their proximal closeness. The Puck Ball photograph is the large-format thirty-six-inch square we have come to expect from the *East Meets West* series and it is, similarly, a gelatin silver print. However, the iconic landscape is replaced by the banality of Tseng's studio, and instead of a vast sweeping landscape are his friends, now famous from New York's downtown club and art scene. Katy K, Keith Haring, Carmel Johnson, John Sex, Bruno Schmidt, Samantha McEwen, Juan Dubose, Dan Friedman, Kenny Scharf, Tereza Goncalves, and Min Thometz join Tseng in a crowd of heterogeneous personalities in the snapshot, and there is an unmistakable sense of belonging in this picture. Where Tseng's ambassador persona stands beside and separate from iconic landmarks, Tseng in this photograph in some ways blends into a group of outsiders. His body fits into the negative space left for him in the group. I turn to this photograph not only to signal to Tseng's versatile oeuvre or a more conventional visualization of his abundant social life as in a group studio portrait but also to contrast his flat affective singularity in his self-portraits as something that was pointedly performed for the series.

In another example of Tseng's group portraiture, this one taken at Riis Beach in Queens, New York, Tseng kneels in his familiar suit, left hand holding the shutter release, glasses on and smile midformed, his right wrist delightfully limp. He kneels surrounded by seven standing beachgoers, some holding drinks, several exposing chests, a couple wearing sweatbands, one crotch being fondled, one man looking like he is about to pat the top of Tseng's head. The Atlantic Ocean waves behind them. Here, the distance is pure camp, is a covered suit beside swimsuits, is sunglasses among other sunglasses. A collage of body parts frames Tseng's face, horizontally between one's rump and arm and a crotch grab, vertically between a man's touch and his own limp wrist. Here, Tseng is not so much performing distance or cheer so much as archiving a moment of myriad possibility, of imagination, in the face of the freedom to be unhappy or foreign.

What I gesture toward in concluding this chapter with examples of Tseng's group portraiture and not the solitude of Tseng's self-portraits is a robust and radiant sociality that pervades his photography. To formulate a theory of distance as queer and feminist aesthetic strategy is also to turn attention to the spectator, the one in the position to view and to judge, one who is beholden to visual hegemonic regimes and must orient ourselves to not only what is visually present but also that which is gestured to in embodied performance. It is to widen the aperture of what is captured on film but also what is opened in each of us when we view an image. In this sense, Tseng models a kind of spectatorial relationship to space and time. The spectator and reader of Asian Americanness, that is, must employ a queer look to be able to see what is not there, to see what the melancholic object indexes and practices in embodiment, the reminder that each of us is a moving archive, necessarily failing but still efforting toward our charge to memorialize, to body forth.

Conclusion

SOMETHING IS MISSING

One cannot witness the lifework without some part of the work being experienced as missing.
—ADRIAN HEATHFIELD and TEHCHING HSIEH, *Out of Now*

Queerness is that thing that lets us feel that this world is not enough, that indeed something is missing.—JOSÉ ESTEBAN MUÑOZ, *Cruising Utopia*

I remember where I sat in the studio in the Performance Studies (PS) wing on the sixth floor of the Tisch building. It was the summer of 2008. I had just moved from the San Francisco Bay Area to take part in this graduate program at New York University. I had no idea what I was getting into. That day, the chair of the department screened a video, a performance document.

The concept of the performance was simple: the artist punched into a work clock every hour, on the hour, for one year. Wearing a utilitarian jumpsuit, the artist took a photograph of himself standing beside the clock immediately after punching in. The year of daily photographs was then compiled into a video, compressing the one-year performance into six minutes. That summer day, with this performance document as the only light source in a windowless room, I learned of Tehching Hsieh's work for the first time. Watching his image flicker, his contour spasm as the video progresses into his year of shallow sleep, I felt my breathing change. I could not put words to the sensation, but Hsieh's virtuosic performance in time moved me. I noticed my heart beating.

I sensed an inscrutable approach to life and creativity, one whose splendor, if not its details, could be shared with others. I felt my face redden in the dark. The artist's Asianness hit me with shameful desire of reflection in performance art. Artist Simon Fujiwara has described his moment of gay recognition upon the viewing of a Mark Rothko color field painting. As I sat in the PS studio, Hsieh's work offered me queer interpellation as an Asian form—hailing me through an open-ended mode of desiring that this book articulates as a surface relation. By way of concluding this book, I will engage another year-long performance by Tehching Hsieh, one fulfilled in collaboration with artist Linda Montano, to think through the forms of sociality that can or cannot be represented in performance, and the productive trouble that inscrutability presents to the thinking of time and the writing of history.

Visualizing Everyday Collaboration in *Rope Piece*

From 1978 to 2000, the artist by the names of 謝德慶, Sam Hsieh, and Tehching Hsieh created and executed six durational works that have defied categorization and comparability in art history. These performance works, which his coauthor Adrian Heathfield calls *lifeworks*, have disrupted conventions of life and art, notions of time and the body, of endurance and vulnerability. The first five pieces were each of one year's length, completed with varying months in between for rest, recovery, and preparation. Like the other artists studied in this book, Hsieh produces work as a solo artist. Solo is significant here not only in the discreteness of his name but also in his virtuosic experiments with isolation.

Experiments with social being were central to Hsieh's endurance art. Hsieh's inaugurating *Cage Piece* was an extreme form of social deprivation, containing himself physically to the confines of a cell and culturally to the absence of media, eye contact, and conversation. The next year was the aforementioned

Clock Piece, in which his time was diligently managed and his social calendar was restricted accordingly. His third year-long performance, *Outdoors Piece*, excluded him from shelters ranging from a cave to a subway train to a building. His environmental security took the form of a sleeping bag. As scholars have noted, this commitment to vagrant living invites commentary on his undocumented status in the United States and the belonging of what Charles Garoian has called his "Asian-alien body."[1]

These sublime endurance works of intense temporal and spatial manipulation gave way to his fourth year-long piece. From July 4, 1983, to July 4, 1984, Hsieh and Linda Montano collaborated for a performance commonly referred to as *Rope Piece* (see figure C.1). This moniker comes from the 8-foot, preshrunk, nylon rope that connected them from the waist, pulling to a taut 5.5 feet between them.[2] A solo artist in her own right, Montano was no stranger to collaborative or endurance work. Their collaboration follows the templates of Hsieh's preceding performances in many respects. Like Hsieh's five other durational works, *Rope Piece* was announced with a contractual statement of the artwork's rules, with Hsieh's signature use of legal templates.[3] Both artists agreed to be in the same room when inside and both artists agreed not to touch for the length of the year. The artists also documented the performance daily. Though the initial statement does not make clear the parameters of art documentation, Hsieh and Montano have since released a photo diary of the year. Hsieh's calculating approach to performance documentation continues in *Rope Piece*, with daily photographs and daily audio recordings of the performance. The photo diary includes photographs of themselves each day of the year as well as photographs of the cassette tapes they recorded whenever one of them spoke.

In the artist monograph *Out of Now*, the year is visualized through two photo series. In the first, the 367 days of the performance (1984 was a leap year) are each represented by one photograph, dated in the bottom right corner (see figure C.2). Eight photos fill a page in the monograph. Often Hsieh and Montano are both figured in the photographs, sometimes with friends and animals, often doing mundane things like sitting on the subway, cleaning the house, lying in bed, standing in the kitchen, or enduring yet another morning bathroom routine. Many appear candid while others are posed with friends seated or standing between the two artists. The artists have since confirmed that they made use of a tripod to take many of the photographs, suggesting the photographs were largely composed by the artists themselves. Other times, the placement of the rope makes clear that one artist is taking a photograph of the other.

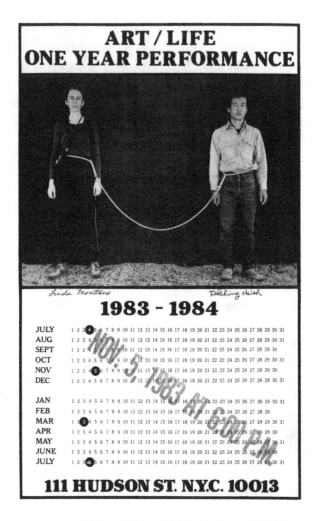

FIGURE C.1. Tehching Hsieh and Linda Montano, *Art/Life One Year Performance 1983–1984*, poster.

Looking at the daily photographs, the minutiae of two lives lived together, never alone, is routine and unsentimental. The eve and day of the 1984 new year are represented by a kitchen workout and TV lounging. Recurring scenes include art galleries and familiar New York backdrops, such as the Brooklyn Bridge, Washington Square Park, or a subway platform. Montano's dog Betty is often pictured, attesting to the trio's three daily walks. These quotidian scenes take on a comedic tone with the rope seen between them: Hsieh trims his toenails while Montano writes at the desk (5/10). Montano

FIGURE C.2. Tehching Hsieh and Linda Montano, *Art/Life One Year Performance 1983–1984*, daily life photos, in *Out of Now: The Lifeworks of Tehching Hsieh*, by Adrian Heathfield and Tehching Hsieh.

sits at the bathroom threshold watching television while Hsieh showers (5/8). Hsieh extends a tape recorder toward the camera (6/15). Hsieh plays arcade games (6/10) and Montano performs a tarot reading (7/2). Montano gets an eye exam and Hsieh takes a photograph (11/23). They look at each other and smile, the rope out of the frame (5/6). They turn their backs to one another in another photograph, the rope pulled taut (1/9). In his underwear, Hsieh drapes a blanket on a sleeping Montano (11/17). The artists prepare (6/19) and post flyers of their studio opening (10/24). They pose with a couple at a party (10/15). They stop at an ATM (9/26). They pick out cereal at the super-market (7/3). They sit before a fire by the river, reminding viewers of Hsieh's *Outdoor Piece* (1/12). They attend street fairs (9/24). He stands at the stove, she at the sink (8/2). They go for a run (7/29 and 5/3); they ride bikes (6/26). They sit at the movies with Martha Wilson and go to the Met. They prepare to board a plane (3/10). They both talk on the phone (3/26). They lie in separate single beds, often. Hsieh enters an elevator while Montano remains outside its threshold (perhaps documenting one of the more dangerous moments the artists later reference, when they arguably broke the rule of being in the same room and faced physical risk) (2/6).

Taken as a group, these photographs give a sense of temporal coverage. There are indications of the activities and people that filled their time, the moments that cumulatively create a life. More simply, taking photography as a form of truth documentation, a viewer can see that, yes, the two artists did as they said they would: they are indeed tied together with this rope, in the same room, not touching. Each photo allows a glimpse, a tiny keyhole through which viewers can briefly sense what that year was about.

Sometimes these glimpses are complicated by the absence of the artists' bodies. Though it is rare in the series, at times neither of the artists is figured. A television monitor and slide projector are featured (11/2), with the artists nowhere to be seen. Children hold onto a many-stringed rope as they cross the street (9/23). These photographs give a sense of looking away from the other and themselves, of focusing on their surroundings. Every so often a dark photo appears, with only the camera's orange date stamp visible in the corner. Other days are explicitly marked with the word "FIGHT," such as on 1/28/84 and 1/29/84, suggesting that the artists were not in the mood for an otherwise composed photograph. These blank photos attest to a mood, a moodiness that affects the performance, even as the performance continues with its visual archive. The photographs without the artists figured trouble the use of the photograph as proof. They point to the omissions and absences that pervade the photography series, gesturing to all that cannot be visualized and recorded through photograph.

What That Year Was Actually Like

The question of what is not captured in the daily life photographs can easily remain unasked because of the abundance of photos and the details they hold. The impressive seriality of photographs is enough to capture a viewer's attention for years. One could get lost in the careful composition of each photograph, and marvel at the recurrence of places, activities, outfits, and people. The visual record allows for a voyeuristic glimpse at the intimacy between the two artists, sparking curiosity for the strange relationality it might have occasioned. What might that year have felt like from a first-person perspective? What were they thinking? What would it be like to have such a physical connection with another, not in the name of desire or love but in the name of art? How did being tied to one another affect their social lives otherwise? The 367 photos are so evocative that the viewer may be disheartened to realize that she actually has no idea what that year was like. Hsieh and Montano's *Rope Piece* gives no shared sense of performance to an audience despite the artists' rigorous documentation.

I am not alone in being entranced by *Rope Piece* or the fact that the quality of Hsieh and Montano's year tied together remains a mystery. Though there are no examples given as evidence, critical reception of *Rope Piece* narrates conflict into the performance. Paul Laster writes, "Montano and Hsieh had to do everything together and disagreed on most."[4] Laster continues, "They documented the piece with daily snapshots and audio recordings, though the latter have not been released."[5] When Emma-Louise Tovey asks Montano about her year with Hsieh, the artist responds: "That's a closed chapter of my life."[6] Tovey writes in *Sleek*: "They didn't always get along. In fact, both sides seem to delicately avoid the subject of what that year was actually like."[7] The juxtaposition of these two sentences suggests a causal relationship between them; that the artists did not always get along is proven by the fact that neither discusses "what that year was actually like." Does a closed chapter indicate conflict or disagreement? Not necessarily, especially when the performance was designed to end from the beginning. Despite—or maybe because of—the abundance of performance documents, viewers want more access, suggesting that documentation not only divulges but also withholds information.

This reception of being left out, of not having access to the actual experience, is reflective of responses to Hsieh's other works. As Frazer Ward writes, "What begins to emerge in *Outdoor Piece* is the insufficiency of the documentary evidence to the brute facts of Hsieh's experience."[8] Ward further comments, "The evidence continues to tell us neither what the experience for Hsieh was 'really like,' nor why Hsieh did it."[9] Ward's and other critics' comments construct a fraught relationship between evidence and experience, one that withholds content and justification. The presentation of format, then, the rigorous documentation of scheduled time and place (whether through a camera's date stamp, a punch clock's hour, a map's red-lined path, a person's hair length, or a calendar's circles), creates a surplus of form. These material structures outline a life lived within its frames, so the work is never presumed empty of meaning. Rather, the shape that meaning could take exists in the visual record, circulates, and is abundantly evident as external matter. At the same time, the content of those years, the interiority of Hsieh's experience, remains unknown.

By reiterating these aesthetics of external display and internal withholding, Hsieh's aggressive documentation practices for his durational performances support what this book has formulated as aesthetic modes of inscrutability, where a social relation is premised on a dynamic of knowing and obfuscating knowledge. Another way to read these critical reviews is to hear the desire there to know, to have access to the pulse of those bodies in time. In this sense, Hsieh's oeuvre teases the viewer. As Ward writes, "'Prefacing an interview with Hsieh and Montano, Alex and Allyson Grey remark of *Rope Piece* that it is 'one of the most highly publicized works of performance art,' but that 'it retains an *impenetrable privacy*. No one will ever know 'what it was like' but the artists themselves.'"[10] Ward describes this withheld information as a "representational shortfall," suggesting it is "a metaphor for the misunderstanding of the plight of those who are socially marginalized, whether illegal aliens, the poor, or the homeless."[11]

The larger question of "what it was like" is perhaps all the more poignant and beguiling with *Rope Piece*, since the constant witness of another (Montano) was instrumental to the performance. The focus shifts, then, not just to Hsieh and *Rope Piece* as one in a series of his works but to the larger question of that plural subjective "we" who writes the artist statement of *Rope Piece*. If Hsieh's performances of inscrutability notoriously withhold more than they reveal and create this "representational shortfall," then how does one make sense of this impenetrability when another person is present? How is it that, even when someone else could theoretically speak to the experience of being "inside" a yearlong performance with Hsieh, viewers still remain "outside" it?

It is remarkable that Ward interprets this representational shortfall as still representing something. With few givens to the piece, reviews of Hsieh's work often defer to the biographical. Ward continues in a similar vein: "If the rope literalized relationality itself, *Rope Piece* was an experiment in sociality, in communication and negotiation, but one posited by an artist who was, in terms of another, larger set of negotiations with the state, still several years away from having a leg to stand on."[12] Ward does not go on to elaborate or clarify his point here or the significance of that "but" in referencing Hsieh's undocumented status and his experiment in sociality. Ward is not alone in foregrounding Hsieh's alien status, one that to me risks relying on his undocumented legal status to interpret the effects of his work. A critic's commitment to an identitarian marker of any sort seems to run short on utility fairly quickly when it comes to Hsieh's work because that representational shortfall is so insistent. As Susette Min writes of Hsieh and Montano, "While their work was not at all intended to be an ethnography, the artists, I want to suggest, were nonetheless interpellated by critics and scholars as native informants and objects of an ethnography of a world of their own making, delineated and bounded by a rope and with each other."[13]

It seems to me that biography, or how we can constellate a person's life under knowable terms, misses the point of Hsieh's project as the artist would have it. This does not mean Hsieh denies relevance of social identifiers. In an interview with Heathfield, Hsieh has said of *Rope Piece*, "The concept made no limitations of gender, race and familiarity, but in executing this it was necessary for me to make some choices. As an Asian male I chose to cooperate with a white female."[14] And, indeed, some social distinctions could be spelled out: Montano uses a female pronoun, Hsieh a male one. Montano is a US citizen and Hsieh was an undocumented immigrant in the United States from Taiwan during the length of *Rope Piece*. Montano grew up in a Roman Catholic tradition, and Hsieh is not self-avowedly religious. Hsieh is photographed reading newspapers in Chinese, Montano in English. Montano cannot speak Mandarin, and Hsieh can speak English. More could be said here to note distinctions that are not without weight. Rather than pursue this line of thought, however, I wish to highlight the limits of the biographical, and, in fact, how normative identity categories constrain the conceptual social work of *Rope Piece*.

Significantly, just as there is a repeated impulse to make sense of *Rope Piece* through artist biography, there is also a desire to make sense of the artists' relationship. Comparing the piece to work between performance artists Marina Abramović and Ulay (Frank Uwe Laysiepen), Heathfield writes, "Hsieh and Montano's piece is less concerned with the torques of desire in heterosexual union and more focused on a terrain of questions to do with other intersecting elemental dynamics of social relation: hospitality, civility and ethics. Hsieh and Montano were not only different genders; they were working from quite distinct perspectives around aesthetics and the social and spiritual functions of art."[15] Common frameworks for understanding couplings emphasize connections forged through sex, romance, and blood. However, Hsieh and Montano were not friends, lovers, life partners, or family. *Rope Piece* troubles the linguistic frameworks we have for social life, reiterating the interpretive trouble of Hsieh's endurance works.

The performance does not provide language for understanding what happened or why. Rather, viewers must rely on the visual through the series of daily photographs for context. The reliance of the visual in performance documentation also gestures to the limits of photography. Joan Kee describes Cheng Wei Kuong's photo of the tally marks for *Cage Piece*: "This close cropping of the photograph indicates that there is something more to the scene than what the picture shows, namely, durational, lived experiences that all still photographs are ill-equipped to relate."[16] The capacity for photography to point to the "something more" takes another form in *Rope Piece*. *Rope Piece* troubles such ocularcentric and textual evidencing, which we will now consider through the second photography series produced: that of the sealed audiotapes.

"Defining but Inaccessible" Witnesses

An observant viewer of these "Daily Life Pictures," as Frazer Ward refers to them, might note that the rope around the artists' waist was not the only string encircling their bodies.[17] Throughout the photo series, one of the two artists is shown wearing a cross-body sling attaching a cassette recorder that hangs at waist level. Viewers catch glimpses of the cassette tapes in the daily photograph series. On January 21, 1984, a row of cassettes is shown with a blurry foreground image of Montano's hand holding a calligraphy pen, perhaps to sign the seal label (the date verifies this assumption). More regularly the image of the recorder appears, a shared weight that transfers from Hsieh's hip to Montano's. These cue an aural archive of *Rope Piece* as well as the second photography archive of this piece in *Out of Now*, showing the 665 cassette tapes, each labeled as "TALKING" as well as by date, tape sequence, and minutes of recording (see figure C.3). One such label reads:

ART/LIFE ONE YEAR PERFORMANCE
LINDA MONTANO & TEHCHING HSIEH
JULY 4, 1983 - 1984, 4 JULY
TAPE: (77A) DATE (9/18) MINS: (224)

The labels combine the artists' names for the piece. (Hsieh's duration works are each officially titled *One Year Performance 19##–19##* and Montano has referred to *Rope Piece* as *Art/Life*.) Note the symmetry in the date presentation, where the hyphen is a sign representative of all that connects one date from the other, a visual mime of the rope between the artists. As the number 665 suggests, most days in the year of *Rope Piece* saw more than one cassette's fill of sound. These cassettes each hold an additional label with the separate date of their subsequent sealing, varyingly done about once a month, with fifteen total sealing dates. The shortest time they went before sealing was seven days (the first sealing) and the longest was from 3/26 to 5/14, for fifty days (the thirteenth sealing).

This second photography series of the sealed cassette tapes is exemplary of the role of withholding in Hsieh and Montano's performance. These tapes are a departure from the documentation in Hsieh's other lifeworks since they materialize and withhold the aural. These tapes insist on the fact of conversation that cannot be shared publicly but must be remembered as something that did in fact take place and take time. In lyrical letters addressed to Hsieh and published in *Out of Now*, Peggy Phelan writes: "You both spoke into a tape recorder, the machine Warhol called the most revolutionary emotional technology of our age, and then sealed the tapes forever. The whispered secret of what they might say reminds us we cannot possess the performance or think we 'understand' it. The tapes put it, permanently, beyond us."[18] The sealed tapes refuse possession and understanding as well as a futurity of possession or understanding. Phelan continues, "'Rope Piece' transferred the thick twine you draped between your body and her body for a year to the thin ribbon between the two bobbins of the tape recorder. That ribbon ages in the archive as we abandon reel to reel in favor of the digital pulse. Archaic and archival, the tapes seal the performance but point to the part we missed."[19] Heathfield writes, "Hsieh and Montano recorded daily testimonies of their yearlong performances on numbered and dated tape cassettes, but their co-signed sealing of each tape withdraws from audition the oral testimony of

FIGURE C.3. Tehching Hsieh and Linda Montano, *Art/Life One Year Performance 1983–1984*, select cassette tapes, in *Out of Now: The Lifeworks of Tehching Hsieh*, by Adrian Heathfield and Tehching Hsieh.

their exchanges within the work, and it does so *for all time.* In withholding this testimony of their exchange of differences, whose presence is keenly felt in its absence, the work calls attention to a defining but inaccessible and now inaudible locus."[20]

Over and again, critics employ these rhetorics of inscrutability: inaccessible, inaudible, withholding, absent. Heathfield describes the "withdrawn oral recordings" as a "self-negating" form and an "extensive spoken disclosure permanently withdrawn from hearing."[21] It is this "zone of insensibility and unrepresentability" that "thereby preserves something of its singularity."[22] Heathfield connects *Rope Piece* to *Cage Piece* in their "enduring presentation of silence" and "through the sealing up, in perpetuity, of the recorded speech acts that are integral to the work."[23] Put into question, he writes, are "the capacities of language to approach the meaningful force of the artwork, which will remain unspeakable."[24]

In an interview with Heathfield, Hsieh has spoken of the audiotapes: "We used tapes to document our conversations across the whole year and sealed them. These tapes are the witness of the 'Rope Piece,' they are like the aircraft's black box. We keep them sealed to keep our privacy, like Pandora's box they cannot be opened. They make a question; they give you imagination."[25] The similes here configure the audiotapes as boxes: "like the aircraft's black box" and "like Pandora's box." These are somewhat contradictory analogies but they both configure the audiotapes as a multidimensional inscrutable space, with reflective exteriority and inaccessible interiority. Unlike an aircraft's black box and Pandora's box, Hsieh and Montano's audiotapes are sealed and not to be heard, ever. By withholding the content of the talking tapes, Hsieh and Montano retain the life of their communication in the time of their recording. By recording the tapes and taking photographs of them, moreover, Hsieh and Montano project a future for their circulation, one that is visually witnessed even if the audio is withheld. The cassette tape photographs offer visual documentation for the year Hsieh and Montano lived and breathed together, whose contents are only for the performers to know.

Ephemera of Inscrutability

José Esteban Muñoz writes, "Queerness has an especially vexed relationship to evidence. Historically, evidence of queerness has been used to penalize and discipline queer desires, connections, and acts."[26] Inscrutability and queerness both account for minoritarian modes of living that navigate regimes of visual surveillance. Hsieh and Montano's withholding *and* prolific documentation constitute a queer act, which Muñoz tasks with those anti-identitarian modes that "contest and rewrite the protocols of critical writing."[27] *Rope Piece* expands an anti-assimilatory sense of historiography, world-making, and sociality, one that cannot be understood as a romantic couple or queer friendship.

If majoritarian cultures cannot recognize Asian American life, it is because of the ephemeral forms of Asian inscrutability. Muñoz writes in *Cruising Utopia* that the "key to queer evidence, and by that I mean the ways in which we prove queerness and read queerness, is by suturing it to the concept of ephemera. Think of ephemera as trace, the remains, the things that are left, hanging in the air like a rumor."[28] Muñoz explains that ephemera is "modality of anti-rigor and anti-evidence that, far from filtering materiality out of cultural studies, reformulates and expands our understandings of materiality."[29] Ephemera "is all of those things that remain after a performance, a kind of evidence of what has transpired but certainly not the thing itself"; "it does not rest on epistemological foundations but is instead interested in following traces, glimmers, residues, and specks of things."[30] Ephemera is a powerful response to critical insistence on evidencing experience. Surely the stakes of such discussion lie in the writing of history and the mattering of life-forms. Joan W. Scott's well-known 1991 article "The Evidence of Experience" critiques a historical strategy that depends on experience as foundational and instead advocates a literary approach to studying the role of experience. Scott writes, "What counts as experience is neither self-evident nor straightforward; it is always contested, and always therefore political. The study of experience, therefore, must call into question its originary status in historical explanation."[31]

Muñoz elsewhere critiques Heather DuBrow's introduction to a PMLA issue on evidence when he notes a belief "complicit with a dominant institutional logic: an imperative to maintain the stability of evidence *despite* the acknowledgment that evidence is always already contingent under the pressure of post-structuralist and post-axiological inquiry."[32] It is politically urgent to insist on ephemera as evidence, Muñoz suggests, because "evidence's limit becomes clearly visible when we attempt to describe and imagine contemporary identities that do not fit into a single preestablished archive of evidence."[33]

I make a point to foreground these critical discussions on ephemera and evidence to make a case for *Rope Piece* as a performance of inscrutable sociality that surface aesthetics make glimpsable. *Rope Piece* is a durational performance made glimpsable through strategic withholding. Following Scott's initial read of Samuel Delany's bathhouse scene, one could interpret the daily life photographs of *Rope Piece* as a kind of ocularcentric truth telling, where the matter of each day is represented and proven by its image. To consider the photographs as their own movement of light, however, following Karen Swann's reading of Delany, is to imagine the photographs as traces, as ephemera of a being in time, being in art, that dislodges a reliance on sight, facticity, and authenticity of experience.

Hsieh asserts that the documentation serves as a trace of the performance; the photographs are not the work itself. In an interview with Karlyn De Jongh, the artist says, "For me the documentation is only a trace of the work."[34] Rather than pursue what the work *is*, I advocate methods of performance studies to consider what it is that *Rope Piece does*. As Muñoz advises, "Performance studies, as a modality of inquiry, can surpass the play of interpretation and the limits of epistemology and open new ground by focusing on what acts and objects do in a social matrix rather than what they might possibly mean."[35] Inscrutability in performance studies is one such modality of inquiry.

Besides, With-holding

What *Rope Piece does*, I argue, is index the inscrutability of being with and beside another, the particularities of all that talking, all that silence, and all that other stuff. Muñoz helpfully distills Jean-Luc Nancy's thesis in *Being Singular Plural* as such: "For Nancy the post-phenomenological category of being singular plural addresses the way in which the singularity that marks a singular existence is always coterminously plural—which is to say that an entity registers as both particular in its difference but at the same time always relational to other singularities. Thus, if one attempts to render the ontological signature of queerness through Nancy's critical apparatus, it needs to be grasped as both antirelational and relational."[36] In this way, we can imagine how inscrutable modes are both antirelational and relational.

The daily life photograph series of *Rope Piece* could be testifying to a sociality between Hsieh and Montano, defending against narratives that conflate singularity with antirelational solitude. Here we may connect impulses across queer theory and Asian American studies that focus on the minority-identified subject as a melancholic agent who can forgo social conscriptions by self-sacrificing or, in the idiom of Lee Edelman, self-shattering. As earlier chapters have discussed, the nonappearance and "productive invisibility" of Asian American visuality could be read as a form of self-sacrifice. At the same time, while *Rope Piece* may be read as a performance of alien sociality, the ephemera of *Rope Piece* is consistent with Hsieh's larger body of work in suggesting that solitude is a fiction and a difficult endurance performance that modern technologies might posture as ontological precondition. The decision to begin and end the performance on July 4, or Independence Day in the United States, is provocative not only for the focus on a rhetoric of independence but also for the history of empire and settler colonialism that Independence Day marks. Of course, Hsieh and Montano depended on one another for the felicity of this performance. But, too, Betty (Montano's dog), their communities who are photographed in some of the daily photographs, and the viewer might be imagined as other collaborators.

Inscrutability as a racialized discourse creates an existential phenomenon that both produces a sense of isolating exceptionalism as well as indexes an a priori relational reading practice. I return to the sealed cassette tapes, those objects whose use value needs to be something other than the designed ability to play sound. The cassette tapes do not need to be heard, for in their objecthood they already register a collective effort—both between the artists in producing these ephemeral traces of the performance and also in giving the viewer some foothold for desire and curiosity. These performance traces of that year, tied together, voice a collective refusal to be satisfied by a product that claims totality or wholeness. The wholeness of experience—the quality of that year, the "what that year was like" that critics refer to time and again—cannot be shared. While there may be grief in its unshareability, the wholeness both exists for itself and renders attempts to engage all the more poignant.

Following Scott's and Muñoz's differing approaches to the "stuff" of experience, then, and the queer historiographic work of ephemera, I suggest that discourses of inscrutability constitute ephemera of relationality. Relationality does not follow singularity. Rather, inscrutability is a critical withholding, and being requires a "with-holding." Singularity, and romances of an isolated solitude, are traces of intimacy that already exist. As Nancy writes, "If Being is being-with, then it is, in its being-with, the 'with' that constitutes Being; the with is not simply an addition."[37] Or, as Donna Haraway writes, "To be one is always to *become with* many."[38]

The being-with or, as I am positing it, the withholding of Hsieh and Montano to me is materialized in the cassette tapes. The sealed tapes render those A sides and B sides visible, locatable, and yet utterly unknowable. There is an aside-ness and a beside-ness to *Rope Piece* that puts pressure on the prepositional becoming of being. Here the a- may resonate with the a- of asexuality and aromanticism, of being to the side without the common social frameworks that render coupledom legible. The rope conjoining Hsieh and Montano, along with the promise to be in the same room at the same time, assured the two would be aside, beside, one another. Eve Kosofsky Sedgwick writes: "*Beside* comprises a wide range of desiring, identifying, representing, repelling, paralleling, differentiating, rivaling, leaning, twisting, mimicking, withdrawing, attracting, aggressing, warping, and other relations."[39] The stakes of complicating relationality lie in insisting on an anti-assimilative method for accounting for difference without essentializing or fixing it through time and space. As Sedgwick reminds us, "A number of elements may lie alongside one another, though not an infinity of them."[40] This spatial preposition of "beside" allows multiple and simultaneous relations without erasing distinctions and contingencies. Sedgwick emphasizes that "its interest does not, however, depend on a fantasy of metonymically egalitarian or even pacific relations, as any child knows who's shared a bed with siblings."[41] Nancy elaborates on "with" as such: "'With' does not indicate the sharing of a common situation any more than the juxtaposition of pure exteriorities does (for example, a bench with a tree with a dog with a passer-by)."[42] The conjoined sameness of temporal and spatial coordinates in *Rope Piece* does not deny difference or insist on a utopic "we" without social context—to be sure, critics' consistent framing of Hsieh's and Montano's national, racial, and gender identities ensure this.

The being aside, being beside, and being with (and Haraway's theories of companion species are relevant here, too, considering the role that Betty played in the year) give "with" much of the prepositional glory. "With" covers a host of relational contingencies, both temporal and spatial. Often "with" indexes something that is everywhere and nowhere indexed. Nancy includes a telling parenthetical in his preface: "(By the way, the logic of 'with' often requires heavy-handed syntax in order to say 'being-with-one-another.' You may suffer from it as you read these pages. But perhaps it is not an accident that language does not easily lend itself to showing the 'with' as such, for it is itself the address and not what must be addressed.)"[43]

A quick definition of *preposition* reminds us that a preposition relates one word to another. This seems nicely vague to me, since it is not that a preposition relates one specific part of speech to another specific part of speech. Prepositions have been described as locators in time and space, something reinforced by Nancy: "'With' is the sharing of time-space; it is the at-the-same-time-in-the-same-place as itself, in itself, shattered."[44] A preposition is a rope, distinct from a conjunction. Beside and aside are spatially evocative. The title of Heathfield and Hsieh's monograph (*Out of Now*) suggests "out" as a central preposition—one that rings relevant to LGBTQ+ discourses of "coming out" but also brings an important confluence between the being-in-time and the possibility of being-out-of-time. Hsieh and Montano's sealed cassette tapes are a kind of dangling preposition, recorded to be heard by another—and yet foreclosed by the same bodies that speak into it: a proposition, the preposition.

Withholding as a minoritarian mode of inscrutability should not be read merely as privacy, insularity, or individualism. Particularly when withholding is attributed to Asian American performance, this mode can be enfolded into white assimilationist narratives of complacency, passivity, and model minoritarian antiblackness. It is all the more important, then, to imagine the social forms of withholding, the social performance that underlines and abets solo performance. Hsieh's endurance works are structured by rigorous documentation and disclosures as well as by the banal passing of time that cannot find external witness. *Rope Piece* is pivotal to consider the work of sociality and witness across his lifeworks. Even when we might imagine that the constant companionship of their work together would allow some measure of witness, *Rope Piece* underscores the impossibility of sharing time/space outside the present as anything other than a document that gestures to but cannot render experience consumable. The social experiment of *Rope Piece* is conjured for the two of the performers through the act of performance. It resists consolidation as a thing to know outside the performance.

In other words, *Rope Piece* is not "about" anything. "It's Not about Anything" is the title of Kandice Chuh's contribution to "Being With," the special issue of *Social Text* in honor of José Esteban Muñoz. Chuh understands Muñoz's concept of disidentification to mean "an intimate but dissident relationship to the given present."[45] To ask about the aboutness of something, including *Rope Piece*, is to miss out on encountering that thing in other ways. Chuh shows how disciplinary distinctions and developments from the Enlightenment forward have reinforced and produced a knowing modern subject, a good productive laboring academic, a racialized model minoritarian worker. As Chuh argues, it's not about anything.

Inscrutable subjectivity is not about a coherent, self-knowing subject whose political and psychic traction lies in studied and quantifiable articulation. Instead, inscrutability as an approximation of an aesthetic category through which these subjects come to the fore is near, nearer. Hsieh teaches me about this nearly as a timely affinity. Time is always about the now, about the endurance of the now through aesthetic practice. For Hsieh, life and performance are both about wasting time, of passing the time. But wasted time is not a threat when it is done "with"—it is okay that the precision of experience will be lost to history, even with rigorous documentation. Withholding honors that some things cannot be captured.

Withholding also opportunes not already knowing the result of something. By performing, one figures out what not-knowing can bring. Hsieh's comments are remarkable: "As artists we [Linda and I] made a powerful piece, but as human beings we were failed collaborators."[46] He asserts that Montano and he were "failed collaborators" in life, drawing a distinction between the terms of collaborative success in and out of the framework of art. There is something to be said about their contractual agreement not to touch during the year. Indeed, the failure of this performance was that, occasionally, Hsieh and Montano touched by accident. The endurance of their year tied together was not like any other sort of union (though juxtapositions have been posed of marriage, sadomasochist relationality, servitude, there alluding to relationalities that are legally, sexually, and economically marked) but was one that aesthetically explored the performativity of being singular-plural. Their privacy comes to feel like something else than property, as in, they are not together because they are legally recognized partners or sexual partners (for they are neither) or legally recognized family, the usual ways in which property is inherited and cosigned and consolidated. No, their reasons for sharing space and sharing life and sharing time are because of art. Social forms belong to artistic practice.

In this book, I have studied the ways in which photography, literature, video art, and performance art can hail an audience-participant precisely through aesthetics of inscrutability; but what Hsieh and Montano do with *Rope Piece* is something else, something about extending the vulnerability of a chance, though staged, encounter where the agreement for a sustained aesthetic project seems to change the feeling of vulnerability and solitude. Subjective experience takes on different possibility. Particularities are not dissolved. These social differences are a deliberate component of the piece. One's view emerges in juxtaposition with another's, whose will may conflict with your own.

As Hsieh has said, he had to "struggle for the value of [his] view."[47] This is an interesting way to put it since the value of one's view (and what constitutes a singular view) is the stuff of aesthetic judgment. The question of aesthetic judgment is in the prospect of there being something wholly subjective without dependence on objective verification. The ability for aesthetic subjectivity, then, depends on having taste and asserting one's view as universally held. Inscrutability upsets this subjective constitution since its terms of aesthetic judgment (this thing is inscrutable!) concede a knowing tasteful subject. As

Sianne Ngai writes in *Our Aesthetic Categories*, an aesthetic "call[s] forth not only specific subjective capacities for feeling and acting but also specific ways of relating to other subjects and the larger social arrangements these ways of relating presuppose. In doing so, they are compelling reminders of the general fact of social difference and conflict underlying the entire system of aesthetic judgment or taste."[48]

The fact that Hsieh and Montano do not elaborate on what their experience was during that year and in the years following, for that matter, gestures to the aesthetic ambiguity of *Rope Piece*. There is no one who has the most official perspective on the piece, not even an agreed-upon collaborative statement to stand by. The "we" of the artist statement is a utopic pronoun. The piece itself, then, is about the incommensurability of their two views, even as they dedicate the year to sharing a view, side by side. This proximity without touching speaks to a mindfulness against assimilation or the liberal impulse to homogenize experience. The rope does not make them one, does not link their bodily systems even as it informs their movements. At the same time, differing views emerge and endure in relation.

Performances of Inscrutability

Hsieh's work can be collectively framed by the concept of inscrutability and his alien tactics. I turn to *Rope Piece* because it makes glimpsable the social ties we hold, temporary though they may be. At the same time as the fact of the rope and the photographs index the unthinkable intimacy of Hsieh and Montano in that one year, the cassette tapes archive the unknowability of that experience. The significance of recognizing its being is incalculable, just as the possibility of its being contained or represented is not one. Being is never exactly being alone; it is always a withholding.

Hsieh is clear about some things. For one, Hsieh insists that performance is the proper medium of his work. He has said: "My work is performance. I created one kind of art form, lived within [it] and passed time: the process of passing time itself is the artwork. There are similarities between the ways I document the performances and the ways conceptual artists document the concepts, but for me documentation is only a trace of the work."[49] Strikingly, he says, "Time is beyond my understanding; I just pass time."[50]

Time, then, is the inscrutable other for Hsieh's work. Some measurements of time contain it, thus the duration of one year. In *Mousse Magazine*, Hsieh is quoted: "One year is the basic unit of how we count time. It takes the earth a year to move around the sun. Three years, four years, is something else.

It is about being human, how we explain time, how we measure our existence."[51] As Heathfield notes, "Duration is constituted here by the giving over of one's time to the time of another. Habituation remains incomplete. Each cannot choose the time of their agency since it is dependent on the other's time. They live therefore in a time frequented by the phenomena of waiting and deferral. A year of two lives is spent in a time attendant to an Other time."[52] Being-with, then, is always about attending to time and about enduring the time of another. Enduring another's time is not about translating it or repurposing it or consuming it. It is about holding it as something one is in relation to. This shared endurance, where *shared* does not suggest an equivalence of experience, cannot be encapsulated. A plural time-being is in the domain not of history, then, but of performance. The ontology of performance is not necessarily in its disappearance, as Peggy Phelan famously asserts, but in its withholding, in its singular and plural being inescapably in time. This withholding is also the utopian hail in inscrutability, where the sounds forever silenced in *Rope Piece*'s audiotapes are gesturing not to a threat but to a hopeful curiosity that the being-with signaled; there is an intimacy beyond present understanding. Understanding does not change the fact of its existence.

In Immanuel Kant's sublime, the overpowering feeling of being at the edge of one's senses is triggered by the figure of a recluse on some island unknown to the rest of the world. This island may be unknown to the rest of the world, as written from the perspective of an outsider, but the person who lives on it knows that world. And the island is not unknown to the rest of the world because an outsider is writing about it, imagining it, fantasizing about it. This primary imaginary reckoning is everything to imagining inscrutability otherwise. Kant seems just as fascinated by this singularity and solitude; it is a towering feeling that could undo you. But it is also that undoing that is pivotal, transformational; it is a brink that Asian racialization confronts you with because that coming to subjectivity is a confrontation with discourses of homogeneity and assimilation. Tehching Hsieh and Linda Montano help me realize that those fictions of homogeneity really are covering an anxiety about the inscrutable social form that Asianness occasions and calls into being. Indeed, as *Rope Piece* shows, there is an open-endedness to the social splendor possible—and no one can ever know all about it.

The charge of withholding information, whether trivial or significant, is often pinned to performances of inscrutability studied throughout this book. A national fear and suspicion toward the silent, the nonvisible, the unreliable, the flat and flexible, and the distant pervades US and Western discourses of modern subjectivity and nation building. But the surface relations of Asian American sociality, as these chapters show, reveal the significant role that Asiatic racialization has played in the long and tenuous American century, where the variously deployed erasure of Asian study has also occasioned more fugitive forms of being, becoming, and writing. By focusing on some details over others, Tehching Hsieh's meticulously documented performance works critique a fetish of material mastery and, instead, expose the endemic inscrutability of life's lived complexity as something that cannot be contained or communicated through language.

I close this book with a meditation on withholding as a different orientation to Asiatic inscrutability to show the ethical and political dimensions of surface relations. Asian racialization in the United States has historically held, and continues in our contemporary world to hold, a space for mutable figures of foreign threat, in the ways that long-standing resource wars, military occupations, exploitative labor-based immigration policies, and representative erasure have become normalized as though the closure or compartmentalization of the Asian other demands these violent practices and ideologies. In turn, Asian subjects are constructed with the function of holding a lot that has little public discourse.

Asian Americans and Asian diasporic subjects, this book suggests, are configured, made socially legible, like a sexual closet, ripe with sexual deviance and necessarily relegated to the periphery while tasked with the storage of what often does not see the light of public consciousness, of what cannot be parted with but equally cannot be shown. Until scholars in gender, race, ethnicity, and American studies grapple with the cultures and histories of Asianness in the United States, Asian Americans will continue to live with this valence of shame and psychic burden of not feeling seen. My contention in this book is not to do away with the shame but to offer it curiosity, space, and time. Instead, I hope to show—particularly for the sake of readers who come into being as Asian Americans and have no choice but to contend with its racializing effects—how surface aesthetics do not only foreclose but also expand possibilities of relationality. As I have shown in these chapters of permissive socialities of Asian inscrutability, actively engaging surface aesthetics need not be merely isolating and depressing. Performing inscrutably may in fact open out other modes and occasion other relationalities that may yet escape language but that exist and create lifeworlds and histories in excess of their identification.

INTRODUCTION

My heartfelt thanks to Courtney Berger and J de Leon for instrumental feedback on this introduction.

1 As Khan writes, "I don't remember a day when I wasn't waiting to take shape, to have a shape that was legible and independent with meaning." Khan, "Acoustic Sound Blanket."

2 Khan, *Acoustic Sound Blankets*, 2018; Khan, *Acoustic Sound Blankets*, 2017.

3 *Oxford English Dictionary*, s.v. "inscrutable, adj. and n.," accessed March 14, 2016, http://www.oed.com.

4 When I use the phrase *racial performativity*, I refer to something that is less about the conscious and omnipotent performance of race and more consistent with the discourse that José Esteban Muñoz describes as the playful "doing" otherwise by racial and sexual minoritarian subjects. I think with Karen Shimakawa's theory of mimetic abjection in Asian American performance and the "insubordinate playfulness" that can arise from provisionally adopting racial tropes. See Muñoz, "Feeling Brown, Feeling Down"; and Shimakawa, *National Abjection*, 104.

5 For instance, the origins of the word *Asia* refer to "east" and "rising," thereby inscribing the word with a geopolitical and spatial orientation. Jack Kuo Wei Tchen shows, T-O maps from 1581 visualize India as the eastern extreme of the Asian landmass, later extended by China as the Far East. Tchen and Yeats, *Yellow Peril!*, 37–48. The reader might think of contemporary idioms of China or Japan as "on the other side of the world," reproducing a visual and spatial understanding of Asian opposition and Euro-American centrality. "Where are you *really* from?" is a quotidian speech act through which Asian American people face this imaginary of being at a perpetual remove.

6 Chow, "How (the) Inscrutable Chinese Led to Globalized Theory," 70. Of course, the coproduction of modern femininity as inscrutable in the age of empire is no coincidence. As Rebecca Schneider writes of Woman, "Even as ['she'] is ubiquitously given to be seen, she simultaneously signifies a flirtatious impossibility of access, a paradoxical 'reality' only of dream, of shadow, always beyond reach, always already lost" (*The Explicit Body in Performance*, 6). Elizabeth Grosz offers, "Woman (upper case and in the singular) remains philosophy's eternal enigma, its mysterious and inscrutable object—this may be a product of the rather mysterious and highly restrained and contained status of the body in

general, and of women's bodies in particular, in the construction of philosophy as a mode of knowledge" (*Volatile Bodies*, 4–5).

7 Chen, *Animacies*.

8 Mae Ngai, *Impossible Subjects*, 2.

9 Robert Chang writes, "Because the broader Asiatic category had yet to come fully into existence, the attribution of foreignness on the racialized Chinese body was extended piecemeal to other Asian groups" ("The Invention of Asian Americans," 954).

10 Shimakawa, *National Abjection*, 15–17.

11 "It's a Modern China That Threatens a Row."

12 Tchen and Yeats describe the contemporaneous, yellow perilist depiction of Fu Manchu (1913) as "bizarre, 'queer,' non-heteronormative" (*Yellow Peril!*, 5). See also Chen's writing on Fu Manchu in *Animacies*.

13 Further, this article's use of the word *powwow* betrays the haunted foundations of the US nation through settler colonialist violence, since this imagined meeting of nations does not name the Indigenous stewards of the land except through appropriation of a word with Narragansett and Massachusett origins.

14 Hong, "The Slur I Never Expected to Hear in 2020."

15 In the time of a global pandemic and necessary face masking, we may consider inscrutability and Asian racial form in the matrix of face covering, inscrutable surfacing, and yellow peril. While COVID-19 and face mask discourse enhanced centuries-old yellow perilism in the United States, once more casting Asian bodies as suspicious and toxic contagion, prominent elected officials refused to promote, let alone mandate, the wearing of face masks despite the fact that it soon became globally recognized as necessary in slowing the transmission of the respiratory disease. In this sense, the historic and contemporary casting of Chinese (and Asians more broadly, as evidenced by panethnic anti-Asian hostilities) as inscrutable threat, and the association of face masks with Chinese and East Asians, informed public health policies that were slow to announce the vitality of face mask use. See Rogin and Nawaz, "'We Have Been through This Before'"; and "Anti-Chinese Rhetoric Tied to Racism against Asian Americans." Rather than address these histories of bias against Chinese and Asian people, Donald Trump issued a presidential proclamation on January 31, 2020, to restrict (unsuccessfully) travel to the United States from China, salting historic wounds when boasting, "We're the ones that kept China out of here." See Eder et al., "430,000 People Have Traveled from China to U.S. since Coronavirus Surfaced."

16 Chow's critique of Derrida's Orientalist hallucination of China as the basis of deconstruction is but one instance of the productive construction of Asian inscrutability for contemporary aesthetic theory. Performative readings of Asian inscrutability contribute to discussions of embodiment, liveness, performativity, and temporality constitutive of performance studies, in ways that seldom acknowledge the relevance of Asian aesthetic form and racialization. For instance, while Brechtian alienation effect is canonized in modern performance

history, the A-effect is often celebrated as an innovative theater device without crediting the Peking Opera performer Mei Lanfang or acknowledging Bertolt Brecht's *relation* to Mei as an alienated viewer. See Kingston, *Tripmaster Monkey*. Special thanks to Colleen Lye for advising my undergraduate English honors thesis on Chinese American performances of alienation.

17 Chow, "How (the) Inscrutable Chinese Led to Globalized Theory," 71.

18 Chow asks whether "simplifying and falsifying the other is not in fact fundamental, indeed indispensable, to the operations of cross-cultural, cross-ethnic representation" ("How (the) Inscrutable Chinese Led to Globalized Theory," 74). Chow argues that the performative reading of Chinese inscrutability occasions globalized critical thought.

19 Chow, "How (the) Inscrutable Chinese Led to Globalized Theory," 72.

20 Amin, Musser, and Pérez, "Queer Form," 235.

21 H. M. Nguyen, "Elegy for the First," in *Not Here*, 17.

22 Much of Asian American history, including wartime Japanese American incarceration and queer desire, can be described as forcefully closeted in US American history. The closeting of Asian American history, culture, and experience is discursively produced through many scales, such as through euphemisms of the Forgotten War or the Cold War. Long T. Bui suggests that the "shadow of exclusion can be interpreted as a kind of metaphorical or literary closet" for Chinese Americans (Bui, "Breaking into the Closet," 133). Indeed, we may consider both the model minority and perpetual foreigner tropes as Asian forms of the closet, as sealed exteriority with unknown interiority. See Sedgwick, *Epistemology of the Closet*. Notably, Sedgwick's literary period is of the late nineteenth and early twentieth centuries, a time of rapid movement in practices of racialization, migration, and empire, including Asian immigration. Yet the reader may notice, as Siobhan B. Somerville does, "the oscillating presence and absence of race" in Sedgwick's analysis ("Feminism, Queer Theory, and the Racial Closet," 198). Citing Sedgwick's example of Esther coming out as Jewish, Somerville writes, "The shimmering function of race in the text, that now-you-see-it-now-you-don't quality, resembles, of course, the very mechanisms of the closet that Sedgwick so powerfully delineates in the book" (198).

23 I think here of Michel Foucault's formulation of *ars erotica* in the foundational first volume of *The History of Sexuality* and Jasbir Puar's critique of it in *Terrorist Assemblages*.

24 Shin, "The Asian American Closet." Shin notes that race, unlike sexuality, cannot be so easily hidden but that Asian Americans may "cover" or minimize markers of ethnic or racial foreignness. Thinking through the protective function of the closet, Shin suggests that the closet takes on a different use for "modern minority groups": "The closet works, not to assist assimilation, but to hinder it, by hiding ethnic practices so that outsider majority group members cannot observe, and by observing, learn to imitate, in misappropriative or denigrating ways" (26). In some ways, *Surface Relations*'s formulation of inscrutability can be understood along Shin's description of a protective closet.

However, the inscrutable closet is not necessarily the utopic "space of comfort, freedom and self-expression" that Shin describes (29). The inscrutable closet can be a crowded stage of negative affect, shot through with shame, loneliness, exhaustion, and intergenerational trauma.

25 Here we may recall Dana Y. Takagi's essay "Maiden Voyage," and her critique that "the field of Asian American Studies is mostly ignorant about the multiple ways that gay identities are often hidden or invisible within Asian American communities. But the irony is that the more we know, the less we know about the ways of knowing" (2).

26 Kim Lee, "Staying In."

27 Kirp, "Diversity Hypocrisy."

28 Eng and Han, "A Dialogue on Racial Melancholia," 353. My thanks to Ann Pellegrini for her graduate seminar on Freud, in which I first read this text and appreciated the role of racial difference in psychoanalytic theory.

29 Quoted in Eng and Han, "A Dialogue on Racial Melancholia," 345.

30 Eng and Han, "A Dialogue on Racial Melancholia," 348. Avery Gordon's writings on haunting as the performance of the ghost in modernization may be helpful here, to remind us that even when we do not know what exactly brings forth the ghost, the ghost has effects, and to be attuned to them is to come to a responsibility, as in an ability to respond. See Gordon, *Ghostly Matters*.

31 Cheng, *The Melancholy of Race*, 17.

32 Ong, *Neoliberalism as Exception*.

33 As Eng and Han observe, for many of Han's gay Asian immigrant patients who struggle in the United States, they often do not consider the toll that racism takes on their lives in a neoliberal post-racial fantasy. Rather, they consider the difficulties of migration, distance from loved ones, and the negotiation of their sexualities.

34 I think here of Ann Pellegrini's offering of psychoanalysis, at its best, as "will to un-know, un-do, and be un-done, practices of un-knowing and un-doing in which no one is or need be the master once and for all" ("Queer Structures of Religious Feeling," 244).

35 I hope this book's ideas on Asian inscrutability will be useful to cross-disciplinary readers as an expansive analytic for racial aesthetics. In *Yellow Peril!*, Tchen and Yeats show how the longer histories of xenophobia, Islamophobia, antisemitism, yellow perilism, and Orientalism must be thought together in the construction of, variously, the Orient, the East, and Asia. I invite readers to make use of these theories of inscrutability when analyzing other signifiers of the East or the Orient.

36 Chuh, *Imagine Otherwise*. Chuh's phrasing of "internal contradiction" might also remind the reader of Sedgwick's language of "internal incoherence and mutual contradiction" to describe sexual common sense (*Epistemology of the Closet*, 1).

37 C. J. Kim, "The Racial Triangulation of Asian Americans."

38 For more on contingency and Asian American feminist relationality, see Huang and Kim Lee, "Performances of Contingency."

39 Collective spaces that center the psychic and emotional well-being of Asian Americans exist. Here we may index the proliferation of resources and workshops for Asian American communities, whether through community organizations like the Asian American Resource Center or The Cosmos or individuals like Leah Lakshmi Piepzna-Samarasinha and Yumi Sukigawa, or look to the meditation and healing practices of various artists, like those featured in the Smithsonian Asian Pacific American Center's online exhibition *Care Package*. These collective spaces are remarkable for addressing Asian American internal life, including for Asian American women, queers, and trans people.

40 Simpson, *Mohawk Interruptus*, 113.

41 Sedgwick, *Touching Feeling*, 149.

42 Best and Marcus, "Surface Reading."

43 Here we may recall Chow's earlier reading of Derrida's alienation at Chinese script and note how subsequent generations of Asian Americans may feel similarly estranged from Asian scripts and "mother tongues." For Eng and Han, this intimate relationship to one's alienation from a sense of the mother, from a sense of endemic belonging, structures Asian American formation. Recall that Eng and Han initially wrote "A Dialogue on Racial Melancholia" with not only second-generation immigrants in mind but also sexual minorities.

44 Shimakawa, *National Abjection*, 125.

45 Amin, Musser, and Pérez, "Queer Form," 238.

46 Muñoz, *Disidentifications*, 188.

47 Here, I refer to the released reports of Harvard College admissions, noting the "negative personality" scores of Asian American applicants. See chapter 5 for more.

48 I think here of and am indebted to the participants of two conference collaborations: the American Studies Association Visual Culture Caucus session, organized by Kyle Frisina, Vivian L. Huang, Christina León, Tina Post, and Sarah Stefana Smith, titled "Visualizing In/Emergence: Race, Aesthetics and the Ethics of Obfuscation," Atlanta, GA, November 2018; and a seminar at the annual Association for the Study of the Arts of the Present (ASAP) meeting called "Surface Aesthetics, Eroticism, and Racial Abstraction in Neofascist Times," organized by Alex Pittman, Amber Jamilla Musser, Pablo Assumpção Barros Costa, and Vivian L. Huang, College Park, MD, October 2019.

49 Shimakawa, *National Abjection*; Gopinath, *Impossible Desires*; Gopinath, *Unruly Visions*; King, *Lost in Translation*; Tongson, *Relocations*.

50 León, "Forms of Opacity," 378.

51 See Post, "Williams, Walker, and Shine"; Smith, "Surface Play"; and Daniher, "Yella Gal."

52 Gordon, *Ghostly Matters*; Chuh, *Imagine Otherwise*.

53 For instance, see Combahee River Collective, "Combahee River Collective Statement"; Lorde, *Sister Outsider*; Woo, "Letter to Ma"; and Anzaldúa, *Borderlands / La Frontera*.

54 Mengesha and Padmanabhan, "Introduction to *Performing Refusal / Refusal to Perform*," 7.

55 Yamada, "Invisibility Is an Unnatural Disaster"; Roshanravan, "Weaponizing Our (In)Visibility."

56 Sedgwick, *Touching Feeling*, 133–36.

57 For more on queer-of-color critique and speculation, see Takemoto, "Looking for Jiro Onuma"; and Nyong'o, *Afro-Fabulations*.

58 Indeed, one could write a book about how Asian inscrutability has been used to leverage some Asian Americans into positions of power, or to leverage certain optics of racial diversity to reinforce white-dominant institutions.

1. INVISIBILITY AND THE VANISHING POINT OF ASIAN/AMERICAN VISUALITY

1 Palumbo-Liu, *Asian/American*, 4; Yamada, "Invisibility Is an Unnatural Disaster," 32; Waxman, "A 'History of Exclusion.'"

2 During my television deep dive during the coronavirus pandemic, it became obvious how formulaic the murder or death of an East Asian woman character still is in moving along the show's plot. For example, see the HBO reboot of *Perry Mason*, Amazon's *The Wilds*, and Peacock's *Girls5eva*.

3 For more about the Orientalist obsession with the self-sacrificing Asian woman as an aesthetic convention that must be identified in order to be problematized, see Huang, "'What Shall We Do?'"; and Huang, "*Endlings* by Celine Song (Review)."

4 See, for instance, Augsberger et al., "Culturally Related Risk Factors of Suicidal Ideation." I examine Asian gender and self-harm in this book's third chapter, on skin surfacing, impenetrability, and trans figuration.

5 "Whether or not they were actually sex workers or self-identified under that label, we know that as massage workers, they were subjected to sexualized violence stemming from the hatred of sex workers, Asian women, working class people, and immigrants" (Red Canary Song, "Red Canary Song Response to Shootings").

6 Mitra, Kang, and Clutario, "It's Time to Reckon with the History of Asian Women in America."

7 Red Canary Song, "Red Canary Song Response to Shootings," 2.

8 D. Rodríguez, "The Asian Exception and the Scramble for Legibility."

9 Consider how the rhetoric of anti-Asian hate became a point of contention within Asian American intellectual and activist circles after Atlanta. As the hashtag #StopAAPIHate circulated and media coverage of anti-Asian racism increased, many scholars advocated for a move away from the language of hate and toward white supremacy, systemic racism, and US militarism. As Dylan

Rodríguez, Jason Wu and James McMaster, and others write, the rhetoric of hate—while viable for public visibility—individuates responsibility and misconstrues white nationalist violence as exceptional to American public life. See Wu and McMaster, "Hate Crime Laws Are Not the Answer." Abolitionist activists were quick to get ahead of the rhetoric of "hate crime" and its concomitant carcerality, rallying Black feminist, queer, and trans political calls to defund the police and refuse enhanced state surveillance of communities of color in particular. As Seulghee Lee submits, anti-Asian racism must be understood as a "direct and singular *expression* of anti-Blackness" and addressed as such ("When Is Asian American Life Grievable?").

10 See Y. Kim, "Respecting the Victims in the Atlanta Spa Shootings."

11 It is worth naming, too—as Ocean Vuong did in his first speaking event after the shooting—the violent economy of attention that renders "race" nationally relevant, and one could say hypervisible, only in proximity to individuated graphic violence and minority tragedy. See Vuong, "Reading and Conversation with Ocean Vuong." For more on the limits of recognition, see Coulthard, *Red Skin, White Masks*.

12 Y. J. Lee, *Songs of the Dragon Flying to Heaven*, 63.

13 Y. J. Lee, *Songs of the Dragon Flying to Heaven*, 64.

14 Young Jean Lee's Theater Company Archive, "Songs of the Dragons Flying to Heaven (2006)."

15 Shimakawa, *National Abjection*, 127.

16 Shimakawa, *National Abjection*, 128. For her work on *Songs of the Dragon*, see Shimakawa, "Young Jean Lee's Ugly Feelings about Race and Gender."

17 The self-sacrifice of the Oriental woman has functioned almost like the flip-side of what Leslie Bow has theorized as Asian American female sexuality's relationship to betrayal, providing her fidelity to the white soldier male hero and thereby reproducing a discursive value system where allegiance to white imperialist nationalism remains protected and asserted as the good. See Bow, *Betrayal and Other Acts of Subversion*.

18 See Jasbir Puar's *Terrorist Assemblages* for her work on the suicide bomber as a queer and Orientalized figure in this sense of perverse self-shattering.

19 Manalansan, "The 'Stuff' of Archives," 103.

20 See, for instance, Yu, "Has Asian American Studies Failed?"

21 Muñoz, "Cruising the Toilet: LeRoi Jones / Amiri Baraka, Radical Black Traditions, and Queer Futurity," in *Cruising Utopia*, 83–96.

22 Muñoz, "Cruising the Toilet," 29.

23 Vuong, "Someday I'll Love Ocean Vuong," 82.

24 Vuong, "Someday I'll Love Ocean Vuong," 82.

25 Eng and Han, "A Dialogue on Racial Melancholia," 348.

26 I think here of Lynn Fujiwara and Shireen Roshanravan's decision to use "Asian American" in their introduction to *Asian American Feminisms and Women of Color Politics* as not holding Asian subjects as exceptional to US accountability.

27 Chuh, *Imagine Otherwise*, 9.

28 Gopinath, *Impossible Desires*, 4.

29 Campt, "Black Visuality and the Practice of Refusal," 80.

30 Glissant, *Poetics of Relation*, 111–20, 189–94; León, "Forms of Opacity," 378.

31 León, "Forms of Opacity," 378.

32 Harper, *Abstractionist Aesthetics*.

33 Harper, *Abstractionist Aesthetics*, 2. As Harper shows, the normalization of abstract aesthetics has created a national image vocabulary where highly stylized visual figures, such as Aunt Jemima and Dragon Lady, are integrated and accepted as realistic images.

34 Smith, "Surface Play," 48.

35 Shimizu, *The Hypersexuality of Race*, 31.

36 Uyehara, "Hello (Sex) Kitty," 401.

37 Uyehara, "Hello (Sex) Kitty," 401.

38 Uyehara, "Hello (Sex) Kitty," 401.

39 Uyehara, "Hello (Sex) Kitty," 402.

40 Uyehara, "Hello (Sex) Kitty," 402.

41 Uyehara, "Hello (Sex) Kitty," 402–3.

42 However, come to think of it, mapping out the anatomy of the vulva is a viable strategy in Diana Oh's performance of *Clairvoyance* in April 2019, part of their yearlong residence at the American Repertory Theater in Cambridge, Massachusetts.

43 Uyehara, "Hello (Sex) Kitty," 403.

44 See Huang, "Whither Asian American Lesbian Feminist Thought?"

45 Kimsooja, *Archive of Mind*.

46 The gallery space was connected to an exhibition on Chinese art, with glass double doors allowing a visual preview of the *Double Happiness* exhibition next door. Billed as an art museum for American and Asian art, the Peabody is also known for its architectural installation of Yu Tang's "The Chinese House." In this sense, the inclusion of Kimsooja's installation is partly justified by her biography as a Korean artist; though Kimsooja's Koreanness is invoked in the wall text introducing the exhibition, however, there is no phenotypic or aesthetic story offered in the exhibition space. The role of race and nationality, then, is not centered in the show as relevant. And, in a sense, one could argue that the lack of clear political or social connection in the exhibition renders it unprovocative or a gallery one could make a quick visit to. As the docent mentioned to me, many visitors step into the gallery space, take a look around, perhaps quickly roll a ball, and then soon after leave the space.

47 Peabody Essex Museum, "PEM Invites Visitors to Participate in a Meditative Sculptural Installation."

48 The interpretive scale of the point reminds me, too, of adrienne maree brown's *Emergent Strategy* and the emphasis on reiterative forms that can be scaled up and multiplied but also exist individually, such as a fern.

49 Smith, "Surface Play," 53.

50 "Is Dot Painting the Remnant of Pointillism?"

51 Snow, "Migration Greeting Card Set."

52 Kim, *The Racial Mundane*; Lowe, *Immigrant Acts*.

2. SILENCE AND PARASITIC HOSPITALITY IN THE WORKS OF YOKO ONO, LAUREL NAKADATE, AND EMMA SULKOWICZ

Special thanks to Karen Shimakawa for her mentorship and feedback on early versions of this chapter. Thanks also to J de Leon; Iván Ramos, Leon Hilton, and the Avant-Gardes, Otherwise working group at the American Society for Theatre Research (ASTR) 2014 conference; Tina Post and the Performance Studies Working Group at Yale; Laurel Nakadate and Leslie Tonkonow Artworks + Projects; Emma Sulkowicz; members of the Unforming Feeling stream at the American Comparative Literature Association (ACLA) 2016 meeting; the editing services of Anitra Grisales and support from the Gaius Charles Bolin Fellowship from Williams College; Susanne Fuchs; E. Hella Tsaconas, Olivia Michiko Gagnon, the peer reviewers, and the board of *Women and Performance* for publishing the article version of this chapter.

1 Ono, *Grapefruit*. The epigraph to this section is from Sean Day-Lewis, "Music," *Daily Telegraph and Morning Post*, September 29, 1966, 80; quoted in Bryan-Wilson, "Remembering Yoko Ono's *Cut Piece*," 120.

2 Bryan-Wilson, "Remembering Yoko Ono's *Cut Piece*," 103; Halberstam, *The Queer Art of Failure*, 123–45.

3 Here I allude to the generative discourse around relational aesthetics and participatory art, particularly Claire Bishop's formulation of "relational antagonism" following Nicolas Bourriaud's *Relational Aesthetics*. See Bishop, "Antagonism and Relational Aesthetics."

4 Munroe, YES *Yoko Ono*, 28.

5 Munroe, YES *Yoko Ono*, 28.

6 Stiles, "Being Undyed," 148.

7 Bryan-Wilson, "Remembering Yoko Ono's *Cut Piece*," 119.

8 Bishop, "Antagonism and Relational Aesthetics," 79.

9 Derrida and Dufourmantelle, *Of Hospitality*, 77.

10 Derrida and Dufourmantelle, *Of Hospitality*, 149.

11 Hamington, *Feminism and Hospitality*, xv.

12 Sander-Staudt, "Su Casa es Mi Casa?," 27.

13 For more on the first Chinese and Japanese immigrants to the United States, as well as early spectacular performances of Asian femininity under the genre of freak show, see Kang, *Compositional Subjects*. For more on Asian female labor in nineteenth-century US immigration, see Sonia Shah's introduction to *Dragon Ladies*, where she notes that "Asian women shouldered much of the cost of subsidizing Asian men's labor" (xv), as well as Bonacich and Cheng, *Labor Immigration under Capitalism*, 5–34.

14 Sander-Staudt, "Su Casa es Mi Casa?," 26.

15 Gopinath, *Impossible Desires*, 6.

16 Shimizu, *The Hypersexuality of Race*; H. T. Nguyen, *A View from the Bottom*.

17 Concannon, "Yoko Ono's *Cut Piece*," 89.

18 Hamington, *Feminism and Hospitality*, xv.

19 I thank Karen Shimakawa for helping me articulate this idea on being held hostage to racializing discourses.

20 Shimakawa, *National Abjection*, 17.

21 *Into Performance*, Midori Yoshimoto's comparative historical study of Japanese female artists in New York, critiques this bias and allows for multiple and heterogeneous Japanese/American femininities that recall Shimakawa's comparative analysis of female characters in Velina Hasu Houston's play *Tea*.

22 Yoshimoto, *Into Performance*, 4.

23 Bryan-Wilson, "Remembering Yoko Ono's *Cut Piece*," 121.

24 Gordon, *Ghostly Matters*; Chuh, *Imagine Otherwise*.

25 See Freeman, *Time Binds*; J. M. Rodríguez, *Sexual Futures, Queer Gestures, and Other Latina Longings*; and brown, *Pleasure Activism*.

26 Indrisek, "Laurel Nakadate."

27 Siegel, "The Provocateur."

28 Kastner, "A Provocateur Who Talks to Strangers."

29 Schehr, preface to *The Parasite*, vii.

30 Serres, *The Parasite*, 3.

31 Serres, *The Parasite*, 3.

32 Serres, *The Parasite*, 64.

33 Serres, *The Parasite*, 64.

34 Serres, *The Parasite*, 24.

35 Fisher, "We Are Parasites," 5.

36 Fisher, "We Are Parasites," 5.

37 Fisher, "Manic Impositions," 223.

38 Fisher, "Manic Impositions," 223.

39 Fisher, "We Are Parasites," 4.

40 Bow, *Betrayal and Other Acts of Subversion*, 37–69.

41 Fleissig, "Laurel Nakadate's 'Only the Lonely' Opens at PS1"; Johnson, "A Burgeoning Film Career Built on Random Encounters"; Schwarting, "You Dirty, Worthless Slut."

42 Saltz, "Whatever Laurel Wants"; Hamilton, "Laurel Nakadate."

43 Hamilton, "Laurel Nakadate."

44 Indrisek, "Laurel Nakadate." We may note how Nakadate echoes the words of Elena Tajima Creef when she writes, "In spite of the current tendency to celebrate and even romanticize multiculturalism, there is a genuine dilemma of where one may place a hybrid body that does not fit into any one simple place on a white American map" (Creef, *Imaging Japanese America*, 177).

45 Scholarship in Asian American and critical mixed-race studies informs my thinking here of racialized performances of inscrutability, in particular Jennifer Ann Ho's *Racial Ambiguity in Asian American Culture* and Colleen Kim

Daniher's "Performing the Racial Ambiguity Act." See also Kina and Dariotis, *War Baby / Love Child*, which includes Nakadate's work.

46 Fisher, "We Are Parasites," 4.

47 I think here of the vital work of Christina León, Iván Ramos, Hentyle Yapp, Katie Brewer Ball, Ren Ellis Neyra, Roy Pérez, and Summer Kim Lee at the panels on racialized negativity at the annual meeting of the American Studies Association in 2015. I am inspired by León's formulation of opacity as "an aesthetic and ethico-political response to the demands for transparency" within Latina/o studies ("Forms of Opacity," 378). Certainly I am indebted to the work of many scholars, including Gayatri Gopinath's theory of impossibility and queer female diasporic subjectivity (*Impossible Desires*), and Martin Manalansan's formulation of disaffection as a temporary affective mode of survival ("Servicing the World").

48 Serres, *The Parasite*, 79.

49 Serres, *The Parasite*, 238.

50 Derrida and Dufourmantelle, *Of Hospitality*, 20.

51 For more on racial aesthetics of silence, see Quashie, *The Sovereignty of Quiet*; and Owen, "Still Nothing," which elegantly theorize quiet and silence as expressive modes of critical resistance in Black culture. My thoughts on silence engage, too, with Mari Ruti's concluding dialogue with Jordan Mulder in *The Ethics of Opting Out*, and "the role that silence plays in the fetishistic production of the exotic other who, by virtue of its unwillingness (or incapacity) to participate in the vocal world of neoliberal agency, functions both as an object of desire and as a site of tremendous anxiety for the urban Western subject" (220).

52 S. Ngai, *Our Aesthetic Categories*, 112–13.

53 S. Ngai, *Our Aesthetic Categories*, 171.

54 Derrida and Dufourmantelle, *Of Hospitality*, 2.

55 Derrida and Dufourmantelle, *Of Hospitality*, 2.

56 Davis, "Columbia Student's Striking Mattress Performance."

57 Sulkowicz, "Rules of Engagement."

58 Van Syckle, "The Columbia Student Carrying a Mattress Everywhere."

59 Duan, "Going from Class to Class."

60 Duan, "Going from Class to Class."

61 Small, "Queer Identity in the MeToo Movement."

62 Fusco, "The Other History of Intercultural Performance."

3. IM/PENETRABILITY, TRANS FIGURATION, AND UNRELIABLE SURFACING

I thank J de Leon for their editorial feedback that revitalized this chapter; Ianna Hawkins Owen, Marshall Green, Christophe Koné, and Feng-Mei Heberer for feedback on early chapter drafts; Iyko Day and the Five Colleges Consortium for Asian/Pacific/American Studies for workshopping an initial draft of this chapter in spring 2018; Cameron Awkward-Rich, Elias D. Krell, Kyla Wazana Tompkins, Treva Ellison, and Ren-yo Hwang for the opportunity to workshop this chapter at the Alliance to Advance Liberal Arts Colleges (AALAC) Queer and Trans of Color Critique retreat; and the students in my Williams College course Feeling Queer and Asian for discussing these books with me.

1 Note Alice O'Grady's use of "edgeplay" in a performance context to consider risk and vulnerability ("Introduction"), which scaffolds performance risks within twenty-first-century structures of risk, fear, and precarity. While sociopolitical contexts are referenced in general, my chapter focuses on Asian diasporic trans and queer people to name forms of precarity that may go unnoticed.

2 Hayward, "More Lessons from a Starfish," 72. My thanks to Cameron Awkward-Rich for bringing this text to my attention.

3 See Morris and Galupo, "'Attempting to Dull the Dysphoria.'"

4 Thom, *Fierce Femmes and Notorious Liars*, 187. Thom does not name the protagonist (though the character's pronoun is "she"), so I will simply refer to the character as "the protagonist" in this chapter.

5 Thom, *Fierce Femmes and Notorious Liars*, 96.

6 Thom, *Fierce Femmes and Notorious Liars*, 187. Note how Thom's writing disidentifies with legal language for truth as something that is a discrete entity and timeless in referencing oath language of "the truth, the whole truth, nothing but the truth," something we will circle back to at this chapter's end.

7 Xiang, "Transdualism," 436.

8 *Oxford English Dictionary*, s.v. "impenetrable, *adj.*," accessed April 2018, http:// www.oed.com.

9 Stryker, "(De)Subjugated Knowledges," 9.

10 Chen, *Animacies*, 121.

11 See Huang, "Whither Asian American Lesbian Feminist Thought?," for my more recent thoughts on these histories and their bearing on Asian American studies.

12 McMillan, "Introduction," 2.

13 Ahmed and Stacey, *Thinking through the Skin*, 1.

14 Ahmed, *The Cultural Politics of Emotion*, 145.

15 Stephens, *Skin Acts*, 2.

16 Stephens, *Skin Acts*, 14.

17 Best and Marcus, "Surface Reading."

18 Truong, *The Book of Salt*, 32.

19 Stephens, *Skin Acts*, 8.

20 See, for instance, Spillers, "Mama's Baby, Papa's Maybe"; and Snorton, *Black on Both Sides*.

21 Ahmed and Stacey, *Thinking through the Skin*, 2.

22 Truong, *The Book of Salt*, 152.

23 Truong, *The Book of Salt*, 142.

24 Truong, *The Book of Salt*, 143.

25 Eng, *Racial Castration*, 150.

26 Fung, "Looking for My Penis."
27 Xiang, "Transdualism," 433.
28 Cheung, "The Woman Warrior versus The Chinaman Pacific."
29 Thom, *Fierce Femmes and Notorious Liars*, 25.
30 Thom, *Fierce Femmes and Notorious Liars*, 25.
31 Thom, *Fierce Femmes and Notorious Liars*, 58.
32 Thom, *Fierce Femmes and Notorious Liars*, 38.
33 Thom, *Fierce Femmes and Notorious Liars*, 87.
34 Notably, this cis-sexist obsession with gaining authority via "remasculinizing" with skin hegemony resounds in Asian American studies, with gender wars that have all but blackballed Frank Chin and the fellow editors of the historic anthology *Aiiieeeee!* for their homophobic and misogynist visions of Asian American cultural nationalism.
35 I will refer to Fu's protagonist as Audrey (she/her), though it is worth noting that the majority of book reviews refer to the character as Peter using he/him pronouns.
36 Fu, *For Today I Am a Boy*, 124, 125.
37 Fu, *For Today I Am a Boy*, 125.
38 Fu, *For Today I Am a Boy*, 127.
39 Fu, *For Today I Am a Boy*, 127.
40 Fu, *For Today I Am a Boy*, 126.
41 Fu, *For Today I Am a Boy*, 135.
42 Fu, *For Today I Am a Boy*, 135.
43 Fu, *For Today I Am a Boy*, 136.
44 Thom, *Fierce Femmes and Notorious Liars*, 59.
45 Thom, *Fierce Femmes and Notorious Liars*, 61.
46 Radi, "On Trans* Epistemology," 46.
47 Thom, *Fierce Femmes and Notorious Liars*, 17.
48 Thom, *Fierce Femmes and Notorious Liars*, 19.
49 Thom, *Fierce Femmes and Notorious Liars*, 19.
50 Stryker, "My Words to Victor Frankenstein," 237.
51 Hahm et al., "Fractured Identity," 65.
52 Peterson et al., "Suicidality, Self-Harm, and Body Dissatisfaction," 475.
53 Adler and Adler, *The Tender Cut*, 1.
54 McDermott, Roen, and Piela, "Explaining Self-Harm," 884.
55 Morris and Galupo, "'Attempting to Dull the Dysphoria,'" 301.
56 Cotten, "Surgery," 205.
57 Adler and Adler, *The Tender Cut*, 3.
58 Stryker and Bettcher, "Introduction," 7.
59 Truong, *The Book of Salt*, 65.
60 Gopinath, *Impossible Desires*, 2.
61 Truong, *The Book of Salt*, 73.
62 Truong, *The Book of Salt*, 142.
63 Truong, *The Book of Salt*, 42.

64 Truong, *The Book of Salt*, 74.

65 Thom, *Fierce Femmes and Notorious Liars*, 156, 127.

66 Thom, *Fierce Femmes and Notorious Liars*, 156.

67 Thom, *Fierce Femmes and Notorious Liars*, 156.

68 Thom, *Fierce Femmes and Notorious Liars*, 179.

69 Thom, *Fierce Femmes and Notorious Liars*, 180.

70 Thom, *Fierce Femmes and Notorious Liars*, 136.

71 Thom, *Fierce Femmes and Notorious Liars*, 174.

72 Thom, *Fierce Femmes and Notorious Liars*, 173.

73 Fu, *For Today I Am a Boy*, 86.

74 Fu, *For Today I Am a Boy*, 83.

75 Fu, *For Today I Am a Boy*, 93.

76 Fu, *For Today I Am a Boy*, 94.

77 Fu, *For Today I Am a Boy*, 94.

78 Fu, *For Today I Am a Boy*, 94.

79 Fu, *For Today I Am a Boy*, 94.

80 Truong, *The Book of Salt*, 142.

81 Thom, *Fierce Femmes and Notorious Liars*, 24.

82 Thom, *Fierce Femmes and Notorious Liars*, 24.

83 Truong, *The Book of Salt*, 240.

84 As the reader later learns, the protagonist and Bão share the same given name. In a way, their sexual encounter is a way for Bình/Bão to create a cleft in which to penetrate his mirror self.

85 Thom, *Fierce Femmes and Notorious Liars*, 187.

86 Thom, *Fierce Femmes and Notorious Liars*, 187.

87 Fu, *For Today I Am a Boy*, 226.

88 Fu, *For Today I Am a Boy*, 235.

89 Truong, *The Book of Salt*, 243.

90 Truong, *The Book of Salt*, 111, 87.

91 Truong, *The Book of Salt*, 239.

92 Truong, *The Book of Salt*, 63.

93 Truong, *The Book of Salt*, 107.

4. FLATNESS, INDUSTRIOUSNESS, AND LABORIOUS FLEXIBILITY

I wish to thank the American Society for Theater Research "Afterlives of the Sixties" working group in November 2013; the organizers and participants at the Living Labor conference at New York University in April 2014; Mika Tajima and Marisa Sánchez; and Anita Mannur and the two anonymous reviewers from the *Journal of Asian American Studies* (*JAAS*) for their generous feedback on different versions of this chapter.

1 Propst, *The Office*, 18.

2 Lye, *America's Asia*, 3, 2.

3 Momin and Huldisch, *Whitney Biennial 2008*, 237.

4 See Machida, *Unsettled Visions*; and Kee, *Contemporary Korean Art*.

5 Machida, *Unsettled Visions*, 17.

6 "Creative Time Presents Mika Tajima."

7 My encounter with Tajima's solo exhibition at the Seattle Art Museum in the winter and spring of 2011/12 informs my writing here. This chapter also benefits from an on-site interview with Marisa Sánchez, assistant curator of the exhibition, and a separate interview with Mika Tajima in her Bushwick studio in the summer of 2013. Marisa Sánchez, interview with the author, June 4, 2012; Mika Tajima, interview with the author, May 24, 2013.

8 See, for example, Crook, "Power, Privacy and Pleasure"; Chanen, "The New Office"; Saval, *Cubed*; and Dillon, "When We Sat on the Floor."

9 Even distractions, however, can prove effective for enhancing worker morale. One need only think of toys and games shared among cubicle teams in tech offices, or the famous Google ball pit for employees. In this way, in late capitalism, the worker may identify with one's workplace as an environment that blurs the lines between personal life and work life.

10 Jana, "Mika Tajima," 117.

11 Tajima cites Albers and a more extensive art genealogy in *After the Martini Shot* by curating several pieces from the Seattle Art Museum's permanent collection in her work *The Extras* (2011).

12 Friedman, "It's a Flat World, after All."

13 Various feminist thinkers have written on this porous ontology. See Cheng, *Ornamentalism* and *Second Skin*; Choi, *Soft Science*; Haraway, "A Cyborg Manifesto"; and Rhee, *Love, Robot*.

14 Art21, "Mika Tajima Wants to Hire Contortionists."

15 Miller, "Mika Tajima and Richard Linklater Are Slackers."

16 See Reddy, *Freedom with Violence*; and Melamed, *Represent and Destroy*.

17 Miller, "Mika Tajima and Richard Linklater Are Slackers."

18 Tajima and Campbell, "500 Words."

19 I reference the Moynihan Report of 1965 to index a governmental document that argued that systemic inequalities could be solved in the private sphere through the upholding of nuclear families. In this sense, the Moynihan Report is a concomitant image of the model minority thesis insofar as it pardons systematic racism and performatively chastises Black communities for not pulling themselves up by the proverbial bootstraps.

20 *U.S. News and World Report*, "Success Story of One Minority Group in the U.S."

21 Suzuki, "Asian American as the 'Model Minority,'" 14.

22 Palumbo-Liu, *Asian/American*, 397.

23 Muñoz, "Feeling Brown, Feeling Down," 675.

24 Bascara, *Model Minority Imperialism*, 18.

25 See Park and Park, *Probationary Americans*, in which the authors note how the US Immigration Act of 1965 brought about major changes in subsequent patterns of Asian immigration, effecting the so-called brain drain of affluent and highly skilled workers in a radical break from previous waves of Asian immigration.

26 Phillips, *Winnicott*, 10.

27 Winnicott, *Playing and Reality*, 118.

28 Palumbo-Liu, *Asian/American*, 397.

29 R. Lee, *Orientals*, 179.

30 Winnicott, *Playing and Reality*, 87.

31 Eng and Han, "A Dialogue on Racial Melancholia," 344.

32 With regard to object-relations theory, Eng and Han have helpfully brought forth a Winnicott-inspired notion of a "racial transitional object" and the prospect of Kleinian "racial reparation" in their coauthored case study of Han's patient Mina, who was born in Korea and adopted by white US American parents. See Eng and Han, "The Prospect of Kinship."

33 For a compelling use of Kleinian reparation for Asian American studies, see Diaz, "Melancholic Maladies," wherein Diaz rehearses scholarship on racial melancholia to identify a hypochondriac-paranoid tendency in Asian Americanist psychoanalytic critique that risks constructing a monolithic white-dominant norm. Modeling and arguing for alternative interpretations of racialized interior life in two canonical Asian American novels (*Woman Warrior* and *Rolling the R's*), Diaz asks what other politics are made possible by disaggregating racial narratives of victim/aggressor and rethinking failure. For more on reparative reading as critical queer methodology, see the work of Sedgwick, especially "Paranoid Reading and Reparative Reading"; and Muñoz, for example, "Feeling Brown, Feeling Down."

34 For critical queer deployments of failure, see Muñoz, *Cruising Utopia*; and Halberstam, *The Queer Art of Failure*.

35 Chiu, Higa, and Min, *One Way or Another*, 118.

36 Eng and Han, "The Prospect of Kinship," 159.

37 Eng and Han, "The Prospect of Kinship," 159.

38 Tajima and the New Humans, *Dead by Third Act*.

39 Tajima and the New Humans, *Dead by Third Act*.

40 Phillips, *Winnicott*, 133.

41 Winnicott, *Playing and Reality*, 121.

42 Winnicott, *Playing and Reality*, 126.

43 Winnicott, *Playing and Reality*, 126.

44 Winnicott, *Playing and Reality*, 126.

45 Phillips, *Winnicott*, 65.

46 Eng and Han, "The Prospect of Kinship," 160, emphasis mine.

5. DISTANCE, NEGATIVITY, AND SLUTTY SOCIALITY IN TSENG KWONG CHI'S PERFORMANCE PHOTOGRAPHS

Thanks to Muna Tseng and the Tseng Kwong Chi Estate; the Grey Art Gallery; and the Creative Center of Photography at the University of Arizona, Tucson, for help with my archival work. Thanks also to the Performance Studies Summer Institute at Northwestern University, the Performance Studies Working

Group at Harvard University, the Association of Asian American Studies conference, the Oakley Center for the Humanities and Social Sciences seminar on Performance Studies in Spring 2019, and the Asian American student activists of Wesleyan University for inviting me to share work from this chapter.

1 Ahmed, "Killing Joy," 588.

2 It is worth noting the common male gendering of both Goofy and the inscrutable Chinese, despite the fact that the actor playing Goofy could, we might imagine, not identify as such outside the costume. The performance of masculine presentation will be further discussed in this chapter.

3 Brandt, "Tseng Kwong Chi and the Politics of Performance," 38.

4 I employ the language of affect through its use in queer theory, following thinkers including Teresa de Lauretis, Brian Massumi, and Jasbir Puar, after Sigmund Freud and Gilles Deleuze, as a visceral and transmittable sensation that limns, escapes, or precedes language. My discursive invocation of affect mimes something of what I suggest Asian American figuration performs, that is, a reproducible form that is useful in its gesture toward that which is not simple to formally assess and is ontologically more ephemeral and dynamic than discourse can allow. Though affect is not strictly material or visible, Eve Kosofsky Sedgwick, via Silvan Tomkins, identifies the familiar choreographies and other bodily performances of affect, notably the downward look or blush of shame (Sedgwick, *Touching Feeling*; Sedgwick and Frank, *Shame and Its Sisters*). Affect, as such, is performative—not in the misrecognition of it being willfully rehearsed and consciously executed but in its reiteration and capacity to form and enact bodies and other material forms in a shared world. Affect can be observed only in relation to something, as a viewer to a photograph, or a reader to a book. Affect is transmitted before language and, relatedly, before the separation of individual from others; thus, as Sedgwick shows, shame is individuating at the same time as it enacts a social form. Affect theory alongside critical ethnic studies is useful for my purposes here for its nuanced entry to conversations of personhood, agency, consciousness, and affect, which are not limited to what can be the static positivism of biology or sociology. As Muñoz writes, affect is "descriptive of the receptors we use to hear each other and the frequencies on which certain subalterns speak and are heard or, more importantly, felt" ("Feeling Brown, Feeling Down," 677). And, following Muñoz, affect allows a discussion of racial performativity and, here, the performative "doing" of Asian Americanness.

5 Eng, *Racial Castration*, 204.

6 Eng, *Racial Castration*, 32.

7 Indeed, this was evidenced by Tseng's presentation of these photographs in various configurations and groupings, rearranging their layout for each gallery installation.

8 Ahmed, "Killing Joy," 581.

9 Schueller, "Claiming Postcolonial America," 177.

10 Santa Ana, *Racial Feelings*, 15, 22. Consider erin Khuê Ninh's description of "the Asian immigrant family" as "a production unit—a sort of cottage industry, for a particular brand of good, capitalist subject" (*Ingratitude*, 2).

11 Muñoz, "Feeling Brown, Feeling Down," 680.

12 Santa Ana, *Racial Feelings*, 14.

13 Bhabha, *The Location of Culture*, 89.

14 Yoon, "Learning Asian American Affect," 296.

15 Yoon, "Learning Asian American Affect," 294.

16 Yoon, "Learning Asian American Affect," 297.

17 Eng and Hom, *Q&A*, 1.

18 Sedgwick, *Touching Feeling*, 8.

19 S. Lee, "An Asian Man Who Likes Math."

20 Okihiro, *Margins and Mainstreams*, 42.

21 Kim Lee, "Staying In," 29.

22 Day, *Alien Capital*, 92.

23 Day, *Alien Capital*, 82.

24 Muñoz, *Cruising Utopia*, 95; Edelman, *No Future*.

25 Perhaps I should clarify that my theory of slutty distance is not based on biography, that is, whether Tseng was or was not in long-distance or polyamorous relationships.

26 Bacalzo, "Portraits of Self and Other," 87.

27 S. Lee, "An Asian Man Who Likes Math."

28 I think of long-distance relationality as in conversation with but not wholly encompassed by what in the social sciences is referred to as a long-distance relationship (LDR).

29 Gopinath, *Unruly Visions*, 92.

30 Tongson, *Relocations*, 23; citing Jennifer Terry, "Proposal: Remote Intimacy," application for the University of California Humanities Research Institute working group seminar "Queer Locations: Race, Space and Sexuality" (Winter/Spring 2004), 2.

31 See also Magat, "Looking After the Filipina Caregiver."

32 Manalansan, "Servicing the World," 217–18.

33 Kim Lee, "Staying In." I also learn from Tina Post's formulation of expressionlessness in relation to shine and Black expressive cultures in her article "Williams, Walker, and Shine." Post formulates expressionlessness as "a certain fungibility of context" that resonates with the work of Asian surface and distant relation in Tseng's photographs (90). Writing of blackbody blackface performers, Post writes that "expressionlessness allowed for a successful performance of black respectability because it allowed subjects to highlight and invest selfhood in the aerials that they wore or surrounded themselves with" (93). Tseng's distance and Post's expressionlessness diverge here as Tseng's performance reads less as self-serious respectability and more about campy foreignness.

34 Pérez, "The Glory That Was Wrong," 281.

35 Pérez, "The Glory That Was Wrong," 281.

36 Chambers-Letson, *After the Party*, 210.

37 Day, *Alien Capital*, 80.

CONCLUSION

1 Garoian, "Performing a Pedagogy of Endurance," 164.

2 Heathfield, "Impress of Time," 47.

3 See Kee, "Orders of Law in the *One Year Performances* of Tehching Hsieh."

4 Laster, "Tehching Hsieh," 119.

5 Laster, "Tehching Hsieh," 119–20.

6 Tovey, "Superstuck," 151.

7 Tovey, "Superstuck," 151.

8 Ward, "Alien Duration," 14.

9 Ward, "Alien Duration," 14.

10 Ward, "Alien Duration," 14, 16, emphasis mine. See also Grey and Grey, "The Year of the Rope," 30.

11 Ward, "Alien Duration," 14.

12 Ward, "Alien Duration," 16.

13 Min, *Unnameable*, 171.

14 Heathfield and Hsieh, *Out of Now*, 335.

15 Heathfield, "Impress of Time," 51.

16 Kee, "Orders of Law in the *One Year Performances* of Tehching Hsieh," 80.

17 Ward, "Alien Duration," 14.

18 Heathfield and Hsieh, *Out of Now*, 347.

19 Heathfield and Hsieh, *Out of Now*, 347.

20 Heathfield, "Impress of Time," 52.

21 Heathfield, "Impress of Time," 52, 53.

22 Heathfield, "Impress of Time," 53.

23 Heathfield, "Impress of Time," 57.

24 Heathfield, "Impress of Time," 57.

25 Heathfield and Hsieh, *Out of Now*, 336.

26 Muñoz, *Cruising Utopia*, 65.

27 Muñoz, "Ephemera as Evidence," 7.

28 Muñoz, *Cruising Utopia*, 65.

29 Muñoz, "Ephemera as Evidence," 10.

30 Muñoz, "Ephemera as Evidence," 10.

31 Scott, "The Evidence of Experience," 797.

32 Muñoz, "Ephemera as Evidence," 8.

33 Muñoz, "Ephemera as Evidence," 9.

34 De Jongh, "Art/Life," 7.

35 Muñoz, "Ephemera as Evidence," 12.

36 Muñoz, *Cruising Utopia*, 11.

37 Nancy, *Being Singular Plural*, 30.

38 Haraway, *When Species Meet*, 4.

39 Sedgwick, *Touching Feeling*, 8.

40 Sedgwick, *Touching Feeling*, 8.

41 Sedgwick, *Touching Feeling*, 8.

42 Nancy, *Being Singular Plural*, 35.

43 Nancy, *Being Singular Plural*, xvi.

44 Nancy, *Being Singular Plural*, 35.

45 Chuh, "It's Not about Anything," 126.

46 Heathfield and Hsieh, *Out of Now*, 335.

47 De Jongh, "Art/Life," 7.

48 S. Ngai, *Our Aesthetic Categories*, 11.

49 De Jongh, "Art/Life," 7.

50 De Jongh, "Art/Life," 5.

51 Ardia, "NYC-Based Artist Tehching Hsieh."

52 Heathfield, "Impress of Time," 49.

Adler, Patricia A., and Peter Adler. *The Tender Cut: Inside the Hidden World of Self-Injury*. New York: New York University Press, 2011.

Ahmed, Sara. *The Cultural Politics of Emotion*. Edinburgh: Edinburgh University Press, 2014.

Ahmed, Sara. "Killing Joy: Feminism and the History of Happiness." *Signs* 35, no. 3 (Spring 2010): 571–92.

Ahmed, Sara, and Jackie Stacey. *Thinking through the Skin*. New York: Routledge, 2001.

Amin, Kadji, Amber Jamilla Musser, and Roy Pérez. "Queer Form: Aesthetics, Race, and the Violences of the Social." *ASAP/Journal* 2, no. 2 (May 2017): 227–39.

"Anti-Chinese Rhetoric Tied to Racism against Asian Americans: Stop AAPI Hate Report." Asian Pacific Policy and Planning Council, June 17, 2020. http://www .asianpacificpolicyandplanningcouncil.org/wp-content/uploads/Anti-China _Rhetoric_Report_6_17_20.pdf.

Anzaldúa, Gloria. *Borderlands / La Frontera: The New Mestiza*. 1987. Reprint, San Francisco: Aunt Lute Books, 2012.

Ardia, Mai. "NYC-Based Artist Tehching Hsieh: When Life Becomes a Performance." *Culture Trip*, January 12, 2017. https://theculturetrip.com/north -america/usa/new-york/new-york-city/articles/tehching-hsieh-when-life -becomes-a-performance/.

Art21. "Mika Tajima Wants to Hire Contortionists." June 17, 2011. https://art21.org /watch/new-york-close-up/mika-tajima-wants-to-hire-contortionists/.

Augsberger, Astraea, et al. "Culturally Related Risk Factors of Suicidal Ideation, Intent, and Behavior among Asian American Women." *Asian American Journal of Psychology* 9, no. 4 (2018): 252–61.

Bacalzo, Dan. "Portraits of Self and Other: *SlutForArt* and the Photographs of Tseng Kwong Chi." *Theatre Journal* 53, no. 1 (March 2001): 73–94.

Bascara, Victor. *Model Minority Imperialism*. Minneapolis: University of Minnesota Press, 2006.

Best, Stephen, and Sharon Marcus. "Surface Reading: An Introduction." *Representations* 108, no. 1 (2009): 1–21.

Bhabha, Homi K. *The Location of Culture*. New York: Routledge, 1994.

Bishop, Claire. "Antagonism and Relational Aesthetics." *October*, no. 110 (Fall 2004): 51–79.

Bonacich, Edna, and Lucie Cheng. *Labor Immigration under Capitalism.* Oakland: University of California Press, 1984.

Bourriaud, Nicolas. *Relational Aesthetics.* Paris: Les Presses du réel, 2006.

Bow, Leslie. *Betrayal and Other Acts of Subversion: Feminism, Sexual Politics, Asian American Women's Literature.* Princeton, NJ: Princeton University Press, 2001.

Brandt, Amy L. "Tseng Kwong Chi and the Politics of Performance." In *Tseng Kwong Chi: Performing for the Camera*, 25–73. Norfolk, VA: Chrysler Museum of Art, 2015.

brown, adrienne maree. *Emergent Strategy: Shaping Change, Changing Worlds.* Chico, CA: AK Press, 2017.

brown, adrienne maree. *Pleasure Activism: The Politics of Feeling Good.* Chico, CA: AK Press, 2019.

Bryan-Wilson, Julia. "Remembering Yoko Ono's *Cut Piece.*" *Oxford Art Journal* 26, no. 1 (2003): 99–123.

Bui, Long T. "Breaking into the Closet: Negotiating the Queer Boundaries of Asian American Masculinity and Domesticity." *Culture, Society and Masculinities* 6, no. 2 (Fall 2014): 129–49.

Campt, Tina Marie. "Black Visuality and the Practice of Refusal." *Women and Performance: a journal of feminist theory* 29, no. 1 (2019): 79–87.

Chambers-Letson, Joshua. *After the Party: A Manifesto for Queer of Color Life.* New York: New York University Press, 2018.

Chanen, Jill Schachner. "The New Office: Today's Interior Design Trends Promote Efficiency, Collegiality—Even Conservation." *ABA Journal* 91, no. 7 (July 2005): 34–41.

Chang, Robert. "The Invention of Asian Americans." *UC Irvine Law Review* 3, no. 4 (2013): 947–64.

Chen, Mel Y. *Animacies: Biopolitics, Racial Mattering, and Queer Affect.* Durham, NC: Duke University Press, 2012.

Cheng, Anne Anlin. *The Melancholy of Race: Psychoanalysis, Assimilation, and Hidden Grief.* New York: Oxford University Press, 2001.

Cheng, Anne Anlin. *Ornamentalism.* New York: Oxford University Press, 2018.

Cheng, Anne Anlin. *Second Skin: Josephine Baker and the Modern Surface.* New York: Oxford University Press, 2013.

Cheung, King-Kok. "The Woman Warrior versus The Chinaman Pacific: Must a Chinese American Critic Choose between Feminism and Heroism?" In *Conflicts in Feminism*, edited by Marianne Hirsch and Evelyn Fox Keller, 234–51. New York: Routledge, 1990.

Chin, Frank, Jeffery Paul Chan, Lawson Fusao Inada, and Shawn Wong, eds. *Aiiieeeee! An Anthology of Asian American Writers.* 3rd ed. Seattle: University of Washington Press, 2019.

Chiu, Melissa, Karin Higa, and Susette S. Min, eds. *One Way or Another: Asian American Art Now.* New York: Asia Society; New Haven, CT: Yale University Press, 2006.

Choi, Franny. "Orientalism (Part I)." In *Floating, Brilliant, Gone*, 33. Austin, TX: Write Bloody Publishing, 2014.

Choi, Franny. *Soft Science*. Farmington, ME: Alice James Books, 2019.

Chow, Rey. "How (the) Inscrutable Chinese Led to Globalized Theory." *PMLA* 116, no. 1 (January 2001): 69–74.

Chuh, Kandice. *Imagine Otherwise: On Asian Americanist Critique*. Durham, NC: Duke University Press, 2003.

Chuh, Kandice. "It's Not about Anything." *Social Text* 32, no. 4 (Winter 2014): 125–34.

The Combahee River Collective. "The Combahee River Collective Statement." 1977. https://www.blackpast.org/african-american-history/combahee-river -collective-statement-1977/.

Concannon, Kevin. "Yoko Ono's *Cut Piece*: From Text to Performance and Back Again." *PAJ: A Journal of Performance and Art* 30, no. 3 (September 2008): 81–93.

Cotten, Trystan T. "Surgery." *TSQ: Transgender Studies Quarterly* 1, nos. 1–2 (May 2014): 205–7.

Coulthard, Glen Sean. *Red Skin, White Masks: Rejecting the Colonial Politics of Recognition*. Minneapolis: University of Minnesota Press, 2014.

"Creative Time Presents Mika Tajima." Creative Time Global Residency Program. 2013. http://creativetime.org/projects/global-residency-2013/mika-tajima/.

Creef, Elena Tajima. *Imaging Japanese America*. New York: New York University Press, 2004.

Crook, Tom. "Power, Privacy and Pleasure." *Cultural Studies* 21, nos. 4–5 (July 2007): 549–69.

Daniher, Colleen Kim. "Performing the Racial Ambiguity Act: Settler Colonialism, Imperialism, and Performance." PhD diss., Northwestern University, 2015.

Daniher, Colleen Kim. "Yella Gal: Eartha Kitt's Racial Modulations." *Women and Performance: a journal of feminist theory* 28, no. 1 (2018): 16–33.

Davis, Ben. "Columbia Student's Striking Mattress Performance." *Artnet*, September 4, 2014. https://news.artnet.com/opinion/columbia-students-striking -mattress-performance-92346.

Day, Iyko. *Alien Capital: Asian Racialization and the Logic of Settler Colonial Capitalism*. Durham, NC: Duke University Press, 2016.

De Jongh, Karlyn. "Art/Life: A Conversation with Tehching Hsieh." *C. Magazine* 105 (Spring 2010): 4–9.

Derrida, Jacques, and Anne Dufourmantelle. *Of Hospitality: Anne Dufourmantelle Invites Jacques Derrida to Respond*. Translated by Rachel Bowlby. Stanford: Stanford University Press, 2000.

Diaz, Robert G. "Melancholic Maladies: Paranoid Ethics, Reparative Envy, and Asian American Critique." *Women and Performance: a journal of feminist theory* 16, no. 2 (2006): 201–19.

Dillon, Jane. "When We Sat on the Floor: Furniture in the Sixties." In "The Sixties: Life: Style: Architecture," edited by Elain Harwood and Alan Powers, special issue, *Twentieth Century Architecture*, no. 6 (2002): 28–34.

Duan, Noel. "Going from Class to Class with Emma Sulkowicz and Her Mattress." *Elle*, September 9, 2014. https://www.elle.com/culture/career-politics/a14546 /columbia-university-sexual-assault-mattress-performance-emma-sulkowicz/.

Duncan, Patti. *Tell This Silence.* Iowa City: University of Iowa Press, 2004.

Edelman, Lee. *No Future: Queer Theory and the Death Drive.* Durham, NC: Duke University Press, 2004.

Eder, Steve, Henry Fountain, Michael H. Keller, Muyi Xiao, and Alexandra Stevenson. "430,000 People Have Traveled from China to U.S. since Coronavirus Surfaced." *New York Times,* April 4, 2020.

Eng, David L. *Racial Castration: Managing Masculinity in Asian America.* Durham, NC: Duke University Press, 2001.

Eng, David L., and Shinhee Han. "A Dialogue on Racial Melancholia." In *Loss: The Politics of Mourning,* edited by David L. Eng and David Kazanjian, 343–71. Berkeley: University of California Press, 2002.

Eng, David L., with Shinhee Han. "The Prospect of Kinship: Transnational Adoption and Racial Reparation." In *The Feeling of Kinship,* by David L. Eng, 138–65. Durham, NC: Duke University Press, 2010.

Eng, David L., and Alice Hom, eds. Q&A: *Queer in Asian America.* Philadelphia: Temple University Press, 1998.

Fisher, Anna Watkins. "Manic Impositions: The Parasitical Art of Chris Kraus and Sophie Calle." WSQ: *Women's Studies Quarterly* 40, nos. 1–2 (Spring/Summer 2012): 223–35.

Fisher, Anna Watkins. "We Are Parasites: On the Politics of Imposition." *Art & Education.* July 15, 2011. Accessed July 2016. www.artandeducation.net/paper /we-are-parasites-on-the-politics-of-imposition/.

Fleissig, Peter. "Laurel Nakadate's 'Only the Lonely' Opens at PS1." *Vogue,* January 20, 2011.

Foucault, Michel. *The History of Sexuality.* Vol. 1, *An Introduction.* Translated by Robert Hurley. New York: Pantheon Books, 1978.

Freeman, Elizabeth. *Time Binds.* Durham, NC: Duke University Press, 2010.

Friedman, Thomas L. "It's a Flat World, after All." *New York Times,* April 3, 2005.

Fu, Kim. *For Today I Am a Boy.* New York: First Mariner Books, 2015.

Fujiwara, Lynn, and Shireen Roshanravan, eds. *Asian American Feminisms and Women of Color Politics.* Seattle: University of Washington Press, 2018.

Fung, Richard. "Looking for My Penis." In *How Do I Look? Queer Film and Video,* edited by Bad Object-Choices, 145–68. Seattle: Bay Press, 1991.

Fusco, Coco. "The Other History of Intercultural Performance." TDR: *The Drama Review* 38, no. 1 (Spring 1994): 143–67.

Garoian, Charles. "Performing a Pedagogy of Endurance." *Teacher Education Quarterly* 29, no. 4 (October 2002): 161–73.

Glissant, Édouard. *Poetics of Relation.* Translated by Betsy Wing. Ann Arbor: University of Michigan Press, 1997.

Gopinath, Gayatri. *Impossible Desires: Queer Diasporas and South Asian Public Cultures.* Durham, NC: Duke University Press, 2005.

Gopinath, Gayatri. *Unruly Visions: The Aesthetic Practices of Queer Diaspora.* Durham, NC: Duke University Press, 2018.

Gordon, Avery. *Ghostly Matters*. Minneapolis: University of Minnesota Press, 1997.

Grey, Alex, and Allyson Grey. "The Year of the Rope: An Interview with Linda Montano and Tehching Hsieh." In *The Citizen Artist: 20 Years of Art in the Public Arena*, edited by Linda Frye Burnham and Steven Durland, 29–40. Gardiner, NY: Critical Press, 1998. Originally published in *High Performance* (Fall 1984).

Grosz, Elizabeth. *Volatile Bodies: Toward a Corporeal Feminism*. Bloomington: Indiana University Press, 1994.

Hahm, Hyeouk Chris, Judith Gonyea, Christine Chiao, and Luca Koritsanszky. "Fractured Identity: A Framework for Understanding Young Asian American Women's Self-Harm and Suicidal Behaviors." *Race and Social Problems* 6, no. 1 (March 2014): 56–68.

Halberstam, Jack. *The Queer Art of Failure*. Durham, NC: Duke University Press, 2011.

Hamilton, Caroline. "Laurel Nakadate." *Art and Australia*, Spring 2007.

Hamington, Maurice. *Feminism and Hospitality: Gender in the Host/Guest Relationship*. Lanham, MD: Lexington Books, 2010.

Haraway, Donna. "A Cyborg Manifesto: Science, Technology, and Socialist-Feminism in the Late Twentieth Century." In *Simians, Cyborgs, and Women: The Reinvention of Nature*, 149–81. New York: Routledge, 1991.

Haraway, Donna. *When Species Meet*. Minneapolis: University of Minnesota Press, 2007.

Harper, Phillip Brian. *Abstractionist Aesthetics*. New York: New York University Press, 2015.

Hartocollis, Anemona. "Harvard Rated Asian-American Applicants Lower on Personality Traits, Suit Says." *New York Times*, June 15, 2018.

Hayward, Eva. "More Lessons from a Starfish: Prefixial Flesh and Transspeciated Selves." *WSQ: Women's Studies Quarterly* 36, nos. 3–4 (Fall/Winter 2008): 64–85.

Heathfield, Adrian. "Impress of Time." In *Out of Now: The Lifeworks of Tehching Hsieh*, by Adrian Heathfield and Tehching Hsieh, 10–61. Cambridge, MA: MIT Press, 2015.

Heathfield, Adrian, and Tehching Hsieh. *Out of Now: The Lifeworks of Tehching Hsieh*. Cambridge, MA: MIT Press, 2015.

Ho, Jennifer Ann. *Racial Ambiguity in Asian American Culture*. New Brunswick, NJ: Rutgers University Press, 2015.

Hong, Cathy Park. "The Slur I Never Expected to Hear in 2020." *New York Times Magazine*, April 12, 2020.

Huang, Vivian L. "*Endlings* by Celine Song (Review)." *Theatre Journal* 72, no. 3 (September 2020): 345–47.

Huang, Vivian L. "'What Shall We Do?': Kathy Change, Soomi Kim, and Asian Feminist Performance on Campus." *TDR: The Drama Review* 62, no. 3 (Fall 2018): 168–74.

Huang, Vivian L. "Whither Asian American Lesbian Feminist Thought?" *Diacritics* 48, no. 3 (2020): 40–58.

Huang, Vivian L., and Summer Kim Lee, eds. "Performances of Contingency: Feminist Relationality and Asian American Studies after the Institution." Special issue, *Women and Performance: a journal of feminist theory* 30, no. 1 (Fall 2020).

Indrisek, Scott. "Laurel Nakadate." *The Believer*, October 2006. https://believermag.com/an-interview-with-laurel-nakadate/.

"Is Dot Painting the Remnant of Pointillism?" *IdeelArt*, November 2, 2016. http://www.ideelart.com/module/csblog/post/300-1-dot-painting.html.

"It's a Modern China That Threatens a Row." *San Francisco Chronicle*, March 18, 1906.

Jana, Reena. "Mika Tajima." In *One Way or Another: Asian American Art Now*, edited by Melissa Chiu, Karin Higa, and Susette S. Min, 116–19. New York: Asia Society; New Haven, CT: Yale University Press, 2006.

Johnson, Ken. "A Burgeoning Film Career Built on Random Encounters." *New York Times*, February 25, 2011.

Kang, Laura Hyun Yi. *Compositional Subjects: Enfiguring Asian/American Women*. Durham, NC: Duke University Press, 1995.

Kastner, Jeffrey. "A Provocateur Who Talks to Strangers." *New York Times*, January 23, 2011.

Kee, Joan. *Contemporary Korean Art: Tansaekhwa and the Urgency of Method*. Minneapolis: University of Minnesota Press, 2013.

Kee, Joan. "Orders of Law in the *One Year Performances* of Tehching Hsieh." *American Art* 30, no. 1 (Spring 2016): 72–91.

Khan, Baseera. "Acoustic Sound Blanket." *Unbag*, "End" (Winter 2018). https://unbag.net/end/acoustic-sound-blanket.

Khan, Baseera. *Acoustic Sound Blankets*. Performance at Gavin Brown, July 13, 2018. https://vimeo.com/296975591.

Khan, Baseera. *Acoustic Sound Blankets*. Performance at the '62 Center for Theatre and Dance Directing Studio, Williams College, Williamstown, MA, September 29, 2017. Organized by Allana Clarke.

Kim, Claire Jean. "The Racial Triangulation of Asian Americans." *Politics and Society* 27, no. 1 (March 1999): 105–38.

Kim, Ju Yon. *The Racial Mundane*. New York: New York University Press, 2015.

Kim, Yerin. "Respecting the Victims in the Atlanta Spa Shootings Means Getting Their Names Right." *Popsugar*, March 24, 2021. https://www.popsugar.com/news/atlanta-spa-shootings-victims-names-matter-essay-48231585.

Kim Lee, Summer. "Staying In: Mitski, Ocean Vuong, and Asian American Asociality." *Social Text* 37, no. 1 (March 2019): 27–50.

Kimsooja. *Archive of Mind*. Peabody Essex Museum, Salem, MA, August 2019.

Kina, Laura, and Wei Ming Dariotis, eds. *War Baby / Love Child: Mixed Race Asian American Art*. Seattle: University of Washington Press, 2013.

King, Homay. *Lost in Translation: Orientalism, Cinema, and the Enigmatic Signifier*. Durham, NC: Duke University Press, 2010.

Kingston, Maxine Hong. *Tripmaster Monkey: His Fake Book*. New York: Alfred A. Knopf, 1989.

Kirp, David L. "Diversity Hypocrisy: The Myriad, and Often Perverse, Implications of Admissions Policies." *National CrossTalk* 15, no. 1 (Winter 2007): 10–11.

Laster, Paul. "Tehching Hsieh: The Art of Survival." *Art Asia Pacific* 56 (November/December 2007): 119–20.

Lee, Robert G. *Orientals: Asian Americans in Popular Culture*. Philadelphia: Temple University Press, 2000.

Lee, Seulghee. "An Asian Man Who Likes Math: Anti-Asian Misandry and Transformative Hospitality." *Tropics of Meta*, March 13, 2020. https://tropicsofmeta .com/2020/03/13/an-asian-man-who-likes-math-anti-asian-misandry-and -transformative-hospitality.

Lee, Seulghee. "When Is Asian American Life Grievable?" *Tropics of Meta*, April 30, 2021. https://tropicsofmeta.com/2021/04/30/when-is-asian-american-life-grievable/.

Lee, Young Jean. *Songs of the Dragon Flying to Heaven*. New York: Theatre Communications Group, 2009.

León, Christina A. "Forms of Opacity: Roaches, Blood, and Being Stuck in Xandra Ibarra's Corpus." *ASAP/Journal* 2, no. 2 (May 2017): 369–94.

Lombard, Christine, dir. *East Meets West: Portrait of Tseng Kwong Chi*. Center for Creative Photography, Tucson, AZ, 1984.

Lorde, Audre. *Sister Outsider: Essays and Speeches*. Berkeley: Crossing Press, 1984.

Lowe, Lisa. *Immigrant Acts: On Asian American Cultural Politics*. Durham, NC: Duke University Press, 1996.

Lye, Colleen. *America's Asia*. Princeton, NJ: Princeton University Press, 2005.

Machida, Margo. *Unsettled Visions: Contemporary Asian American Artists and the Social Imaginary*. Durham, NC: Duke University Press, 2008.

Magat, Jonathan. "Looking After the Filipina Caregiver: Ambiguity and Unknowability across Jenifer K Wofford's *Nurse Drawings*." *Women and Performance: a journal of feminist theory* 30, no. 1 (September 2020): 70–92.

Manalansan, Martin F. "Servicing the World: Flexible Filipinos and the Unsecured Life." In *Political Emotions*, edited by Ann Cvetkovich, Janet Staiger, and Ann Reynolds, 215–28. New York: Routledge, 2010.

Manalansan, Martin F. "The 'Stuff' of Archives: Mess, Migration, and Queer Lives." *Radical History Review* 120 (Fall 2014): 94–107.

McDermott, Elizabeth, Katrina Roen, and Anna Piela. "Explaining Self-Harm: Youth Cybertalk and Marginalized Sexualities and Genders." *Youth and Society* 47, no. 1 (November 2015): 873–89.

McMillan, Uri. "Introduction: Skin, Surface, Sensorium." *Women and Performance: a journal of feminist theory* 28, no. 1 (Spring 2018): 1–15.

Melamed, Jodi. *Represent and Destroy: Rationalizing Violence in the New Racial Capitalism*. Minneapolis: University of Minnesota Press, 2011.

Mengesha, Lilian G., and Lakshmi Padmanabhan. "Introduction to *Performing Refusal / Refusal to Perform*." *Women and Performance: a journal of feminist theory* 29, no. 1 (2019): 1–8.

Miller, Wesley. "Mika Tajima and Richard Linklater Are Slackers." *New York Close Up: A Documentary Series on Art and Life in the City*, October 25, 2011. Accessed

February 2015. http://www.art21.org/newyorkcloseup/2011/10/25/mika-tajima
-richard-linklater-are-slackers/.

Min, Susette. *Unnameable: The Ends of Asian American Art.* New York: New York
University Press, 2018.

Mitra, Durba, Sara Kang, and Genevieve Clutario. "It's Time to Reckon with the
History of Asian Women in America." *Harper's Bazaar,* March 23, 2021.

Momin, Shamim M., and Henriette Huldisch. *Whitney Biennial 2008.* New Haven,
CT: Yale University Press, 2008.

Morris, Ezra R., and M. Paz Galupo. "'Attempting to Dull the Dysphoria': Nonsuicidal Self-Injury among Transgender Individuals." *Psychology of Sexual Orientation and Gender Diversity* 6, no. 3 (2019): 296–307.

Muñoz, José Esteban. *Cruising Utopia: The Then and There of Queer Futurity.* New
York: New York University Press, 2009.

Muñoz, José Esteban. *Disidentifications: Queers of Color and the Performance of
Politics.* Minneapolis: University of Minnesota Press, 1999.

Muñoz, José Esteban. "Ephemera as Evidence: Introductory Notes to Queer
Acts." *Women and Performance: a journal of feminist theory* 8, no. 2 (1996):
5–16.

Muñoz, José Esteban. "Feeling Brown, Feeling Down: Latina Affect, the Performativity of Race, and the Depressive Position." *Signs* 31, no. 3 (Spring 2006):
675–88.

Munroe, Alexandra, with Jon Hendricks et al. *YES Yoko Ono.* New York: Henry N.
Abrams, 2000.

Nancy, Jean-Luc. *Being Singular Plural.* Translated by Robert Richardson and
Anne O'Byrne. Stanford: Stanford University Press, 2000.

Ngai, Mae. *Impossible Subjects: Illegal Aliens and the Making of Modern America.*
Princeton, NJ: Princeton University Press, 2004.

Ngai, Sianne. *Our Aesthetic Categories.* Cambridge, MA: Harvard University Press,
2012.

Nguyen, Hieu Minh. *Not Here: Poems.* Minneapolis Coffee House Press, 2018.

Nguyen, Hoang Tan. *A View from the Bottom: Asian American Masculinity and
Sexual Representation.* Durham, NC: Duke University Press, 2014.

Ninh, erin Khuê. *Ingratitude: The Debt-Bound Daughter in Asian American Literature.* New York: New York University Press, 2011.

Nyong'o, Tavia. *Afro-Fabulations: The Queer Drama of Black Life.* New York: New
York University Press, 2018.

O'Grady, Alice. "Introduction: Risky Aesthetics, Critical Vulnerabilities, and
Edgeplay: Tactical Performances of the Unknown." In *Risk, Participation, and
Performance Practice: Critical Vulnerabilities in a Precarious World,* edited by
Alice O'Grady, 1–29. New York: Palgrave Macmillan, 2017.

Oh, Diana. *Clairvoyance.* American Repertory Theater, Cambridge, MA,
April 2019.

Okihiro, Gary. *Margins and Mainstreams: Asians in American History and Culture.* Seattle: University of Washington Press, 1994.

Ong, Aihwa. *Neoliberalism as Exception: Mutations in Citizenship and Sovereignty.* Durham, NC: Duke University Press, 2006.

Ono, Yoko. *Grapefruit.* New York: Simon and Schuster, 1964.

Owen, Ianna Hawkins. "Still, Nothing: Mammy and Black Asexual Possibility." *Feminist Review* 120 (2018): 70–84.

Palumbo-Liu, David. *Asian/American: Historical Crossings of a Racial Frontier.* Stanford: Stanford University Press, 1999.

Park, Edward J. W., and John S. W. Park. *Probationary Americans.* New York: Routledge, 2005.

Peabody Essex Museum. "PEM Invites Visitors to Participate in a Meditative Sculptural Installation by World-Renowned Korean Artist." Press release, April 11, 2019. https://www.pem.org/press-news/pem-invites-visitors-to-participate-in-a-meditative-sculptural-installation-by-world-renowned-korean-artist.

Pellegrini, Ann. "Queer Structures of Religious Feeling: What Time Is Now?" In *Sexual Disorientations: Queer Temporalities, Affects, Theologies,* edited by Kent L. Brintnall, Joseph A. Marchal, and Stephen D. Moore, 240–57. New York: Fordham University Press, 2017.

Pérez, Roy. "The Glory That Was Wrong: El 'Chino Malo' Approximates Nuyorico." *Women and Performance: a journal of feminist theory* 25, no. 3 (April 2016): 277–97.

Peterson, Claire M., Abigail Matthews, Emily Copps-Smith, and Lee Ann Conard. "Suicidality, Self-Harm, and Body Dissatisfaction in Transgender Adolescents and Emerging Adults with Gender Dysphoria." *Suicide and Life-Threatening Behavior* 47, no. 4 (August 2017): 475–82.

Phillips, Adam. *Winnicott.* Cambridge, MA: Harvard University Press, 1988.

Post, Tina. "Williams, Walker, and Shine: Blackbody Blackface, or the Importance of Being Surface." *TDR: The Drama Review* 59, no. 4 (Winter 2015): 83–100.

Propst, Robert. *The Office: A Facility Based on Change.* Elmhurst, IL: Business Press, 1968.

Puar, Jasbir. *Terrorist Assemblages.* Durham, NC: Duke University Press, 2007.

Quashie, Kevin. *The Sovereignty of Quiet.* Newark, NJ: Rutgers University Press, 2012.

Radi, Blas. "On Trans* Epistemology: Critiques, Contributions, and Challenges." *TSQ: Transgender Studies Quarterly* 6, no. 1 (February 2019): 43–63.

Red Canary Song. "Red Canary Song Response to Shootings at Gold Massage Spa, Young's Asian Massage, and Aroma Therapy Spa." March 17, 2021. https://docs.google.com/document/d/1_QomFJnivTZL5fcCS7eUZn9EhOJ1XHtFBGOGqVaUY_8/edit.

Reddy, Chandan. *Freedom with Violence: Race, Sexuality, and the U.S. State.* Durham, NC: Duke University Press, 2011.

Rhee, Margaret. *Love, Robot.* Brooklyn, NY: the operating system, 2017.

Rodríguez, Dylan. "The Asian Exception and the Scramble for Legibility: Toward an Abolitionist Approach to Anti-Asian Violence." *Society + Space,* April 8,

2021. https://societyandspace.webflow.io/articles/the-asian-exception-and
-the-scramble-for-legibility-toward-an-abolitionist-approach-to-anti-asian
-violence.

Rodríguez, Juana María. *Sexual Futures, Queer Gestures, and Other Latina Long-ings*. New York: New York University Press, 2014.

Rogin, Ali, and Amna Nawaz. "'We Have Been through This Before': Why Anti-Asian Hate Crimes Are Rising amid Coronavirus." PBS, June 25, 2020. https://www.pbs.org/newshour/nation/we-have-been-through-this-before-why-anti-asian-hate-crimes-are-rising-amid-coronavirus.

Roshanravan, Shireen. "Weaponizing Our (In)Visibility: Asian American Feminist Ruptures of the Model-Minority Optic." In *Asian American Feminisms and Women of Color Politics*, edited by Lynn Fujiwara and Shireen Roshanravan, 261–82. Seattle: University of Washington Press, 2019.

Ruti, Mari. *The Ethics of Opting Out*. With Jordan Mulder. New York: Columbia University Press, 2017.

Saltz, Jerry. "Whatever Laurel Wants." *Village Voice*, April 26, 2005.

Sánchez, Marisa. Interview with the author, June 4, 2012.

Sander-Staudt, Maureen. "Su Casa es Mi Casa? Hospitality, Feminist Care Ethics and Reciprocity." In *Feminism and Hospitality: Gender in the Host/Guest Relationship*, 19–38. Lanham, MD: Lexington Books, 2010.

Santa Ana, Jeffrey. *Racial Feelings: Asian America in a Capitalist Culture of Emotion*. Philadelphia: Temple University Press, 2015.

Saval, Nikil. *Cubed: A Secret History of the Workplace*. New York: Doubleday, 2014.

Schehr, Lawrence R. Preface to *The Parasite*, vii. Baltimore: Johns Hopkins University Press, 1982.

Schneider, Rebecca. *The Explicit Body in Performance*. New York: Routledge, 2013.

Schueller, Malini Johar. "Claiming Postcolonial America: The Hybrid Asian-American Performances of Tseng Kwong Chi." In *Asian North American Identities: Beyond the Hyphen*, edited by Eleanor Ty and Donald C. Goellnicht, 170–86. Bloomington: Indiana University Press, 2004.

Schwarting, Jen. "You Dirty, Worthless Slut." *Paper Monument* 2. Accessed July 2016. http://www.papermonument.com/post/you-dirty-worthless-slut.

Scott, Joan. "The Evidence of Experience." *Critical Inquiry* 17, no. 4 (Summer 1991): 773–97.

Sedgwick, Eve Kosofsky. *Epistemology of the Closet*. Berkeley: University of California Press, 1990.

Sedgwick, Eve Kosofsky. *Touching Feeling*. Durham, NC: Duke University Press, 2003.

Sedgwick, Eve Kosofsky, and Adam Frank, eds. *Shame and Its Sisters: A Silvan Tomkins Reader*. Durham, NC: Duke University Press, 1995.

Serres, Michel. *The Parasite*. Translated by Lawrence R. Schehr. Baltimore: Johns Hopkins University Press, 1982.

Shah, Sonia, ed. *Dragon Ladies: Asian American Feminists Breathe Fire*. Boston: South End, 1997.

Shimakawa, Karen. *National Abjection: The Asian American Body on Stage.* Durham, NC: Duke University Press, 2002.

Shimakawa, Karen. "Young Jean Lee's Ugly Feelings about Race and Gender." *Women and Performance: a journal of feminist theory* 17, no. 1 (March 2007): 89–102.

Shimizu, Celine Parreñas. *The Hypersexuality of Race.* Durham, NC: Duke University Press, 2007.

Shin, Jean. "The Asian American Closet." *Asian American Law Journal* 11, no. 1 (January 2004): 1–30.

Siegel, Miranda. "The Provocateur: Laurel Nakadate." *New York Magazine*, December 4, 2011.

Simpson, Audra. *Mohawk Interruptus.* Durham, NC: Duke University Press, 2014.

Small, Zachary. "Queer Identity in the MeToo Movement: A Conversation with Emma Sulkowicz." *Hyperallergic*, August 31, 2018. https://hyperallergic.com/458257/conversation-with-emma-sulkowicz/.

Smith, Sarah Stefana. "Surface Play: Rewriting Black Interiorities through Camouflage and Abstraction in Mickalene Thomas's Oeuvre." *Women and Performance: a journal of feminist theory* 28, no. 1 (2018): 46–64.

Snorton, C. Riley. *Black on Both Sides: A Racial History of Trans Identity.* Minneapolis: University of Minnesota Press, 2017.

Snow, Jess X. "Migration Greeting Card Set." JustSeeds. Accessed November 2018. https://justseeds.org/product/migration-greeting-card-set/.

Somerville, Siobhan S. "Feminism, Queer Theory, and the Racial Closet." *Criticism* 52, no. 2 (Spring 2010): 191–200.

Spillers, Hortense. "Mama's Baby, Papa's Maybe: An American Grammar Book." *Diacritics* 17, no. 2 (Summer 1987): 64–81.

Stephens, Michelle Ann. *Skin Acts: Race, Psychoanalysis, and the Black Male Performer.* Durham, NC: Duke University Press, 2014.

Stiles, Kristine. "Being Undyed: The Meeting of Mind and Matter in Yoko Ono's Events." In *YES Yoko Ono*, by Alexandra Munroe, with John Hendricks, 145–49. New York: Henry N. Abrams, 2000.

Stryker, Susan. "(De)Subjugated Knowledges: An Introduction to Transgender Studies." In *The Transgender Studies Reader*, edited by Susan Stryker and Stephen Whittle, 1–17. New York: Routledge, 2006.

Stryker, Susan. "My Words to Victor Frankenstein above the Village of Chamounix: Performing Transgender Rage." *GLQ: A Journal of Lesbian and Gay Studies* 1, no. 3 (1994): 237–54.

Stryker, Susan, and Talia M. Bettcher. "Introduction: Trans/Feminisms." *TSQ: Transgender Studies Quarterly* 3, nos. 1–2 (May 2016): 5–14.

Sulkowicz, Emma. "Rules of Engagement." Artist website. Accessed December 9, 2020. emmasulkowicz.com/mattress-performance-carry-that-weight-1.

Suzuki, Bob H. "Asian Americans as the 'Model Minority': Outdoing Whites? Or Media Hype?" *Change* 21, no. 6 (1989): 13–19.

Tajima, Mika. Interview with the author, May 24, 2013.

Tajima, Mika, and Andy Campbell. "500 Words." *Artforum*, September 28, 2011. http://artforum.com/words/id=29072.

Tajima, Mika, and the New Humans. *Dead by Third Act*. 14:40 min. Produced by Artissima, 2009. http://www.ubu.com/film/tajima_dead.html.

Takagi, Dana Y. "Maiden Voyage: Excursion into Sexuality and Identity Politics in Asian America." *Amerasia Journal* 20, no. 1 (1994): 1–17.

Takemoto, Tina. "Looking for Jiro Onuma: A Queer Meditation on the Incarceration of Japanese Americans during World War II." GLQ: *A Journal of Lesbian and Gay Studies* 20, no. 3 (2014): 241–75.

Tchen, John Kuo Wei, and Dylan Yeats. *Yellow Peril! An Archive of Anti-Asian Fear*. New York: Verso Books, 2014.

Thom, Kai Cheng. *Fierce Femmes and Notorious Liars: A Dangerous Trans Girl's Confabulous Memoir*. Montreal: Metonymy Press, 2016.

Tongson, Karen. *Relocations: Queer Suburban Imaginaries*. New York: New York University Press, 2011.

Tovey, Emma-Louise. "Superstuck." *Sleek*, Summer 2012, 150–53.

Truong, Monique. *The Book of Salt*. Boston: Houghton Mifflin, 2003.

Tseng, Muna, and Ping Chong. "SlutForArt." PAJ: *A Journal of Performance and Art* 22, no. 1 (January 2000): 111–28.

U.S. News and World Report. "Success Story of One Minority Group in the U.S." December 26, 1966.

Uyehara, Denise. "Hello (Sex) Kitty: Mad Asian Bitch on Wheels." In *O Solo Homo: The New Queer Performance*, edited by Holly Hughes and David Román, 375–409. New York: Grove, 1998.

Van Syckle, Katie. "The Columbia Student Carrying a Mattress Everywhere Says Reporters Are Triggering Rape Memories." *New York Magazine*, September 4, 2014.

Vuong, Ocean. "Reading and Conversation with Ocean Vuong." Harvard Radcliffe Institute, Cambridge, MA, April 8, 2021.

Vuong, Ocean. "Someday I'll Love Ocean Vuong." In *Night Sky with Exit Wounds*, 82–83. Port Townsend, WA: Copper Canyon, 2016.

Ward, Frazer. "Alien Duration: Tehching Hsieh, 1978–99." *Art Journal* 65, no. 3 (2006): 6–19.

Waxman, Olivia B. "A 'History of Exclusion, of Erasure, of Invisibility': Why the Asian-American Story Is Missing from Many U.S. Classrooms." *Time*, March 30, 2021.

Winnicott, D. W. *Playing and Reality*. New York: Routledge, 2005.

Woo, Merle. "Letter to Ma." In *This Bridge Called My Back: Writings by Radical Women of Color*, edited by Cherríe Moraga and Gloria Anzaldúa, 138–45. Albany: State University of New York Press, 2015.

Wu, Jason, and James McMaster. "Hate Crime Laws Are Not the Answer to Anti-Asian Violence, Abolition Is." *Teen Vogue*, April 28, 2021.

Xiang, Zairong. "Transdualism: Toward a Materio-Discursive Embodiment." TSQ: *Transgender Studies Quarterly* 5, no. 3 (August 2018): 425–42.

Yamada, Mitsuye. "Invisibility Is an Unnatural Disaster." In *This Bridge Called My Back: Writings by Radical Women of Color*, edited by Cherríe Moraga and Gloria Anzaldúa, 35–40. Albany: State University of New York Press, 2015.

Yoon, K. Hyoejin. "Learning Asian American Affect." In *Representations: Doing Asian American Rhetoric*, edited by Luming Mao and Morris Young, 293–322. Logan: Utah State University Press, 2008.

Yoshimoto, Midori. *Into Performance: Japanese Women Artists in New York.* Newark, NJ: Rutgers University Press, 2005.

Young Jean Lee's Theater Company Archive. "Songs of the Dragons Flying to Heaven (2006)." Accessed August 2017. https://youngjeanlee.org/work/songs -dragons-flying-heaven/.

Yu, Timothy. "Has Asian American Studies Failed?" In *Flashpoints for Asian American Studies*, edited by Cathy J. Schlund-Vials, 36–47. New York: Fordham University Press, 2017.

Foucault, Michel, 111, 189n23
Freeman, Elizabeth, 56
Fresh off the Boat, 26
Freud, Sigmund, 12, 122
Friedman, Thomas L., 113
Fu, Kim, 77, 85, 87, 89
Fujiwara, Simon, 166
Fung, Richard, 82–83
Fusco, Coco, 70

Garoian, Charles, 167
gender binary, 73, 78, 80, 83, 95
gender neutrality, 132
gender performances, 38
genitalia, 78–79, 82–83, 88, 94. *See also* bodies; skin
Ghost in the Shell, 26
gift economy, 54
Glissant, Édouard, 18, 33
globalization, 113, 121
Gopinath, Gayatri, 18, 32–33, 155
Gordon, Avery, 55, 190n30
Grapefruit (Ono), 48
Grey, Alex, 172
Grey, Allyson, 172

Hahm, Hyeouk Chris, 91–92
Halberstam, Jack, 48
Hamington, Maurice, 52, 54
Han, Shinhee, 11–12, 15, 31, 91, 124, 127, 131, 190n33, 202n32
Happy Birthday (Nakadate), 56–58, 63
Haraway, Donna, 180
Harper, Phillip Brian, 34
Harvard admissions scandal, 22, 136, 191n47
Hayward, Eva, 74
Heathfield, Adrian, 165–66, 181–82, 185
Hello (Sex) Kitty (Uyehara), 35–38
Herman Miller Research Corporation, 106, 109–11, 113, 119, 121. *See also* Action Office furniture
heteronormativity, 80
heterosexuality, 26, 73, 78
Holding Your Breath (New Humans), 112
Hom, Alice, 145
homophobia, 88, 98, 141
Hong, Cathy Park, 7

hospitality, 21, 48–49, 51–54, 60. *See also* host/guest dialectic; parasitic hospitality
host/guest dialectic, 61–62. *See also* hospitality; parasitic femininity
Hsieh, Tehching, 22, 165–85

Ibarra, Xandra, 33
illegibility, 4–5, 88–89, 149. *See also* legibility
immigration, 6, 167, 173, 186, 195n13. *See also* citizenship
impenetrability, 74, 78–79, 102, 105, 172. *See also* inscrutability; penetration; unreliable surfacing
Impossible Desires (Gopinath), 32–33
individualism, 40, 111
inscrutability: aesthetics of, 3–5, 7, 11, 20, 68, 126, 172, 183; and discipline, 68; perceptions of, 7, 30–31, 80, 114, 133; performances of, 4, 14–17, 140, 178, 196n45; and political expression, 19–20; and privacy, 182; as productive, 5, 10, 13, 23, 42–43, 89, 148, 180, 186; as queer performance, 162–63; and relationality, 62; and visuality, 33; and vulnerability, 71. *See also* impenetrability; invisibility; silence
insularity, 153, 161
interiority, 49–50
intersubjective becoming, 15
invisibility, 13, 20, 25, 27–29, 32, 44, 152, 186. *See also* inscrutability
I Will Never Stop Reaching for You (Snow), 44–45

Jana, Reena, 112
Japan, 52, 187n5
Japanese American incarceration, 189n22
Jung, Moon-Ho, 150

Kang, Sara, 27
Kant, Immanuel, 185
Kee, Joan, 174
Khan, Baseera, 1–3
Kim, Ju Yon, 45
Kim Lee, Summer, 10, 152, 156
Kimsooja, 39–41, 194n46
King, Homay, 18
Kingston, Maxine Hong, 76, 145
Klein, Melanie, 122

Ward, Frazer, 172, 174
Warhol, Andy, 109, 117
Western knowledge, 2, 8, 14
"Where are you really from?," 30, 32, 45, 187n5. *See also* national belonging
whiteness, 6, 13, 85–86, 118, 144–45, 148, 154, 162. *See also* Asianness
White on White (Malevich), 117–18, 125
white supremacy, 18, 48, 146, 154. *See also* racism
Williams College, 71
Winnicott, D. W., 106, 122–32
Woman Warrior, The (Kingston), 75
women: disappearance of, 30; invisibility of, 20–21; in orientalist narratives, 26–27; sexualization of, 38, 52. *See also* femininity

Wong, Martin, 160
World is Flat, The (Friedman), 113

xenophobia, 4–5
Xiang, Zairong, 83

Yamada, Mitsuye, 19, 25–26
Yamaoka, Kristi, 145
Yeats, Dylan, 190n35
Yeh, C. Spencer, 108
yellowface, 26, 34
yellow peril rhetoric, 5, 17, 55, 106, 188n12, 188n15
Yoon, K. Hyoejin, 136, 145
Yoshimoto, Midori, 55
Young, Anne Liv, 60

CPSIA information can be obtained
at www.ICGtesting.com
Printed in the USA
BVHW050339100623
665694BV00005B/13